Nonprofit Law & Governance For Dummies®

Cheat Sheet

D0783407

A Checklist for Forming a New Nonprofit

✔ **Clearly define your mission and its scope:** Every nonprofit has a mission. Make sure your nonprofit's mission is clearly defined and concisely written. It should reflect the shared goals of everyone involved in establishing the organization.

✔ **Put together a business plan and system:** The organization should identify the sources and uses of its funds. It should also figure out whether it can be viable in the long run.

✔ **Adopt a set of bylaws:** Bylaws serve as the constitution of your organization. You might start by using standard forms, but do make sure that issues of major importance to your organization are clearly addressed.

✔ **Recruit a board:** Nonprofit organizations are run by boards of directors or trustees. Recruiting the right board can mean the difference between success or failure of a nonprofit's mission.

✔ **Hold an organizational meeting and define duties and responsibilities:** This step is important to do early on because it allows you to make sure that formalities are dealt with before the organization becomes engrossed in fulfilling its mission.

✔ **File for tax-exempt status with the IRS:** Tax-exempt status is *not* automatic. It must be awarded by the IRS. Your organization must file the necessary paperwork and qualify under the law for exempt status.

✔ **Register with your state:** State requirements vary, but most require you to follow a certain registration process so that the states can track which nonprofits exist within their borders. Most states also require a separate registration process if funds will be solicited within their borders.

✔ **Get staff and volunteers in place:** If your organization has day-to-day operations to perform, it's important to figure out who will do the actual work. More importantly, you have to figure out who will supervise operations and be held accountable.

Nonprofit Law & Governance For Dummies®

Cheat Sheet

Tax Traps for Nonprofits

Many nonprofits make the mistake of assuming that because the federal government doesn't tax most nonprofit income, it doesn't require nonprofits to comply with tax-reporting requirements. This isn't the case at all. Nonprofits must file documentation to ensure that their special status isn't being used to confer benefits on private individuals or to further non-exempt purposes. Here are a few tax traps that many nonprofits fall into:

- ✔ **Not filing required returns and reports:** The Internal Revenue Service (IRS) carefully monitors the revenue, expenses, and activities of nonprofit organizations and requires them to file annual returns and reports to retain their tax-exempt status. Fines can be stiff for organizations that fail to comply.

- ✔ **Not filing complete or accurate returns:** Not all duties in nonprofit organizations can be safely delegated to well-meaning volunteers. Tax forms are technical documents that require the attention of someone skilled in completing them.

- ✔ **Paying unreasonable compensation:** Paying board members and executives more than what's justified by the market can result in a prompt loss of your organization's tax-exempt status and in penalties for all those involved.

- ✔ **Deviating from the tax-exempt mission:** The IRS grants nonprofit organizations exempt status to carry out specific missions. So, if you engage in non-exempt activities your organization's exempt status may be terminated.

- ✔ **Allowing the organization's property to be used personally by employees:** Nonprofit assets must be used for nonprofit purposes (and only nonprofit purposes). For example, it isn't alright to decide that land for a youth camp program should instead be used as the site for a vacation home for board members.

- ✔ **Entering into transactions where a clear conflict of interest exists:** Nonprofit funds should never be diverted to lucrative business transactions that benefit board members or executives (or their families). Nor should the organization's assets be used for other types of loans or perks.

- ✔ **Not filing state tax returns in all states in which the nonprofit does business:** States can be picky about what occurs within their borders. So, they have their own reporting requirements that must be satisfied.

- ✔ **Engaging in activities that generate income from sources unrelated to the organization's mission:** When nonprofits compete with private-sector businesses, they must pay taxes on the activities that generate the unrelated business income.

- ✔ **Ignoring or not responding to correspondence from the IRS:** Volunteer staffing and overlapping duties can cause critical notices to fall through the cracks. Don't let this happen to your organization.

For Dummies: Bestselling Book Series for Beginners

Nonprofit Law & Governance
FOR DUMMIES®

by Jill Gilbert Welytok, JD, CPA and
Daniel S. Welytok, JD

Foreword by U.S. Senator Chuck Grassley of Iowa

Wiley Publishing, Inc.

Nonprofit Law & Governance For Dummies®

Published by
Wiley Publishing, Inc.
111 River St.
Hoboken, NJ 07030-5774
www.wiley.com

Copyright © 2007 by Wiley Publishing, Inc., Indianapolis, Indiana

Published by Wiley Publishing, Inc., Indianapolis, Indiana

Published simultaneously in Canada

For general information on our other products and services, please contact our Customer Care Department within the U.S. at 800-762-2974, outside the U.S. at 317-572-3993, or fax 317-572-4002.

For technical support, please visit www.wiley.com/techsupport.

Wiley also publishes its books in a variety of electronic formats. Some content that appears in print may not be available in electronic books.

Library of Congress Control Number: 2007924229

ISBN: 978-0-470-08789-3

Manufactured in the United States of America

10 9 8 7 6 5 4 3 2 1

WILEY

About the Authors

Jill Gilbert Welytok, JD, CPA, LLM, practices in the areas of corporate law, nonprofit law, and intellectual property. She is the founder of Absolute Technology Law Group, LLC (www.abtechlaw.com). She went to law school at DePaul University in Chicago, where she was on the Law Review, and picked up a Masters Degree in Computer Science from Marquette University in Wisconsin where she now lives. Ms. Welytok also has an LLM in Taxation from DePaul. She was formerly a tax consultant with the predecessor firm to Ernst & Young. She frequently speaks on nonprofit, corporate governance–taxation issues and will probably come to speak to your company or organization if you invite her. You may e-mail her with questions you have about Sarbanes-Oxley or anything else in this book at jwelytok@abtechlaw.com. You can find updates to this book and ongoing information about SOX developments at the author's website located at www.abtechlaw.com.

Daniel S. Welytok, JD, LLM, is a partner in the business practice group of Whyte Hirschboeck Dudek S.C., where he concentrates in the areas of taxation and business law. Dan advises clients on strategic planning, federal and state tax issues, transactional matters, and employee benefits. He represents clients before the IRS and state taxing authorities concerning audits, tax controversies, and offers in compromise. He has served in various leadership roles in the American Bar Association and as Great Lakes Area liaison with the IRS. He can be reached at dsw@whdlaw.com.

Dedication

To Tara, Julia, and Daniel Welytok

Authors' Acknowledgments

We would like to thank the following people:

Judith Steininger, nonprofit consultant. Judy is a professor emeritus at the Milwaukee School of Engineering and a former Peace Corps volunteer. She has served on numerous nonprofit boards, including Hoan Foundation, Patrick & Beatrice Haggerty Art Museum, Dominican High School, Girls Scouts, Milwaukee County Council, and Milwaukee Chamber Theater. Judy is a great philanthropist and a Milwaukee treasure, and her perspective on this book has been invaluable.

Amy Seibel, technical editor, attorney, CPA. Amy is an AV-rated attorney with more than two decades of experience in the nonprofit and corporate governance realm. We have been very fortunate to have her as a technical editor on this book.

Donna Mortara, school board member, community volunteer. Donna is one of those influential community members who quietly seems to be everywhere getting things done and balancing community interests. She is approachable with concerns and creative in addressing them. We are fortunate that she has shared here perspective with us as a responsive community volunteer over the years.

We would also like to thank **Ron Jones** and **Dan Steininger** for their kind words about the book. And we're especially grateful to **Senator Chuck Grassley** for taking time out of his busy schedule to write the foreword.

Publisher's Acknowledgments

We're proud of this book; please send us your comments through our Dummies online registration form located at www.dummies.com/register/.

Some of the people who helped bring this book to market include the following:

Acquisitions, Editorial, and Media Development

Senior Project Editor: Tim Gallan

Acquisitions Editor: Lindsay Lefevere

Copy Editor: Jessica Smith

Technical Editor: Amy Seibel

Editorial Manager: Christine Meloy Beck

Editorial Assistants: Erin Calligan, Joe Niesen, David Lutton

Cartoons: Rich Tennant (www.the5thwave.com)

Composition Services

Project Coordinator: Jennifer Theriot

Layout and Graphics: Claudia Bell, Carl Byers, Joyce Haughey, Laura Pence, Alicia B. South

Anniversary Logo Design: Richard Pacifico

Proofreaders: Laura Albert, Aptara

Indexer: Aptara

Publishing and Editorial for Consumer Dummies

 Diane Graves Steele, Vice President and Publisher, Consumer Dummies

 Joyce Pepple, Acquisitions Director, Consumer Dummies

 Kristin A. Cocks, Product Development Director, Consumer Dummies

 Michael Spring, Vice President and Publisher, Travel

 Kelly Regan, Editorial Director, Travel

Publishing for Technology Dummies

 Andy Cummings, Vice President and Publisher, Dummies Technology/General User

Composition Services

 Gerry Fahey, Vice President of Production Services

 Debbie Stailey, Director of Composition Services

Contents at a Glance

Foreword xix

Introduction 1

Part 1: Nonprofits in the 21st Century 7
Chapter 1: Defining and Scrutinizing the Nonprofit Sector...9
Chapter 2: Regulating Nonprofits: Who's in Charge? 21
Chapter 3: The State of the Nation's Nonprofits 33

Part 11: The Nuts and Bolts of Nonprofits......................45
Chapter 4: Starting Up and Staying True to the Mission 47
Chapter 5: Getting Tax-Exempt Status 69
Chapter 6: Paying Nonprofit Directors, Officers, Staff, and Volunteers 87

Part 111: Structuring a Nonprofit to Meet 1ts Mission ...101
Chapter 7: Filing the Dreaded Form 990 103
Chapter 8: The Responsibilities of the Board 117
Chapter 9: Creating the Right Committee Structure 135
Chapter 10: All About Audit Committees 141

Part 1V: Some Special Types of Nonprofits 151
Chapter 11: Forming a Solid Foundation 153
Chapter 12: Capitalizing on Cooperatives..165

Part V: Legal Landmines 179
Chapter 13: Existing in a World of Sarbanes-Oxley 181
Chapter 14: Some Sticky Accounting Issues That All Nonprofits Face....................199
Chapter 15: Communicating Comfortably with the IRS..217

Part V1: The Part of Tens 227
Chapter 16: More Than Ten Web Sites Every Nonprofit Should Visit......................229
Chapter 17: Ten Questions to Ask Before Agreeing to Join a Nonprofit Board 235
Chapter 18: Ten Ways to Lose Tax-Exempt Status 243
Chapter 19: Ten Tips for Dealing with the Media..249

Part VII: Appendixes 255

Appendix A: Sample Nonprofit Bylaws 257

Appendix B: Sample Audit Committee Report 261

Appendix C: State Regulatory Authorities for Nonprofits 263

Appendix D: Selections from the Revised Model
Nonprofit Corporation Act (1987) 275

Index 325

Table of Contents

Foreword...xix

Introduction 1
    About This Book...1
    Conventions Used in This Book 2
    What You're Not to Read 2
    What We Assume About You 2
    How This Book Is Organized...3
        Part I: Nonprofits in the 21st Century..............................3
        Part II: The Nuts and Bolts of Nonprofits 4
        Part III: Structuring a Nonprofit to Meet Its Mission.......4
        Part IV: Some Special Types of Nonprofits.......................4
        Part V: Legal Landmines 4
        Part VI: The Part of Tens 5
        Part VII: Appendixes 5
    Icons Used in This Book 5
    Where to Go from Here..6
    Feedback, Please 6

Part 1: Nonprofits in the 21st Century.............................7

Chapter 1: Defining and Scrutinizing the Nonprofit Sector 9
    Characteristics That Nonprofits Share.....................................10
        Stakeholders 10
        Documentation 11
        Funding and financing...12
        Tax-exempt status 12
        The bottom line 13
        Limitations 13
    Comparing Small Nonprofits to Small For-Profit Businesses 14
        The similarities 14
        The differences 15
    Surveying the Latest Legal Landscape.....................................15
        New legal scrutiny over nonprofits................................16
        The Pension Protection Act of 2006 18
    Focusing on Good Governance 20

Chapter 2: Regulating Nonprofits: Who's in Charge? 21

The IRS: The Primary Federal Regulator...21
U.S. Postal Regulations...23
Federal Election Laws...23
State Regulations...24
Fifty laws for fifty states 25
Model acts: Templates for good behavior...26
Regulations in Counties and Municipalities 32

Chapter 3: The State of the Nation's Nonprofits 33

Unprecedented Scrutiny 33
Lessons from Nonprofits in the News 34
Lesson #1: Spend donations only for the intended purposes 35
Lesson #2: Exercise oversight in distributing program funds........36
Lesson #3: Compensate nonprofit executives reasonably..............37
Lesson #4: Discourage donors from taking
grossly inflated deductions 38
Lesson #5: Have more than one person authorize expenditures...39
Lesson #6: Operate under established
and well-documented standards 39
Lesson #7: Steer clear of illegal lobbying activities 40
New Federal Legislation: The Pension Protection Act of 2006................41
New incentives for giving 41
Tax relief for charitable organizations...42
Requiring written records 42
The end of some charitable loopholes 43

Part II: The Nuts and Bolts of Nonprofits 45

Chapter 4: Starting Up and Staying True to the Mission 47

Making the Mission Matter 47
Using the mission statement as a roadmap 48
Summing it up in a single statement 48
Picking up ideas from some model mission statements 49
Drafting the mission statement 50
Getting Tax-Exempt Status...50
Classifying your organization: Section 501(c) 51
"Tax exempt" doesn't mean contributions are "tax deductible"....52
Filling out the forms 54
Gathering the right documents 55
Receiving acknowledgment..56
Withdrawing your application 56
Opening up to public inspection 56
Seeing your exempt status request through the review process...57
Keeping your tax-exempt status once you get it...............................58

Choosing an Entity Type 59
    Corporations 59
    Limited liability companies 60
    Unincorporated associations 60
    Trusts 61
    Cooperatives 61
Incorporating as a Nonprofit 62
    Drafting articles of incorporation 62
    Writing the bylaws 63
Getting Leaders on the Board 64
    Profiling candidates 65
    Persuading candidates 65
    Conducting meaningful meetings 66

Chapter 5: Getting Tax-Exempt Status 69

Checking Out the "Eligible" List for Tax-Exempt Status 69
    Skimming Internal Revenue Code Section 501(c) 70
    Exemptions in other parts of the Code 77
Applying for Tax-Exempt Status 79
    Filling out the forms 79
    Paying the fees 80
    Providing additional documents 80
    Understanding the approval process 81
    Applying if your organization hasn't begun operating 82
    Getting a determination 83
Appealing an Adverse Determination with the IRS 83
    Doing the paperwork 84
    Taking it to court: An exhausting process 84

**Chapter 6: Paying Nonprofit Directors, Officers,
Staff, and Volunteers 87**

Convening a Compensation Committee 87
    Setting the officers' salaries 88
    Comparing salaries paid at other nonprofits 89
    The buck stops with the board 90
Following IRS Guidelines 91
    Determining what's "reasonable" 91
    Documenting the decision process in the minutes 92
Cooking Up a Compensation Package 93
    Identifying the additional ingredients of a compensation package ...94
    Putting the compensation recipe in writing 94
    Looking at the consequences of paying
       unreasonable compensation 95
Governance Issues and Compensation 97
    Identifying best practices 98
    Weighing all the factors 99

Avoiding Tax for Volunteers 99
    Keeping track with an accountable plan 99
    Opting for a non-accountable plan 100

Part III: Structuring a Nonprofit to Meet Its Mission 101

Chapter 7: Filing the Dreaded Form 990 103

Introducing Form 990: What It Is and Who Has to File It 103
    Organizations that must file a 990 without fail 104
    Organizations that don't have to file a 990 105
    Filing deadlines and extensions 106
Figuring Out Which Form to File 106
    Form 990 versus 990-EZ 106
    A private matter: The 990-PF 107
    Monitoring unrelated business income with the Form 990-T 107
Satisfying the States with Form 990 108
    Scoping out state statutes 108
    Avoiding some sticky state issues 109
Avoiding Common 990 Nightmares 109
Researching Form 990s Online 110
Sampling Some Form 990s 112
    Finding answers on the Form 990 112
    Breezing through Form 990-EZ 115

Chapter 8: The Responsibilities of the Board 117

Introducing the Basics of the Board of Directors 117
    Striking a balance: Strategic boards versus meddlesome ones ...118
    Electing the board of directors 119
    Governing as a body 119
    The key functions of a board 120
    The legal obligations of directors 120
Understanding a Director's Responsibilities 121
    Directors' common-law duties 121
    Other important board of director duties 125
    Going above and beyond the scope of authority 126
    Extra obligations for directors who are trustees 127
Your Rights as a Director 128
    Protection under the business judgment rule 128
    Access to corporate books and records 129
    Access to the minutes 129
    Communication with management 129
    The right to dissention from board actions 129
SOX Policies and Nonprofit Boards 130
    Policies that nonprofit boards are required to adopt after SOX ...130
    Following the trend toward independent boards 131
    Other savvy SOX moves for directors 133

Chapter 9: Creating the Right Committee Structure 135

Basic Committee Structures 135
Forming a Committee 136
  When committees are formed 137
  Who sits on a committee..137
  What a committee's process looks like 137
Types of Committees 138
  Establishing an executive committee 138
  Appointing a nominating committee 138
  Adding an audit committee..139
  Creating a compensation committee 140
  Initiating an investment committee 140

Chapter 10: All About Audit Committees 141

The Role of the Audit Committee..142
  Using an independent accounting firm....................................142
  Developing audit committee standards 143
  Starting with a charter...144
  Interfacing with management 144
Audit Committee Membership Guidelines..................................145
  Independence is key 145
  Figure in a financial expert..146
Serving on an Audit Committee 146
  Monitoring events and policing policies 146
  Interfacing with the auditors 147
  Preapproving nonaudit services 147
  Handling complaints...148
  Considering CEO and CFO certifications.................................148
  Ferreting out improper influence 149
  Rotating the audit partners 149
  Engaging advisors 150

Part 1V: Some Special Types of Nonprofits **151**

Chapter 11: Forming a Solid Foundation 153

Why Form a Foundation? 153
  Keeping it all in the family..154
  Maintaining privacy and control 154
Comparing Private Foundations to Public Charities 155
The Types of Private Foundations 156
  Private operating foundations 156
  Grant-making foundations 158
Establishing a Foundation: Time to Jump Through Some Legal Hoops....159
  Federal-level compliance..159
  State-level compliance 161
Running Your Foundation 162

Terminating a Private Foundation 163
    Giving it away..163
    Having it taken away 163

Chapter 12: Capitalizing on Cooperatives 165

Cashing In on Collaboration: How Cooperatives Work 166
    Banding together to meet business objectives 166
    Buying and selling in bulk 166
    Making a margin for the members 167
Categorizing Cooperatives...167
    Consumer cooperatives 168
    Housing and condominium cooperatives 168
    Electric, telephone, and utility cooperatives................168
    Health cooperatives: Nothing to sneeze at 169
    Marketing as a cooperative 170
    Purchasing cooperatives 170
    Workers' cooperatives 170
    Financial cooperatives 171
Members Only: Who Can Be Part of a Cooperative? 171
Collaborating for Tax Benefits...172
    Distributing the dividends: Cash and equity credits 172
    Special requirements for special types of cooperatives 173
Forming a Cooperative in Five Easy Steps............................173
    Step one: Check your state's statutes...........................173
    Step two: File articles of incorporation 174
    Step three: Adopt some bylaws....................................174
    Step four: Make some rules and policies.......................174
    Step five: Issue member shares and certificates 174
Running a Cooperative: Is It Any Different Than a Corporation?...........175
    Profit distribution...175
    Share transfer restrictions 175
The Typical Operations of a Cooperative 176
Dealing with Some Cooperative Conundrums.........................177

Part V: Legal Landmines 179

Chapter 13: Existing in a World of Sarbanes-Oxley 181

A Quick and Clean Overview of Sarbanes-Oxley....................182
    Four squeaky-clean SOX objectives 183
    The major provisions of SOX 184
Applying SOX to the Nonprofit Arena...................................188
    Specific SOX provisions for nonprofits.........................189
    What most nonprofits are actually doing.......................190
    Determining the impact of required SOX provisions
        on nonprofits 193
Implementing Standards Logically: A Balanced Approach....................194
How SOX-Savvy Is Your Nonprofit?.....................................195

**Chapter 14: Some Sticky Accounting Issues
That All Nonprofits Face** **199**
    "Tax Exempt" Doesn't Mean "Tax Free" 199
        Distinguishing between earned and unearned income 200
        Understanding unrelated business income 201
    Valuing Donations Realistically 205
        Figuring out if your donors are reporting realistic values 206
        Predicting the unpredictable 210
    Dealing with Donations, Deductions, and Donors
        Who Overvalue Their Items 211
        Handing out deductions 212
        Penalizing donors who overvalue 213
    The Requirements of the Pension Protection Act 213
        Cash contributions 214
        Clothing and household items 214
        Appreciated personal property 214
        Fractional interests 214
        Facade easements 215

Chapter 15: Communicating Comfortably with the IRS **217**
    The Tax Exempt and Government Entities Division of the IRS 217
    Soft Contacts: Friendly Notes from the IRS 219
        Knowing a soft contact when you see one 219
        Responding to a soft contact 220
        Contacting TE/GE Customer Account Services .220
        Deciding when to get a lawyer 221
    Sending a Determination Letter 221
    Surviving an IRS Audit 222
        Looking at things from the auditor's perspective 222
        Identifying any errors 223
        Studying filings from other tax years 223
        Getting your ducks and digits in a row 223
        Meeting face to face 225
        Following up with the auditor 226
        Ending on a good note 226

Part VI: The Part of Tens **227**

**Chapter 16: More Than Ten Web Sites
Every Nonprofit Should Visit** **229**
    Guidestar 229
    The Internet Nonprofit Center 230
    USA.gov 231
    CompassPoint 232
    NASCOnet.org 232
    Other Worthwhile Sites 232

**Chapter 17: Ten Questions to Ask Before Agreeing
to Join a Nonprofit Board** **235**

Who's on the Current Board and How Did They Get There?.................235
How Long Are the Director's Terms?..236
How Many Board Members Does It Take to Get Anything Done?..........237
What Committees Does the Board Control?..237
Can I See the Books and Records of the Organization?..........................238
What's the Organization's Financial Situation? 238
Is the Organization Current on Its Payroll Taxes?...................................239
What Are the Responsibilities of the Directors? 240
When, Where, and How Often Does the Board Meet? 241
Is the Board Being Sued or Has It Ever Been Sued?................................242

Chapter 18: Ten Ways to Lose Tax-Exempt Status **243**

Engage in Plenty of Nonexempt Activities 243
Get Involved in Prohibited Political Activities 244
Become a Partnership 245
Divert Some of Your Organization's Earnings to Private Individuals 245
Farm Out Control of Your Operations 246
Fail to Limit Your Commercial Activities 246
Require Donations in Exchange for Your Organization's Services 246
Skip Filing IRS Form 990 for Three Years in a Row.................................247
Support Terrorist Activities...247
Pay Your Executives Exorbitant Salaries 248

Chapter 19: Ten Tips for Dealing with the Media **249**

Acquaint Yourself with Your Local Media..249
Create Your Message 250
Be Prepared When Being Interviewed..250
Keep Control of the Story 250
Don't Avoid the Press 251
Hire Professional PR Help When Necessary..251
Remember That Nothing Is Ever "Off the Record" 252
Gather the Forces When Appropriate 252
Know the Difference between News and Advertising 252
Surf the 'Net 253

Part VII: Appendixes. *255*

Appendix A: Sample Nonprofit Bylaws **257**

Appendix B: Sample Audit Committee Report **261**

Appendix C: State Regulatory Authorities for Nonprofits **263**

**Appendix D: Selections from the Revised Model
Nonprofit Corporation Act (1987)** 275
    Chapter 2: Organization 275
    Chapter 7: Members' Meetings and Voting.............................277
        Subchapter A: Meetings and Action Without Meetings................277
    Chapter 8: Directors and Officers 278
        Subchapter A: Board of Directors 278
        Subchapter C: Standards of Conduct...................................280
        Subchapter D: Officers...283
        Subchapter E: Indemnification 285
    Chapter 10: Amendment of Articles of Incorporation and Bylaws........289
        Subchapter A: Articles of Incorporation 289
        Subchapter B: Bylaws 295
        Subchapter C: Articles of Incorporation and Bylaws 297
    Chapter 11: Merger 297
    Chapter 12: Sale Of Assets 302
    Chapter 13: Distributions...304
    Chapter 14: Dissolution 304
        Subchapter A: Voluntary Dissolution 304
        Subchapter B: Administrative Dissolution.......................310
        Subchapter C: Judicial Dissolution 312
        Subchapter D: Miscellaneous 315
    Chapter 15: Foreign Corporations.......................................316
        Subchapter A: Certificate of Authority 316
        Subchapter B: Withdrawal 322
        Subchapter C: Revocation of Certificate of Authority..................322

Index *325*

Foreword

I can't imagine American society without nonprofit work, and I sure don't want to. Disaster relief, sheltering the homeless, feeding the poor, mentoring young people, and after-school programs are all in a day's work for charities and churches in every community.

Helping a neighbor is as ingrained in our culture as freedom of speech and the right to vote. Many spend precious leisure hours driving the elderly to doctor appointments or building houses for deserving families. And many Americans find an extra dollar for the Salvation Army kettle or cancer research. Some people can give more than others. Regardless, all Americans reap incalculable benefit from charities.

Reflecting these values, the federal tax code gives generous tax breaks to non-profit groups. Each year, the federal government foregoes the collection of about $280 billion in taxes from non-profit groups.

For decades, Congress handed out these tax breaks without much thought. But then some headlines grabbed our attention. The foundation executive in Boston who dipped into the charity's funds to pay for his daughter's expensive wedding. Organizations that were charities in name only because they were used as tax shelters by self-enriching individuals. The car owner who deducted thousands of dollars for donating to charity his 1976 AMC Pacer that goes only in reverse. The well-traveled safari hunter who wrote off his entire trip to South Africa by donating a dusty stuffed ibex head to a museum that never cared to display its prize.

These abuses of American generosity — as reflected in the federal tax code — were outrageous. They threatened the good reputation of charities. They mocked honest taxpayers. Congress needed to act, and we did. We made clear that favorable tax treatment is a privilege, not a right. With this privilege comes a great responsibility — by both the government and individual nonprofit organizations — to safeguard the public trust. We need to protect donors by ensuring contributions are used appropriately. We need to protect taxpayers by guaranteeing that tax benefits given to public charities correlate with the benefits that public charities provide to society. Government officials fulfill this responsibility to both donors and taxpayers with effective oversight and with laws that minimize the potential for abuse while also providing incentives for charitable giving.

As chairman of the Senate Committee on Finance, I worked to reform the laws that relate to nonprofit organizations. In my current capacity as the senior-most Republican on the Finance Committee, I'll continue that work. We need to make nonprofit operations more transparent and improve nonprofit governance. Among all charities, of those that have failed their mission, I've found that poor board governance unites all of them. A vigilant and committed board is key to making sure charities stay focused on the goals that encourage people to give.

Nonprofit organizations play an important role in safeguarding the public trust. They need to be guided by the best practices in the charitable field. Those put forward by the Independent Sector's Nonprofit Panel and the Better Business Bureau Wise Giving Alliance are two good examples among many others. This book is another important resource for nonprofit organizations. It's a road map on how to meet legal obligations and further the good work of the charitable missions that are an essential part of the fabric of American life.

Chuck Grassley
United States Senator, Iowa

Introduction

· ·

*W*elcome to *Nonprofit Law & Governance For Dummies*. This book takes you on a tour of the nation's nonprofits in the world of Sarbanes-Oxley and enhanced financial oversight. Whether you're a board member, officer, volunteer, employee, or donor, this book is for you. It's designed to tell you where you fit into the gears of the nonprofit sector (which incidentally employs one out of seven Americans).

Having the big picture straight in your mind helps ensure that you won't lose track of the mission of your organization in the details of daily administration or the pressure of public scrutiny.

About This Book

In the wake of the Sarbanes-Oxley Act, or SOX, questions have been raised about the overall health of the nation's nonprofit sector. In addition, in the wake of the September 11, 2001, terrorist attacks and Hurricane Katrina in 2005, questions have been raised as to the financial fitness and oversight of this important sector of our economy. The sector itself has taken an approach of proactively governing itself and working with legislators to bring about reasoned reforms.

The goal of *Nonprofit Law & Governance For Dummies* is to give you a helicopter view of the regulatory terrain, while giving you enough detail to spot the legal landmines within your own organization. This book is also intended to give you the level of insight you need for practical, cost-effective decision making.

For example, this book can help you do the following:

- ✔ **Understand what types of organizations make up the United States nonprofit sector:** The nonprofit sector of the U.S. economy is larger than the economies of many small countries. It consists of organizations ranging from informal community groups to private foundations and complex corporate structures with multiple divisions and subsidiaries.

- ✔ **Understand the role of the Internal Revenue Service:** The Internal Revenue Service, or IRS, is the primary federal organization that regulates nonprofit organizations. It wields the power to grant, deny, or revoke organizations' tax-exempt status.

- **Comply with state laws and regulations:** Even though the federal government is the primary arbiter of tax-exempt status, states take an avid interest in what types of entities are formed, how funds are solicited, and other activities that are conducted within their borders.

- **Avoid lawsuits and adverse regulatory actions:** This book, although not intended as a substitute for a good securities lawyer or certified public accountant, takes a hard look at the types of liability that board members, officers, employees, and other volunteers can incur when they're involved in carrying out the mission of a nonprofit organization. It also gives you an idea of who incurs liability under SOX and how you can avoid having your company (or yourself) added to the list of litigants.

- **Anticipate future rules and trends:** Regulation of the nonprofit sector is constantly evolving, and it has gained momentum following the highly publicized scandals involving such organizations as the Red Cross and the United Way. This book takes a look at how new regulations and scrutiny may affect nonprofits at all levels.

Conventions Used in This Book

It's unfortunate, but true: Understanding the nonprofit sector and the laws that apply to these organizations means that you're going to run into lots of legal jargon and accounting minutiae. To give you a jump-start, we define some legal and accounting terms in this book and use *italics* to make such terms stand out a bit.

Also, so that they're easy to spot and easy to read, we have placed all Web sites (and there are plenty!) in `monofont`.

What You're Not to Read

We occasionally wander off-topic to discuss something historical, technical, or interesting (or, at least, interesting to us!). In these instances, we set the discussions apart by placing them in sidebars, which are the gray boxes that you'll see from time to time throughout the book. Because the text in sidebars is nonessential, feel free to skip it if it doesn't interest you.

What We Assume About You

In writing this book, we had to make a few assumptions about who our readers would be and what kind of information they'd be looking for. First of all, we assume that you want to understand the legal and regulatory issues facing nonprofits in a way that you can't achieve by suffering through the thousands of pages of statutes and regulations, including the Internal Revenue Code. We also assume that you want to keep up with the most important legislation and standards regarding nonprofits and that you want to figure out exactly how they affect your organization.

Whether you're a board member, executive director, staff person, volunteer, donor, or you head up a private foundation, this book is for you. Nearly everyone in the United States has some sort of stake in the vitality of our nation's nonprofit sector. This book helps you understand some of the following issues, which are universal concerns to nonprofit stakeholders:

- ✔ How an effective nonprofit should operate
- ✔ The complex overlay of federal and state laws that apply to nonprofits, including IRS regulations
- ✔ What standards should be voluntarily adopted by your organization
- ✔ How to maintain an effective and smoothly functioning nonprofit board
- ✔ The best ways to stay true to the mission of your organization

How This Book Is Organized

Nonprofit organizations vary widely in size, mission, organizational structure, and practices. The index and table of contents can help you find your way to the parts of the book that are most relevant to your organization. The chapters in this book treat each topic independently without assuming you've read previous chapters (as a textbook might), so you can use them as references and jump around to find what you need. *Nonprofit Law & Governance* is divided into six parts, which we explain in the following sections.

Part 1: Nonprofits in the 21st Century

This part of the book looks at the historical mission of nonprofits and the role that they have played in the United States economy over the last 200 years. It explains why the government gives these organizations a "free ride" by exempting them from federal and state taxes. It explains how the Internal Revenue Service and the states work in tandem to weave a regulatory framework that protects donors, stakeholders, and intended beneficiaries of nonprofit organizations.

Part II: The Nuts and Bolts of Nonprofits

This part of the book delves into the basics of how nonprofits are organized and the critical characteristics they all share. It also explains the legal and regulatory environments in which all nonprofits operate, and the administrative and organizational structures they must have in place to carry out their missions. This part ends with a chapter that can guide you through the sticky subject of compensating officers and directors.

Part III: Structuring a Nonprofit to Meet Its Mission

This part explores some of the different types of legal entities (such as trusts and corporations) that can be formed to operate nonprofits. It also explains the duties that you'll assume if you agree to become part of a nonprofit board of directors, and it explores the difficulties in recruiting, compensating, and keeping good board members. Finally, it delves into the area of creating effective committees and delegating board functions to them (with an entire chapter devoted to audit committees).

Part IV: Some Special Types of Nonprofits

This part of the book takes you on a tour of the types of organizations that make up the nonprofit sector. They range from small, unincorporated associations and community groups to large private foundations, cooperatives, and multimillion-dollar corporations that rival their private sector counterparts in terms of their impact and influence on the American economy.

Part V: Legal Landmines

It's a sad fact that a few nonprofits run astray of their missions and encounter lawsuits, regulatory actions, and negative publicity. This part looks at the common mistakes that even some of the nation's largest nonprofits have made. This peek at the common mistakes can help you identify strategies so that your organization can avoid suffering the same fate.

For example, this part explains how to avoid common tax traps (such as failing to pay tax on unrelated business income) and activities that may cause your organization to lose its tax-exempt status. It also offers information on communicating effectively with the IRS in case questions arise, and gives you some tips for the sticky situations that even the most conscientious nonprofit organizations might encounter.

Part VI: The Part of Tens

The short chapters in this part offer checklists on important topics that can help board members and organizations avoid difficult situations. It suggests questions to ask before agreeing to serve on a nonprofit board, summarizes common ways that organizations lose their tax-exempt status, and provides a list of good Web site resources that can help you and your organization on a daily basis. We round out this part with a chapter on the ten ways you can use the media to your advantage.

Part VII: Appendixes

The appendixes in this book contain useful reference materials that you can actually put to use in your organization. You'll find sample nonprofit bylaws and a sample audit committee report. You'll also find a directory of contact information for state and regulatory authorities and select articles from the Model Nonprofit Corporation Act of 1987.

Icons Used in This Book

For Dummies books use little pictures, called *icons,* to flag parts of the text that stand out from the rest for one reason or another. Here's what the icons in this book mean:

Time is money. When you see this icon, your attention's being directed to a compliance shortcut or timesaving tip.

This icon signals the type of advice you may get in a lawyer's office if your organization were paying the exorbitant going rates. Of course, the information highlighted by this icon is no substitute for sound legal advice from your organization's attorney, who actually knows the facts of your individual situation.

This icon indicates that you're getting the kind of tip your audit or CPA firm might dispense. But remember, you should actually consult a real accounting professional before acting on anything that follows this icon.

This is a heads-up warning to help you avoid compliance mistakes, legal traps, and audit imbroglios.

This icon flags particularly noteworthy information — stuff you shouldn't forget.

Where to Go from Here

Because we wrote each chapter of this book as a stand-alone treatment of the topic covered, you can start with Chapter 1 and read the whole book, or you can skip around and brush up on only the topics that interest you at the moment. If you're new to the nonprofit sector, we recommend that you start with Part I. If you're hip to nonprofit governance issues, skip ahead to the parts in the book that address your particular needs or concerns.

Feedback, Please

We're always interested in your comments, suggestions, or questions, so we'd love to hear from you. Send Jill an e-mail message at `jwelytok@ abtechlaw.com`, or send Dan one at `dsw@whdlaw.com`. You can also visit `abtechlaw.com`. On this site, you'll find contact information for all the great legal and accounting professionals who helped with this book (I've included their credentials and accomplishments on the acknowledgments page).

Part I
Nonprofits in the 21st Century

The 5th Wave   By Rich Tennant

"Thanks to Sarbanes—Oxley, we've got more internal controls than a warehouse full of Imodium."

In this part . . .

This part provides the basics on nonprofits, including what they are, what legislation has recently changed their governance, and who regulates them. We round out the part with a chapter that explains the state of today's nonprofits.

Chapter 1

Defining and Scrutinizing the Nonprofit Sector

- -

In This Chapter

▶ Discovering what nonprofits have in common

▶ Looking at nonprofits and small businesses side by side

▶ Understanding the recent legal changes regarding nonprofit governance

▶ Concentrating on governing positively and effectively

- -

*T*he United States nonprofit sector workforce consists of about 11 million people, or 7 percent of the entire U.S. workforce. Numbers like these make the U.S. nonprofit sector the sixth largest economy in the world — larger even than the economies of Canada or Russia.

To give you a closer look at this booming workforce, this chapter reviews some of the core characteristics of U.S nonprofits: why so many exist and the policy reasons that justify granting millions of them tax-immunity.

But there's even more to this opening chapter. Those people who are running nonprofits also need to be aware of recent scrutiny and legislation in the nonprofit world. Inspired by tales of fundraising fraud, conflicts of interest, bloated compensation, and careless accounting, state and federal legislators are hard at work creating new laws to restore public confidence. After cracking down on corporate America by enacting the Sarbanes-Oxley Act (which lays down the restrictions, limitations, and requirements for the for-profit sector), lawmakers and enforcement officials are beginning to target the country's 1.8 million nonprofits for legislation. This chapter discusses the ramifications of this attention.

The vastness of the nonprofit sector

The nonprofit sector is pervades nearly every aspect of American culture. Virtually every U.S. citizen has some type of regular interaction or relationship with a nonprofit entity. Here are a few statistics to help you appreciate the enormity of the nonprofit sector:

✔ **Charities make up about half of it:** Of the approximately 1.8 million nonprofits in the United States, more than half of them (about 780,000) are charitable. The other half fulfill other missions (such as promoting arts, culture, business cooperation, social interractions or public and communtiy goals).

✔ **It's multiplying like gerbils:** The number of nonprofits in this country has tripled since 1963. It's estimated that 20,000 to 30,000 new nonprofits are started each year.

✔ **It has financial strength in numbers:** The vast majority of nonprofits are small, just like the majority of U.S. for-profit businesses are. For example, most nonprofits have an annual gross revenue of less than $25,000 a year. However, the cumulative revenues of these organizations are $710 billion, or about 9 percent of the U.S. gross domestic product (which is the total value of all goods and services produced and sold by the United States).

Characteristics That Nonprofits Share

A nonprofit organization is an organization with a purpose. The purpose, known as its *mission,* is an overriding goal other than making a profit. For example, a nonprofit may promote cancer research, improve access to goods services for low-income individuals or foster arts such as opera and ballet, All nonprofits have a reason for their existence.

For profit entities (such as corporations and other businesses ultimately answer to shareholders, owners, and partners. Unlike their for-profit counterparts, nonprofits do not exist to generate revenue for owners or shareholders. Nonprofits do not even have owners and shareholders. Rather, all nonprofits have *stakeholders.*

Stakeholders

A stakeholder, as the term inplies, is a individual or group with an interest in having the nonprofit fulfill its mission. Stakeholders include anyone who's interested or affected by the nonprofit organization and its services. Stakeholders in the nonprofit sector include the following:

- ✔ **Users:** By users, I mean the people and parties who actually use the services and goods created, distributed, or allocated by the nonprofit organization.

- ✔ **Donors and funding sources:** This group includes the people and entities (including the government) that help fund the operations of the nonprofit.

- ✔ **Community:** Often the surrounding community as a whole will have a stake in how well a nonprofit organization meets its mission and objectives.

Documentation

Each nonprofit has its own DNA-like uniqueness. However, three particular types of documentation link most nonprofits: mission statements, charters, and bylaws.

Mission statements

A *mission statement* isn't a legal document, but it's the document that defines a nonprofit organization's goals and reasons for existing. All nonprofits should have a clear mission statement that's reviewed periodically to make sure that it reflects the organization's current objectives. Not only does a mission statement help keep the nonprofit on track, it also informs the public of what that organization's objectives are. (See Chapter 4 for more on mission statements, including information on creating and drafting your organization's statement.) Nonprofits generally fulfill their missions by creating and managing an organizational structure that's staffed and organized to meet their day-to-day goals.

When an organization has outlived its mission (or in other words, if the issues for which it was formed no longer exist), the nonprofit itself may cease to exist. Or, if the nonprofit isn't fulfilling its mission, it may be rightfully questioned by its stakeholders.

Charters

A *charter* is the prerequisite for official status as a nonprofit corporation within a state. In other words, it's the constitution of the organization. This document, which is sometimes also called a *certificate of incorporation,* is typically filed with the secretary of state. Changes to the charter require a formal amendment.

Most states require organizations to file annual reports to keep their non-profit status.

Bylaws

For nonprofit corporations, *bylaws* outline the basic operating rules for your organization and spell out how it's governed. Bylaws include rules pertaining to directors, officers, meetings, and voting. (Flip to Chapter 4 for more on this document.)

Funding and financing

Most nonprofits don't generally conduct their own operations to generate income. In fact, as Chapter 5 explains, nonprofits are not allowed to compete with the private sector businesses. Rather, nonprofits typically depend on the following sources to finance activities consistent with their missions:

- ✔ **Donations:** Private citizens can sometimes get tax deductions when they donate money to nonprofits. (The specifics of tax-deductibility of donations are covered in Chapter 14.)

- ✔ **Fundraising activities:** Nonprofits may carry out certain income-generating activities such as food drives, charity balls, and booster clubs, but may have to pay taxes on the earnings if they compete in certain ways with private businesses as discussed in Chapter 14.

- ✔ **Nonprofit foundations:** Individuals and organizations may establish private foundations (see Chapter 11 for more on foundations). These are special tax-exempt entities generally run by private individuals to accomplish tax-exempt purposes.

- ✔ **The government:** Nonprofit organizations are often established to carry out state, federal, and local government programs. These organizations may receive tax revenues that are allocated for such programs.

Tax-exempt status

Nonprofits generally don't have to pay federal income taxes on the funds that they receive from the sources listed in the preceding section. This is referred to as *tax-exempt status*. The requirements for obtaining tax-exempt status are discussed in more detail in Chapter 5.

To receive tax-exempt status, an organization must be operated exclusively for one or more of the following purposes:

- Charitable
- Religious
- Educational
- Scientific
- Literary
- Public safety
- The fostering of national or international amateur sports competition
- The prevention of cruelty to children or animals

There are instances where nonprofits are required to pay taxes on some activities that legally compete with the private or for-profit sector. For example, if an organization holds a weekly spaghetti dinner, it's considered to be competing with the local restaurants and therefore must pay taxes on the income from the fundraiser. The money it receives from this fundraiser is called *unrelated taxable business income.* (You can find more information about this type of income in Chapter 14.)

The bottom line

Even though nonprofits don't exist to generate a profit, they still must keep their eye on the bottom line. They generally have strict budgetary constraints. Nonprofit organizations may accept, hold, and disburse money and may enter into all sorts of commercial transactions. Money and how to manage it is a day-to-day issue for nonprofits.

A more precise term is not-for-profit, rather than nonprofit, and this is often used in legislation and texts.

Limitations

Because of their privileged tax-exempt status, nonprofits are prohibited from doing certain things that are completely acceptable for their private sector, for-profit counterparts. For example, nonprofit organizations usually lose their coveted exempt status if they do any of the following:

Why don't charitable organizations pay taxes?

The rationale that the courts have long used in exempting charitable organizations from taxation is that such entities often relieve the government of having to provide many similar services (feeding the poor, providing health and safety services, educating the public and promoting business cooperation). In particular, Congress figures that charitable organizations also relieve taxpayers of having to pay additional taxes for such services.

Each year thousands of organizations in the United States apply for and receive tax-exempt status from the Internal Revenue Service under Internal Revenue Code Section 501(c)(3), which is discussed more fully in Chapter 5.

- ✔ **Engage in prohibited political activities:** Nonprofits are prohibited from political campaign activity.
- ✔ **Change their operations on a whim:** Nonprofits must adhere to the purposes for which they were established. So, unlike their corporate counterparts, they can't diversify and evolve freely to reflect changing markets or community needs.
- ✔ **Farm out control of their operations:** Nonprofits must be governed by their own boards, and can't have outside management teams.

Ten of the most common ways that nonprofits can lose tax-exempt status are discussed in Chapter 18.

Comparing Small Nonprofits to Small For-Profit Businesses

Many nonprofits have huge missions and relatively small budgets to accomplish them. This imbalance isn't all that different from many private sector businesses, particularly small start-up companies with big future goals. To help you understand how nonprofits function, this section compares them to small businesses, with which you may be more familiar.

The similarities

If you work in a nonprofit environment, you may notice that your organization has the following similarities to a typical small business environment:

✓ **Well-defined goals and missions:** Everyone knows what the organization's product or services are.

✓ **Limited resources to accomplish goals:** The organization doesn't have unlimited resources, so it must accomplish its goals with the available funds.

✓ **Accountability for achieving the mission:** Organizations that fail in their missions generally aren't funded indefinitely.

✓ **Criteria for assessing whether goals are met:** Healthy for-profit and nonprofit organizations have created a way of self-evaluating to determine whether the organization is meeting its own goals.

✓ **A defined management or governing structure:** Like private corporations and commercial business entities, most nonprofit organizations have boards, management, and various levels of staff that help keep the organization afloat.

✓ **Identifiable stakeholders:** Just as private companies must know who their customers are and serve them accordingly, nonprofits must ultimately satisfy the objectives and needs of their various stakeholders.

The differences

Just as there are similarities between nonprofits and for-profits, there are also a few differences. For example, consider the following items, which you'll find in a nonprofit but not in a for-profit:

✓ **Third-party funding:** It's rare for someone to just give money to a for-profit business. However donations, grants, and government funding are the norm in the nonprofit world.

✓ **Participation of volunteers:** For-profit companies are generally staffed by employees who are hired at competitive wages. However, nonprofit organizations typically rely heavily on the donated time of volunteers.

✓ **Stakeholders who don't contribute financially to the organization:** Many of the people who are directly served by nonprofits contribute nothing financially to these organizations. There's a disconnect between the financial viability of a nonprofit organization and the perceived quality of the services or goods that it provides.

Surveying the Latest Legal Landscape

Congressional and Internal Revenue Services (IRS) initiatives, along with more stringent legislation, are causing nonprofits across the country to assess their compliance with the law and to reconsider decades-old practices. At the helm of this push for change is Republican Senator Charles Grassley of Iowa, who asked the IRS to look more closely at the inner workings of nonprofits. The Pension Protection Act of 2006, which contains provisions that nonprofits need to be aware of, is also an important part of the sweeping change that's occurring in the nonprofit sector.

New legal scrutiny over nonprofits

In 2004, Senator Grassley prodded the Senate Finance Committee to propose legislation that would dramatically increase federal government oversight of nonprofits.

He charged that nonprofit groups and individuals are "exploiting" a vacuum "in the enforcement of the laws governing tax-exempt groups to enrich themselves rather than serve the public." To this end, Grassley publicly requested that both the Chief Counsel of the IRS and the Commissioner of the IRS's tax-exempt entities division look into what is happening in the nonprofit sector more closely. To regain nonprofit service to the public, Senator Grassley specifically asked requested that the IRS scrutinize the following:

- **Charges of excessive compensation:** Senator Grassley urged the IRS to aggressively pursue cases where it appears that board members or trustees are receiving overly generous paychecks when taking into account what they actually do. (Flip to Chapter 6 to find out what compensation is appropriate for those who work for a nonprofit organization.)

- **Unrelated business income:** Senator Grassley questioned whether exempt organizations are abusing tax-exempt status by not paying taxes on income that's unrelated to their exempt purposes. (You can read more about unrelated business income in Chapter 14.)

- **The tax-exempt status of nonprofit hospitals:** Senator Grassley focused public attention on the issue of whether nonprofit hospitals provide enough charity care or other benefits to deserve their tax-exempt status.

- **Compliance with reporting requirements by large nonprofits:** Senator Grassley wanted to know how well charities with total assets of $100 million or more are complying with the requirement that they file their federal informational returns electronically.

Despite this aggressive to-do list, Grassley has not been overly critical of the IRS' efforts to date. In fact, he has publicly praised the agency for its efforts to ensure that charities are complying with the federal law that prohibits them from getting involved in partisan politics.

At Senator Grassley's prodding and after several well-publicized hearings on the subject, the Senate Finance Committee issued draft legislation in 2005. The Committee also agreed to receive legislative recommendations from the Panel on the Nonprofit Sector, which is a prestigious independent group of individuals with expertise in administering tax-exempt entities. The panel's Web site is located at www.nonprofitpanel.org.

Some of the ideas from Congress and other sources that the Committee discussed included the following:

- **Increasing IRS authority:** The Committee considered granting the IRS greater enforcement powers to address the perceived violations of tax-exempt status.

- **Ratcheting up Form 990 filing requirements:** By enhancing Form 990 filing requirements, the committee hoped to increase the transparency of tax-exempt organizations. (Form 990 is discussed in greater detail in Chapter 7.)

- **Requiring nonprofits to periodically reconfirm their tax-exempt status.**

Shining the spotlight on some specific charities

Some of the groups that Senator Grassley targeted in his scrutiny of nonprofits include the Edward Orton Jr. Ceramic Foundation in Westerville, Ohio, the Musculoskeletal Transplant Foundation in Edison, N.J., and the National Association of Investors Corporation in Madison Heights, Mich.

According to Senate Finance Committee findings, the organizations generated significant amounts of income that were unrelated to their tax-exempt purpose, but they didn't pay taxes on those funds. Senator Grassley further alleged that key officials of the organizations appeared to be overpaid.

J. Gary Childress, the Orton Foundation's general manager, steadfastly defended his organization's tax-exempt status in the media. Childress denied that Orton violated any laws or overpaid any employees. He explained that the court had affirmed the IRS's determination of Orton's tax-exempt status in 1971. He explained that Orton didn't have to pay tax on its sales of ceramics because they were related to its charitable purpose of furthering research in the field of industrial ceramics.

Similarly, representatives of the Musculoskeletal Transplant Foundation defended its tax-exempt status by explaining that their organization provides products that for-profit companies do not. "Given the altruistic nature of tissue donation, MTF strongly believes that its tissue banking is a tax-exempt activity that should continue to be performed by nonprofit, charitable organizations and should not be not subject to taxes as an unrelated business activity."

The Red Cross versus Senator Grassley

In December 2006, Senator Grassley took aim at one of the largest and most established nonprofit targets in the United States: the American Red Cross. In a well-publicized letter, he asked the Red Cross to explain in detail how its board operates. He requested copies of all board meeting minutes for the past five years, a description of the duties of the board, correspondence and e-mails between board members and its chief executive officer, and copies of the agency's internal evaluations.

In his letter and accompanying press statements, Senator Grassley questioned the effectiveness of the governing board. His demand for an investigation came in response to charges that the agency had responded slowly and inefficiently to Hurricane Katrina and had mismanaged funds meant for victims of the September 11 terrorist attacks.

Finally, Senator Grassley explained that "the name and notoriety of the Red Cross make it essential for those governing the organization to go the extra mile to ensure public confidence not only in the Red Cross but in the nonprofit sector generally."

Here's the Red Cross's response to the publicity:

"We are fully cooperating with the Senate Finance Committee and Chairman Grassley in response to their questions regarding the operations of the American Red Cross. The American Red Cross is committed to learning from our prior challenges and making the necessary changes to improve the delivery of services to the American people.

The Red Cross wants to implement the best corporate governance practices found in the charitable and for-profit sectors. We are encouraged that Senator Grassley, in his letter today, agrees that "there is no daylight between us in that common goal." To that end, the American Red Cross has initiated an independent governance review and will soon host a summit on corporate governance best practices, all with the purpose of developing concrete recommendations.

Because the Red Cross exists to fulfill a vital national mission, we bear an exceptional burden to ensure that we meet and exceed the expectations of those whom we serve and of those who selflessly donate their time, money and blood."

The Pension Protection Act of 2006

The federal Pension Protection Act of 2006 is the newest legislation that's designed to protect workers' pension rights. This Act contains many embedded provisions for nonprofits, some of which are actually welcomed by the organizations.

Ease of revoking tax-exempt status

Prior to the Pension Protection Act, once an organization received its determination from the IRS that it had qualified for tax-exempt status under Section 501(c)(3) of the Internal Revenue Code, that status remained in effect forever unless revoked by the IRS. Now, under Section 1223(b) of the Pension Protection Act, tax status is automatically revoked if the organization fails to file Form 990 three years in a row. Form 990 is the informational return that the IRS requires nonprofit organizations to file. (This form and all its requirements are discussed in Chapter 7.)

Record-keeping requirements

Save your receipts! Under the new law, no tax deductions are allowed for cash contributions without a receipt, canceled check, or credit card statement. You don't need to mail these things in with your tax returns, but you do need to keep the receipts and other documentation with your copy of the return in case you're stuck with an IRS audit.

The new law also toughens the rules for noncash donations. If you donate items such as cars, clothing, and household goods to a charity, they must be in good condition.

New tracking of tiny nonprofits

For the last 40 years, the IRS has exempted small organizations from having to maneuver the complexities of IRS Form 990. This exemption meant that the local church bake sale and other programs with annual revenues under $25,000 didn't have to file anything with the IRS. However, they were still required to comply with state laws. This is no longer true.

With the new Pension Protection Act, these small nonprofit groups are now required to provide the following information to the IRS:

- ✔ The legal name of the organization
- ✔ Any name under which such organization operates or does business
- ✔ The organization's mailing address and Web address (if any)
- ✔ The organization's taxpayer identification number
- ✔ The name and address of a principal officer
- ✔ Evidence of the continuing basis for the organization's exemption from the filing requirements (such as documents verifying its status with state governments)

It remains to be seen what the new IRS "notice" form for small organizations will include. The requirement that organizations offer up "evidence" pretty much assures that some new type of IRS form will be created and required even for the smallest organizations.

The implications of revocation

The IRS publishes a new shaming list of the organizations that have had their tax-exempt status revoked due to failure to file returns or notices, which means that donors who make gifts after the lists are published will be denied a deduction. And you know what that means: You'll have some angry donors who will spread the negative news far and wide. As you can imagine, that's not good for an organization's bottom line. As if that bad publicity weren't enough, the organizations also have to reapply for tax-exempt status (not a fun weekend task). If an organization can show "reasonable cause" for failure to file the return or notice, exemption *may be* granted retroactively to the date of the loss of exemption.

Focusing on Good Governance

Institutes and seminars have sprung up across the country to help nonprofits govern themselves more effectively. Many nonprofit organizations are also voluntarily complying with Sarbanes-Oxley, a stringent law passed to govern for-profit corporations. This law was passed in response to the bankruptcies of Enron and Worldcom and was aimed at corporate corruption. Corporations have spent billions to comply with this law. Nonprofits, though legally exempt from most of Sarbanes-Oxley, are facing a confidence crisis of their own due to this far-reaching law. Desperate to avoid the public scrutiny bestowed on the Red Cross and United Way (both of which were caught up in nasty scandals), many nonprofits are adopting Sarbanes-Oxley standards on a voluntary basis. Check out Chapter 13 for more on these corporate standards in the nonprofit sector.

Chapter 2

Regulating Nonprofits: Who's in Charge?

In This Chapter

▶ Looking at the IRS's enforcement role

▶ Understanding how the USPS regulates nonprofits

▶ Checking out the federal election requirements

▶ Surveying state and local laws and model acts

Approximately 1.4 million charitable, religious, scientific, educational, and cultural organizations in the United States compete for funds and government support to carry out their operations. The nonprofit sector holds assets of more than $2 trillion and receives about $241 billion in support from individuals, corporations, and foundations. Compared to private businesses (particularly after the Sarbanes-Oxley Act was passed, as discussed in Chapter 13), nonprofits have been allowed to operate in this country with a surprising amount of freedom. However, the size of the sector and the support it receives from the public points to the need for effective regulation. So, in this chapter, I show you how the layers of regulation are imposed at the federal, state, and local levels.

The IRS: The Primary Federal Regulator

The Internal Revenue Service (IRS) isn't only the collection arm of the federal government; it's also the chief regulator of larger nonprofit organizations. In particular, it's the arm of the government that holds the responsibility for granting and taking away the tax-exempt status of public charities (see Chapter 5 for more details on getting tax-exempt status).

A brief history of philanthropy

The concept of charitable giving dates back to biblical times. The ancient Romans also were quite the community philanthropists. They founded hospitals, asylums, and nursing homes throughout the empire. In the middle ages, churches administered many programs that bear remarkable similarity to modern-day government programs. Plato established the equivalent of a modern-day private foundation to support an educational academy after his death.

And, finally, philanthropy got a real boost in the United States during the Industrial Revolution, when benevolent and socially conscious organizations began springing up to stem the tide of misery that accompanied the wave of economic progress. These societies and organizations have remained important though the years. Some retain the informal structures typical of smaller nonprofits, whereas others have grown to huge national and even multinational enterprises that are subject to complex laws and regulations.

Because the IRS is the agency that confers tax-exempt status, it has come to play a dominant role in regulating what charities can and can't do. Without tax-exempt status, organizations must pay federal (and in some cases state) income taxes on the funds that they receive. And to top it all off, the people who donate to these charities can't take a charitable deduction when paying their own taxes.

The IRS has a specific, highly trained Tax Exempt and Government Entities Division (TE/GE) that's staffed by specialists in the nonprofit area. These specialists view their roles less as tax collectors and more as nonprofit watchdogs. Their publicly stated role is to make sure that exempt organizations continue to make the contributions to society that justify their coveted tax-exempt status. (The role of the TE/GE is discussed more fully in Chapter 15.)

According to the way the IRS looks things, Public charities fall into two categories:

✔ **Private foundations:** *Private foundations* are a special type of charity established by a small number of private donors so that they can direct how the charitable funds are spent. The private foundation is eligible for tax-exempt status if it complies with the rules found in Section of the Internal Revenue Code. (Private foundations are discussed more extensively in Chapter 11.)

   Stricter rules apply to private foundations because in theory they aren't subject to regulations or required to be responsive to the public in the same way as churches, government programs, schools, hospitals, and organizations that get their support from the government.

✔ **Other kinds of public charities:** Charities that are not managed by private individuals (which are the vast majority of charities) fall into this category. Traditional types of public charities include churches, research facilities and publicly funded heath care institutions.

U.S. Postal Regulations

Because many nonprofits depend so heavily on U.S. mail for their fundraising appeals, the postmaster of the U.S. Postal Service (USPS) serves as another resource for regulating them.

For example, in the last few years, the USPS has really stepped up its efforts in enforcing nonprofit postal regulations more vigorously than ever before. It's mainly concerned with fraudulent or misleading direct-mail pieces and in cracking down on for-profit firms that try to send mail using nonprofit permits.

In order to effectively monitor and regulate nonprofit postal regulations, the USPS is authorized, by federal laws and regulation, to do the following:

✔ Spot-check bulk mail (for things like drugs and explosives)

✔ Impose fines if abuses are uncovered, such as mailing illegal substances or using the mail to run a scam

✔ Require changes in the content of the mailing, such as a disclaimer so that the content is not misleading

✔ Revoke nonprofit mailing permits

The bulk mail coordinator at your local or regional post office can be helpful in answering questions about obtaining and properly using a nonprofit postal permit.

Federal Election Laws

Nonprofit organizations are limited in the type and scope of the political activities in which they can engage because of their tax-exempt status under Section 501(c)(3) of the Internal Revenue Code. The government's rationale for this limitation is simple: It doesn't make any sense for the government to subsidize organizations by granting tax-exempt status so that the nonprofits can advocate for their own political interests.

The following is a quick rundown of political activities that tax-exempt organizations *can* do:

- ✔ Lobby (within a certain limit) on specific issues
- ✔ Conduct nonpartisan public education and training sessions about participation in the political process
- ✔ Educate political candidates on issues of public interest
- ✔ Publish information about political candidates' positions on issues
- ✔ Rent their mailing lists to political organizations that pay fair market value for the information
- ✔ Conduct voter registration and participation drives
- ✔ Work with political parties on formulating their platforms

The following is a skull-and-crossbones list of activities that 501(c)(3) tax-exempt nonprofit organizations *can't* do:

- ✔ Endorse candidates for public office
- ✔ Make any campaign contributions
- ✔ Restrict the rental of their mailing lists to certain political candidates
- ✔ Ask candidates to directly endorse a specific issue in exchange for the organization's support
- ✔ Step up their criticism of the actions of incumbent candidates immediately before an election
- ✔ Publish or communicate anything that explicitly or implicitly favors or opposes a candidate

Organizations who engage in these prohibited activities face the loss of their tax-exempt status, and all of the negative publicity that is associated with such a loss. Donors may be prohibited from taking deductions on future returns.

Chapter 3 provides accounts of organizations that have lost their tax-exempt status after engaging in prohibited political activity.

State Regulations

Most states are active in policing the charities and organizations within their borders. For example, states generally determine which organizations can represent themselves as nonprofits, and they make sure that the nonprofits have a valid purpose. The states also police the solicitation and fundraising that takes place within their borders.

State attorneys also play an important enforcement role in interpreting the laws for various states and bringing lawsuits against errant nonprofits in court. During these lawsuits, state courts have the power and discretion to correct abuses in the nonprofit sector by rendering in decisions and handing down orders that deal with specific infractions.

There are no legal constraints on the sharing of information between the IRS and state revenue departments. This means they can both audit you or your organization more efficiently!

Fifty laws for fifty states

Where there's a state, there's a statute. In other words, most states have their own ideas and laws about what constitutes proper behavior by a nonprofit organization. These laws address issues like the following:

- **Registration:** States need to keep tabs on who's operating nonprofit organizations within their borders. To get this information, states usually require nonprofits to fill out some type of current registration document.

- **State taxation:** States are responsible for deciding whether organizations within their borders are required to pay income, sales and use, and property taxes.

- **Regulation of solicitation:** States want to know who's knocking on doors, sending flyers, or telephoning people for money within their borders. Most states have a division of a consumer affairs organization that monitors charitable solicitation activities. At a minimum, states usually require organizations that are soliciting funds to identify themselves and their purpose.

- **Immunity of directors and trustees:** Because many nonprofit organizations depend on volunteers, it's important for states to have laws in place that address the issue of whether directors and trustees can be sued for the liabilities of the organization.

  In most states, if registrations are kept current, the directors and trustees of the organization will be immune from civil suits unless they commit outright fraud.

✔ **Fraud prevention:** State attorneys general play an active role in making sure that sham organizations aren't used to dupe consumers into contributing to bogus causes.

✔ **Governance issues:** The federal government leaves day-to-day governance issues to the states. These issues include things like how many board members need to be present before an organization can vote on an issue and the terms of board members and how they're selected.

Does it seem incomprehensible that nonprofit organizations have to pass through a gauntlet of fifty state laws?

Fortunately, there are some basic similarities in the regulatory frameworks adopted in each state. These similarities exist for two reasons:

✔ Nonprofit organizations across the country tend to face similar issues (for example, the ones listed in the previous bulleted list). This means that all the states usually cover the same topics.

✔ Many states borrow heavily from prewritten sets of laws called *model acts,* which are covered in the next section.

Model acts: Templates for good behavior

It may seem odd to think that many state legislatures simply cut-and-paste from another document in passing important statutes that affect nonprofit organizations within their borders. But process in a number of states, thanks to the existence of many "model acts" available to states as crib sheets.

Most states have nonprofit laws that are based on a *model nonprofit corporation act* and several other types of laws that are based on *model acts.* These model acts are scholarly, well-thought-out documents that are created by special government panels, expert committees, and specially convened commissions that think through the important issues and come up with the best possible legal language to cover them.

After the model acts are written, they're made available as a sample set of laws that states are free to literally copy into their own laws, in whole or in part.

If you become familiar with a model act (or the laws of at least one state that are based on the act), you'll have a good understanding of how the laws in most other states work.

Because each of the fifty states has thousands of nonprofits within its borders, it's inevitable that legislators and regulators are going to search for these types of shortcuts to deal with the most common issues. For this reason, several model acts have sprung up to help states grapple with complicated nonprofit issues, the most important of which is the Model Nonprofit Corporation Act. This section takes you on a tour of some of the more commonly relied upon model acts, and alerts you to the issues that they attempt to address.

The Model Nonprofit Corporation Act

The Model Nonprofit Corporation Act is a set of sample statutes that can be adopted by states to regulate the nonprofits that operate within their borders. The Revised Model Nonprofit Corporation Act was adopted in 1987 by a subcommittee of the American Bar Association. This revised Act contains sample laws on many issues, including the following:

- ✔ Requirements for registration with the state
- ✔ Requirements for what must be included in an acceptable set of Articles of Incorporation
- ✔ Requirements for what belongs in a nonprofit's bylaws

The Revised Model Nonprofit Corporation Act is the most important model act for nonprofits. Its most important provisions are reproduced in Appendix D.

There have been no updates since 1987. So it's important to keep in mind that many of the provisions of the Model Nonprofit Corporation Act don't take into account current tax laws and the more recent trends in federal and state legislation.

While most states have adopted key portions of this Act in some form, not *all* states have. And the states that have done so invariably make at least some modifications. So it's only a starting point in getting an overview of state law. To find out what the law is in a particular state, you need to consult that state's statute or an attorney who practices law within the state.

The states that have adopted the entire model

Parts of the Revised Model Corporation Act have been applied pretty much word-for-word, in whole or in part, in the following states:

- ✔ Arkansas
- ✔ Indiana
- ✔ Mississippi

 ✔ Montana

 ✔ North Carolina

 ✔ South Carolina

 ✔ Tennessee

 ✔ Washington

States that have rejected the model

Some states have formally rejected the Revised Model Nonprofit Corporation Act. For example, Wyoming, Georgia, and Ohio have explicitly rejected the Act, and have stated that they will draft their own laws from scratch, thank you very much. This means that even if you're generally familiar with the Model Nonprofit Corporation Act, you need to look carefully at what these states have in their statutes without assuming any similarities with the model act.

States that have taken a middle ground

Nearly half the states that haven't formally adopted the Revised Model Corporation Act as their own state statutory scheme have nevertheless adopted some of its most important provisions. These states usually have laws that follow the Act's guidance on issues like the duty of care that directors owe to an organization (see Chapter 8 for more on the duty of care).

The Model Charitable Solicitations Act

The Model Charitable Solicitations Act is another set of prewritten sample statutes that states can adopt to regulate organizations that *solicit* (ask for money) within their borders.

The Model Charitable Solicitations Act was developed by the National Association of Attorneys General (NAAG), the National Association of State Charity Officials (NASCO), and a bunch of representatives from the nonprofit sector. It was drafted in 1986 and hasn't been updated since 1986 (which means there are plenty of things in it that are either obsolete or don't make sense to follow in the context of other legislation that has been enacted over the last two decades).

The Model Charitable Solicitations Act has one major notable bug. In 1988, the U.S. Supreme Court struck down parts of the Act as unconstitutional. In particular, the Supreme Court took issue with the provisions of the Act that required professional solicitors to register with the state and provide financial details about their services. So, as you can imagine, states haven't and won't be adopting these financial provisions.

However, states can (and most do) require organizations and individuals who solicit funds within their borders to register and meet certain minimal requirements. These requirements are intended to ensure that state residents aren't duped into donating money to fraudulent fundraising scams.

Many states also require professional solicitors to register. These states may have specific requirements for the solicitation material as well.

Some states exempt organizations that solicit contributions below a certain dollar amount. In some states, the threshold exception doesn't apply if the solicitation activities are conducted by anyone other than volunteers.

The Uniform Unincorporated Nonprofit Association Act: Regulating small nonprofits

No laws require a nonprofit organization to incorporate, or even to adopt any type of formal business structure. However, many states strongly believe that some sort of rules should apply to those informally organized nonprofits that are operating within their borders.

Accordingly, the Uniform Unincorporated Nonprofit Association Act (UUNAA) was drafted by a National Conference of Commissioners on Uniform State Laws.

This particular model act addresses the following sticky questions:

- Who has the authority to acquire, hold, and transfer property on behalf of an unincorporated association?
- Who can sue on behalf of the entity?
- Who can be sued if the entity engages in actions that result in civil liability?
- Who has the right to enter into contracts on behalf of the entity?

The UUNAA was drafted with the small, informal associations in mind. If your nonprofit falls into this category, it may not have ready access to legal advice. So the UUNAA is a good source of legal answers for your organization. You can find a copy of the Act at www.muridae.com/nporegulation/documents/unincorp_assoc_act.html.

The model standards for charitable gift annuities

An *annuity* is a type of investment that you purchase for a lump sum and then receive principal and interest payments over a period of time. States have long been in charge of regulating the insurance and annuity industries. Annuities are particularly relevant to charities because charities invest large donations that they receive in annuities, or they may receive donations in the form of an annuity (such as a grant that's paid out over time). Sometimes charities even sell *gift annuities*, which are contractual arrangements between donors and charities where the charity makes fixed periodic payments to one or two individuals (annuitants) in exchange for money or assets transferred to the charity.

Having your cake and eating it too: Charitable gift annuities

Charitable gift annuities are a flexible way for wealthy individuals to make a gift of valuable property to charity during their life, get a big tax deduction for doing it, and keep a stream of income from the property that they can use during their lives.

For example, suppose you want to make a $100,000 gift to a charity that has a program for making charitable gift annuities. Here's how a typical program might work:

1. You complete a special annuity agreement contract with the charity, which specifies the gift and the income stream that you'll receive each year.

2. You transfer $100,000 worth of cash or other assets to the charity.

3. You receive fixed payments annually (or more frequently if desired) in an amount specified in the agreement. (The amount of the payment is a percentage of the gift based on your age and other factors at the time of the gift.)

4. The IRS allows you to take an immediate charitable income tax deduction in the year you make the gift. In addition to this deduction, part of the annual annuity payment you get each year is tax-free for the number of years equal to your life expectancy.

5. As yet another bonus, in addition to the income tax deduction you get, the assets used to fund your gift annuity aren't included in your estate for estate tax purposes.

In some cases, if the annuity contract you sign with the charity allows it, you can choose another person (typically a spouse, parent, or sibling) to receive payments if you don't live out your life expectancy.

The charitable annuity strategy is particularly effective if you're giving a charity a gift of some sort of property that's increased in value a lot since you got it. Normally, you'd have to pay income tax on all that gain (which is called *capital gains tax*) all in one year. However, if you make the gift, you can pay that nasty capital gains tax a little bit each year for the duration of your life expectancy (instead of taking a big tax hit in a single year).

Also, because the initial income tax deduction is based on the current value of the property (rather than what you paid for it), the tax incentives for entering into charitable gift annuities are huge. At the end of the process you get to bypass capital gains tax, you get a current income tax charitable deduction, and you get to report a portion of your annuity payment at reduced rates. Plus you get to help a worthy charity!

Nonprofits and the laws of other countries

With the Internet, it isn't uncommon for a non-profit organization to attract the attention of donors (and regulatory authorities) outside of the United States. But you have to be cautious because many foreign governments are stricter about regulating the solicitation of nonprofits than U.S authorities, whereas others are considerably more lenient.

In many countries, nonprofits are referred to as *non-government organizations,* or NGOs. A complete discussion of the laws of every country in the world, are obviously beyond the scope of this (or any) book. However, the overall picture is a complicated patchwork of laws, culminating at least one account of a U.S. citizen traveling as a tourist being arrested in another country for material appearing on a Web site.

The National Association of Insurance Commissioners has drafted two model acts to help states regulate the so-called "planned giving" industry (planned giving is a method of making a charitable contribution where some or all gift components are only distributed, or have their ownership finally resolved, after some event has passed).

The first model act on this subject is the Charitable Gift Annuities Model Act, which has a lot of requirements for charities that use annuities as a tool for funding their operations. (For more information about charitable gift annuities, see the sidebar "Having your cake and eating it too: Charitable gift annuities." This act requires charities that offer gift annuities to notify state officials that they do so. The model act also requires that the charities have at least $300,000 in available assets. You can view a copy of the act at www. pgresources.com/draft2.html.

The model acts that regulate charitable investments

Many nonprofit organizations hold the money they get from donations, grants, and other sources in a trust. They invest the trust assets and use the income they get from the investments to help fund their operations and fulfill their missions. The responsibility for making sensible investments rests with the boards of the charitable organizations, which are deemed to be acting as trustees (see Chapter 8 for more on the duties of board members who are considered trustees). Accordingly, the boards are held to special standards that apply to trustees. The following model acts help states deal with these issues:

- **The Uniform Prudent Investor Act:** This Act covers issues like what care trustees and fiduciaries need to exercise in choosing investments and what standards are acceptable in terms of risk and potential return.

- ✔ **The Uniform Management of Institutional Funds Act:** This model act explains the rights of governing boards to invest the funds of specific types of institutions such as hospitals and colleges.

- ✔ **The Uniform Principal and Income Act:** This Act, which was created by the National Conference of Commissioners on Uniform State Laws in 1997, is a good starting point if you want to discover the duties that trustees are responsible for when investing funds held in trust.

- ✔ **The Uniform Trust Act:** This particular model act contains sample laws that apply to the administration of trusts, such as accounting for principal and interest. The Uniform Trust Act is still under development.

Regulations in Counties and Municipalities

Government regulation of nonprofits doesn't end at the state level. Counties and municipalities also have a say as to what goes on within their borders, and so they add another layer of regulation in the form of local ordinances and regulations.

Typically these local ordinances address issues like door-to-door solicitation, signage, and activities that affect the community. These county and municipal ordinances may also provide for local property tax exemptions in that jurisdiction's authority.

Counties and municipalities may require special permits and licensing for nonprofits to conduct activities within their borders. To find out what requirements are in effect in your area, check with the local county or municipal office or police department.

Adhering to the fundraising standards of watchdog groups

In the world of nonprofits, watchdog agencies pay a special role in protecting the public and in maintaining the credibility of nonprofits. One such group is the Council of Better Business Bureaus' Philanthropic Advisory Service. This group has created some comprehensive fundraising standards for nonprofit organizations. According to these standards, squeaky clean nonprofit organizations should spend at least 50 percent of the funds they get from consumers on the activities described in the initial solicitation.

Chapter 3

The State of the Nation's Nonprofits

In This Chapter

▶ Understanding the current level of scrutiny

▶ Looking at missteps made by some high-profile nonprofits

▶ Summarizing the Pension Protection Act of 2006

*I*nspired by tales of fundraising fraud, conflicts of interest, bloated compensation, and excessive overhead, state and federal legislators are hard at work creating new laws to restore public confidence. This time, it isn't corporations like Enron or Worldcom provoking public outrage; rather it's the nation's nonprofit organizations that are gaining negative attention. This chapter presents several lessons you can learn from recent scandals.

After cracking down on corporate America by enacting the Sarbanes-Oxley Act (SOX) in 2002, lawmakers and enforcement officials are now setting their sights on the country's 1.8 million nonprofits. As discussed later in this chapter, many provisions in the Pension Protection Act of 2006 are a direct response to high-profile scandals in the nonprofit sector.

Unprecedented Scrutiny

U.S. nonprofits are entering an era of the most intense federal and state regulation in history. The following are examples of developments currently converging into a perfect legal storm for the nation's nonprofits:

✔ **Federal legislation:** On August 17, 2006, President Bush signed into law the Pension Protection Act of 2006 (PPA), which includes a package of charitable giving incentives and safeguard measures as well as a series of reforms designed to deter individuals from using public charities for private benefit. The specific provisions of the PPA are discussed in more detail later in this chapter in the section "New Federal Legislation: The Pension Protection Act of 2006."

✔ **Sweeping state reforms:** States are passing tough new laws, such as California's Nonprofit Integrity Act of 2004, which is rapidly becoming a template for other state initiatives. The act requires charities with at least $2 million in revenue to conduct annual audits, to follow certain procedures in compensating executives, to establish a board-level audit committee, and to work with the attorney general's office before fundraising. Similar bills cracking down on nonprofits have also been proposed in at least a dozen other states, including New York, Arizona, and Maine. West Virginia recently started funding programs to educate board members who oversee the state's nonprofit organizations. (See the sidebar "One state's experiment in teaching board members how to read financial statements.")

Many states already have stringent laws on the books, and nonprofits anticipate them being enforced with new vigor. Fortunately, most state laws contain common elements for accountability and governance, and it's possible for nonprofits, which often operate and solicit donations in many states, to adopt policies and governance structures that will fulfill all emerging state requirements.

✔ **IRS initiatives:** The Internal Revenue Service (IRS), which grants tax exemptions to nonprofits, is dedicating more auditors to its tax-exempt unit. The IRS is currently auditing about 500 large foundations, which control billions of dollars in assets, to determine their compensation practices. Various legislative initiatives have been proposed to increase the resources available to the IRS to monitor nonprofits, and would require the IRS to pass more stringent regulations for nonprofits. (See the sidebar "A new era of nonprofit audits" for more on how the IRS is more closely monitoring nonprofit organizations.)

Under these emerging state and federal regulatory schemes, nonprofits not only face new regulatory requirements, but they also face much higher risks of litigation. Regardless of whether a lawsuit or an investigation is meritorious, the associated publicity can place nonprofits in peril, as donors awaiting the outcome withdraw critical financial support.

Lessons from Nonprofits in the News

An alarming study by the Brookings Institute found that roughly a third of Americans expressed confidence in how U.S. nonprofits are run. This climate placed the nonprofit community on high alert, particularly charitable nonprofits, which survive on donations and public confidence. Because nonprofits must maintain public confidence to survive, many have embarked on a course of voluntary self-reform.

One state's experiment in teaching board members how to read financial statements

In West Virginia, a scandal at a nonprofit senior center made headlines when it was revealed that the board members, who didn't understand how to interpret financial statements, had been duped into allowing the director to earn nearly half a million dollars in salary and benefits. State officials realized that many nonprofit members didn't have a clue as to how to read a financial statement, and decided to take action.

The Secretary of State's office teamed up with the private company to provide training seminars for nonprofit board members throughout the state. Secretary of State Spokesman Ben Beakes told reporters that state officials may eventually push to make financial and ethics training mandatory for all nonprofit volunteers.

In a survey by the law firm Foley & Lardner, 93 percent of charitable nonprofits reported that they have implemented or are in the process of implementing programs of self-regulation to mirror the Sarbanes-Oxley requirements (discussed in Chapter 13) that are imposed on their private sector counterparts. However, few resources are available to guide nonprofits in complying with the barrage of new laws being passed to make such reform mandatory.

Because many nonprofits rely on public donations and political goodwill, negative publicity can be extremely damaging. Even if your nonprofit organization is publicly vindicated, or some bad publicity is unfair, donor confidence can be diminished. Moreover, confidence in the organizations' leadership may be lost, which leads to turnover that diverts the board's attention from its mission for an extended period of time.

This section looks at some missteps that have plagued prominent nonprofits and that have been reported in the press. These missteps offer you insight as to how your nonprofit organization can avoid a similar fate.

Lesson #1: Spend donations only for the intended purposes

Even if no funds turned up missing and every dollar is used for a positive purpose, your nonprofit can become embroiled in a scandal if funds are spent on anything other than what donors gave the money for. Public confidence in the nation's charities plummeted when questions arose as to how the Red Cross and other prominent nonprofit groups administered the more than $2 billion that poured in for the victims of the September 11, 2001, terrorist attacks.

A new era of nonprofit audits

Internal Revenue Service (IRS) statistics show that in 2005 the number of nonprofit agencies nationwide that file annual tax returns grew by more than 100,000. There are now approximately 648,600 agencies in the United States. The IRS expects to get nearly 90,000 applications from organizations applying for charitable status in 2006 alone.

To keep pace, the IRS now has a total of 905 workers assigned to monitor the compliance of tax-exempt organizations. IRS audits of non-profit groups have increased by 12.3 percent since 2001, and more than 6,000 audits are projected for the 2006 tax year.

The IRS has targeted mostly larger nonprofits with assets of $10 million or more so that the agency can monitor the greatest amount of non-profit assets with its own limited audit resources. The agency is paying special attention to entities that receive large government grants.

While many of the donations had no legal restrictions attached to them, most donors believed that their donations were specifically for 9/11 relief. Some organizations used funds for other arguably good purposes. But, this misuse of funds put them in clear violation of federal and state law standards.

Media accounts focused, in particular, on the Red Cross, which admittedly used funds designated by donors for 9/11 relief to fund other projects. Senator Charles E. Grassley of Iowa, of the Senate Finance Committee, publicly demanded that the Red Cross turn over a comprehensive accounting of its finances. New York Attorney General Eliot Spitzer, threatened to sue the charity. Previous to this misstep, the Red Cross had enjoyed the status of a quasi-government agency, with virtually no oversight.

The controversy prompted calls for oversight that have reverberated at every level of the nonprofit community. It also resulted in leadership change at the Red Cross.

Your organization needs to carefully track restrictions to which donations are subject and account for its programs separately, as appropriate. You must maintain separate accounts to ensure that funds from donors and granting authorities are used for designated purposes.

Lesson #2: Exercise oversight in distributing program funds

In the aftermath of the Hurricane Katrina disaster of 2005, Federal Emergency Management Agency (FEMA) executives and charitable employees were arrested on federal bribery charges for inflating the number and cost of meals served at Hurricane Katrina relief centers. The Red Cross also made headlines by distributing $6.2 million in funds to a town that was barely touched by the Hurricane. National media reported that town residents formed long lines to receive $2,400 payments, which they then used to buy jewelry and other nonessential items.

Your nonprofit organization must take reasonable steps to identify who is actually benefiting from its programs and how. This means that boards and management can't simply issue policies, but they have to take a realistic hands-on look at how they're actually working.

Lesson #3: Compensate nonprofit executives reasonably

Excessive executive compensation (as discussed more fully in Chapter 6) is yet another reason that nonprofits find themselves the subject of unwelcome media scrutiny.

For example, did you know that the New York Stock Exchange (NYSE) is a nonprofit? New York Attorney General Eliot Spitzer knew, and he sued NYSE Chairman Richard A. Grasso over his $187 million compensation package. The suit said that the NYSE failed to ensure compliance with New York's nonprofit corporation law. Publicity over the lawsuit ultimately forced Grasso out of office.

Universities also have been frequently questioned regarding their compensation policies in recent years. For example, the press picked up on the fact that Harvard University was questioned regarding its management of a $19 billion endowment after it paid a $1.8 million severance package to a former university president. Following the media reports, Massachusetts Attorney General Michael A. Hatch ordered an audit of the last year of the fund.

The healthcare industry, dominated by nonprofits, is another favorite focus of the media. For instance, in 2005, Minneapolis-based HealthPartners, Inc., a nonprofit healthcare company, was embarrassed by revelations of inflated compensation packages, contracts between insiders, and excessive travel and entertainment costs. HealthPartners underwent an audit, and says it readily implemented all audit recommendations.

Excessive compensation at nonprofits will likely be in the news with even more regularity, as the IRS ratchets up its audit ratio. The agency has already identified as many as 200 nonprofits that pay an executive or board member more than $1 million a year. The IRS has pledged to investigate them and follow up with audits.

Nonprofits and the bankruptcy law

Among other scandals in the nonprofit sector, there has been an increase in organizations filing for bankruptcy under Chapter 11. A *Chapter 11 bankruptcy* is a type of proceeding that allows an organization to "reorganize" and pay its debts under a plan. Organizations that want to continue must file Chapter 11–type bankruptcies instead of filing under other sections of the bankruptcy code that allow the entity to fold and discharge its debts.

Usually a nonprofit that's financially troubled will fold instead of opting to pay its debts under a bankruptcy plan that allows it to continue. Successful Chapter 11 filings aren't common because it's difficult for an organization to rebound.

Unlike for-profit businesses, nonprofits can't be forced to convert from Chapter 11 to Chapter 7 bankruptcy, which is a liquidation proceeding. If a donation is made to a nonprofit that has filed for Chapter 11, it's generally considered part of the bankruptcy estate unless the donor places restrictions on the gift.

Among the more prominent Chapter 11 bankruptcy filings is a private New York high school. This school proposed to change the valuation on a property, purchased for $4.25 million, to its true market value, which it believed to be $1.2 million. Several Roman Catholic dioceses have also filed for bankruptcy in the wake of abuse scandals. Chapter 11 filings also occur in the nonprofit hospital sector.

Compensation must be reasonable. Boards should have some knowledge of market rates paid to management in similar positions in both the private and nonprofit sector. If the board doesn't have this information, it should establish a compensation committee to research the issue and make appropriate compensation recommendations (as discussed in Chapter 6).

Lesson #4: Discourage donors from taking grossly inflated deductions

Allowing donors to take inflated deductions for property that they donate to your organization is another good way to attract negative media attention. (Chapter 14 gives you guidelines for keeping your donors in line with respect to the values they place on what they give to your organization.)

In 2006, many newspapers across the country picked up on the fact that tax deductions for vehicle donations cost the government hundreds of millions of dollars. Senator Charles E. Grassley of Iowa said that his concerns went well beyond cars. "Donations of land, art, and intellectual property are all raising concerns," he said. "The Finance Committee will look at significant reforms in this area."

Even though your organization isn't legally responsible for valuing donations, failing to look into the issue can cause some embarrassing media moments. (Check out Chapter 14 for more on donation valuation.)

Lesson #5: Have more than one person authorize expenditures

The United Way's image was tarnished by failing to exercise effective control over how its funds were disbursed. In 2005, the United Way of the National Capital Area, which raises money in the District of Columbia and its suburbs in Maryland and Virginia, was caught up in a scandal involving allegations of financial mismanagement and excessive expenses and management compensation. Upon further investigation, it was revealed that management had sidestepped audits and board oversight.

The former chief executive of the local United Way of the National Capital Area pled guilty to defrauding the charity of almost $500,000. Prosecutors said Oral Suer, who had served as CEO of nearly 20 years, charged the organization for personal expenses, such as bowling equipment and trips to Las Vegas, paid himself $333,000 for annual leave, and misappropriated $94,000 from the charity's pension plan, leaving the public to wonder what kind of oversight was in place when checks were cut.

Another scandal involved PipeVine, a San Francisco nonprofit corporation that processed more than $100 million a year in charitable donations for several United Way organizations and Fortune 500 companies. It was abruptly shut down in 2006 after it had mistakenly spent some donations on its own operating expenses.

Always have several people in your nonprofit reviewing the signing of checks and the payment of expenditures to ferret out improper payments before the press does.

Lesson #6: Operate under established and well-documented standards

Though accused of misdeeds, the Liberty-Ellis Island Foundation, which oversaw the restoration of the Statue of Liberty, stood tall. The agency was accused of failing to properly oversee the millions it collected, and after the September 11, 2001, terrorist attacks, it was accused of delaying to spend the funds to promptly reopen the Statue of Liberty. The agency fully cooperated with the Senate Finance Committee Investigation and was able to point to its own written standards regarding management of its funds. Ultimately, an investigation by the state Attorney General concluded that the foundation was prudent to not dip into its endowment to finance the project. It noted that although the group's bylaws didn't restrict it from using its endowment, the foundation had a clearly documented policy of preserving the principal.

The Liberty-Ellis Island Foundation provides an excellent example of a non-profit board that documented its policies and decision-making process so that when a controversy ensued it had a paper trail to support its decisions.

So, the point is, whenever possible, document your organization's policies, goals, and objectives in the minutes of its meetings or in a memo. This is a savvy public relations move. If your organization's actions on a specific matter are specifically questioned, it will help point out that your board is acting consistently with pre-established policies.

Lesson #7: Steer clear of illegal lobbying activities

On January 3, 2006, Washington lobbyist Jack Abramoff pled guilty to three criminal felony counts, and then his name stayed in the news throughout the year. The felonies were related to defrauding of American Indian tribes and corruption of public officials through Abramoff's actions as a lobbyist. Several prominent nonprofit organizations have become linked to the Abramoff scandal.

As discussed in Chapter 18, federal law prohibits tax-exempt groups from being paid to lobby or perform public relations, and organizations may lose their tax-exempt status by violating this rule.

Nevertheless, five conservative nonprofit groups managed to splash their organizations' names across the front page by taking money from Abramoff in exchange for writing newspaper columns and calling legislators on his behalf. For example, if Abramoff wanted Congress to bestow a tax break on one of his clients, say a whiskey manufacture, he knew that a newspaper editorial written by him wouldn't influence lawmakers. But, editorials by prominent leaders of high-profile nonprofits might do the trick. Abramoff would prevail upon his nonprofit friends to write op-ed pieces and make phone calls to legislators. In return, Abramoff "donated" several thousands of dollars to the nonprofit organizations.

In the end, be wary of large-scale contributors who want to donate money to your organization because of your willingness to take a public position on a specific issue.

New Federal Legislation: The Pension Protection Act of 2006

The Pension Protection Act of 2006 (PPA) contains plenty of provisions that affect public and private charities, despite its seemingly unrelated name. The PPA includes incentives, record-keeping requirements, and limits on deductions. As is the case with any major legislation, it reflects compromises and negotiations.

New incentives for giving

The PPA includes four new tax incentives to encourage greater charitable contributions. These contributions may be short-lived, however, depending on the legislative climate in the coming years. Currently, these incentives are for contributions made during 2006 and 2007 tax years.

Legislative action in 2007 will be necessary to extend these incentives for future years.

At present, these four new incentives include the following:

- **IRA rollovers:** This perk permits taxpayers 70½ years or older to make tax-free distributions of up to $100,000 from traditional Individual Retirement Accounts (IRAs) or Roth IRAs directly to many types of public charities (except certain types of private foundations).

  Several high-profile nonprofit advocacy groups (such as the Independent Sector and the Council on Foundations) are working with the IRS to clarify what happens if a taxpayer accidentally makes an IRA charitable rollover to a private foundation rather than a public charity.

- **Food donations by businesses:** The PPA extends to all businesses a deduction for donating food inventory. However, the deduction is less than the fair market value of the food.

- **Book donations:** A provision of the PPA gives an incentive to businesses to donate book inventories to public schools. According to the law, the businesses taking this deduction must be corporations.

- **Contributions of property for conservation purposes:** This PPA provision provides incentives for taxpayers to donate land that can be used for environmental preservation and conservation purposes. It raises the charitable deduction limit from 30 percent of adjusted gross income to 50 percent of adjusted gross income for qualified conservation contributions. *Adjusted gross income* is a donor's income taking into account certain expenses and adjustments. So, this amount is less than the taxpayer's total income.

  The charitable deduction limit is raised to 100 percent of adjusted gross income for eligible farmers and ranchers, provided that the farmers and ranchers don't put a restriction on the gift to prevent the use of the donated land for farming or ranching purposes.

Tax relief for charitable organizations

It's important to remember that "tax exempt" doesn't necessarily mean "tax free." Nonprofit organizations do have to pay taxes on some of their income, particularly when they engage in activities that compete with the private sector. (Flip to Chapter 14 for more details.)

However, the following provisions in the PPA reduce the tax burden for some charitable organizations:

- **Unrelated business income tax rules:** A charitable organization that controls a subsidiary organization will no longer be required to pay unrelated business income tax (as discussed in Chapter 14) on certain payments it receives from subsidiary organizations if the payments are meant to cover interest, rent, and certain other types of payments.

- **Excise tax exemption for blood collector organizations:** It may seem odd to think that donated blood was ever subject to a tax. However, the PPA now specifically exempts some blood collector organizations from certain excise taxes with respect to activities related to blood donations.

Requiring written records

The PPA cracks down on undocumented deductions. For example, under the new law, charitable deductions for contributions made in the form of cash or check must be accompanied by one of the following forms of documentation if they're going to be treated as deductible:

- A cancelled check
- A receipt or letter from the charity
- Some other reliable written records showing the name of the charity, the nature of the contribution, and the amount of the donation

The rule for requiring a written receipt from the charity for cash contributions of $250 or more (which existed prior to the PPA) is still in effect.

The end of some charitable loopholes

There's seemingly no end to the ways that private individuals will attempt to profit from charitable transactions. Fortunately, the PPA cracks down on some specific loopholes that have been identified, largely as a result of media attention. Some of these provisions that are designed to sew up existing loopholes include those in the following categories:

- **Self-dealing:** Effective for tax years beginning after August 17, 2006, fines and penalties are doubled for violations by private foundations and their managers of self-dealing and other rules designed to keep private individuals from setting up charitable foundations to orchestrate transactions. In these transactions, wealthy individuals rather than needy charities profit.

- **Facade easements:** The PPA cracks down on deductions taken for donations of buildings that are subsequently adapted for use by for-profit businesses or donated in such dilapidated condition that the charities can't possibly afford to restore them. The PPA also provides that no portion of the building exterior donated may be changed or altered in a manner that's inconsistent with its historical character. The taxpayer must also have a written agreement with the charity receiving the donation certifying that the charity

  - Is a qualified public charity whose purpose is environmental or historic preservation or protection

  - Has the resources to manage and enforce the easement restrictions as well as the commitment to do so

  The taxpayer must also submit an objective appraisal of the value of the donated property. (Check out Chapter 14 for more on facade easements.)

- **S-corporations:** Under the PPA, if an *S-corporation* (a special type of small business corporation with less than 75 shareholders) makes a charitable contribution, its shareholders must reduce the *basis* of their stock by the amount of their contribution. The basis is the cost or value of the stock for tax purposes, and it's the amount used to figure out how much gain a taxpayer needs to report when the stock is ultimately sold. The result of this rule is that when S-corporation stock is sold, the shareholders may pay more tax when they sell the stock because of the lower basis.

Part II

The Nuts and Bolts of Nonprofits

The 5th Wave   By Rich Tennant

"Have someone in accounting do a cash flow statement, a basic EPS, and finish this Sudoku puzzle for me."

In this part . . .

In this part, you can find out how nonprofits are organized and what critical characteristics they all share. It also explains how to apply for and maintain tax-exempt status. Finally, because compensation is a hot-button item for nonprofits, we give you a clue on how to maneuver the subject.

Chapter 4

Starting Up and Staying True to the Mission

In This Chapter

▶ Documenting the mission of your organization

▶ Filling out the forms for tax-exempt status

▶ Agreeing on the right entity

▶ Becoming an incorporated organization

▶ Looking for leadership

*E*very nonprofit organization has a reason for being. That is, every organization has a goal and a purpose. Unfortunately, not everyone within your organization or within the Internal Revenue Service may agree on what that purpose is. Add into the mix the expectations of donors and the people behind the causes that your organization is supposed to serve, and you can probably embroil even the most well-conceived nonprofit into a controversy that will keep it from ever establishing a single goal.

So that your organization doesn't suffer the same fate, this chapter helps you create a mission statement (which will publicly identify your nonprofit's goals and purposes), qualify for your initial tax-exempt status, and create the basic legal paperwork you need to remain credible and controversy-free in the start-up stages.

Making the Mission Matter

A *mission statement* tells the world why your organization exists and what it hopes to accomplish in the future. Donors and granting authorities, in particular, want to know what you plan to do with the funds they give you. For this reason alone, the mission statement is the most important public relations release your organization will ever make.

Using the mission statement as a roadmap

Marketing isn't the only reason to have a mission statement. Among other things, the mission statement provides a roadmap that can be critical to an organization in times of turmoil.

Failure to clearly state and communicate your organization's mission can cause your organization to

- **Be confused about the organization's goals:** Boards need direction and stated objectives. If the objectives aren't stated at the outset, the potential for internal controversy and strife increases exponentially.

- **Miss the real mission:** If the mission is too narrowly stated, the board may construe the organization's objectives cautiously (and therefore too narrowly), which can cause it to miss some of the possibilities for best achieving its goals.

- **Outlive its purpose:** Sometimes organizations cease to serve the purpose for which they were created. If the board members realize that their organization has outlived its mission, they may need to make a logical decision as to whether the organization should continue to exist.

Summing it up in a single statement

A mission statement is generally a sentence not a speech. Its goal is to sum up the purpose of your organization in a way that's easily remembered and often repeated. The mission statement of your organization should be a single sentence stating the following:

- **The full name of your organization:** Because the name of your organization alone may not reflect its goals, the mission statement should always include the name of the organization so that it becomes inextricably associated with the organization's goals and objective.

  Some organizational names don't provide much information until the organization becomes well-known. For example both "Big Brothers/Big Sisters of America" and "Red Cross" don't provide the same information as a name like "American Cancer Society." If your organization isn't well-known initially, and its name isn't particularly descriptive, you want your mission statement to be particularly clear and you want to strive to have it appear whenever your organization receives press coverage, publicity, or acknowledgment.

✔ **What your organization does:** Use positive, goal-oriented terms to encompass the broadest objectives of your organization. For example, the goal of Big Brothers/Big Sisters of America is to make a "positive difference in the lives of youth . . ."

✔ **Who your organization impacts:** The human and economic impact of a benevolent organization often extends well beyond the people it directly serves. Accordingly, your mission statement should reflect the broadest community impact of the organization's programs and services, while still identifying the targeted nature of its services.

For example, the Big Brothers/Big Sisters of America mission statement identifies children and youth as its scope. Note, however, that it doesn't narrow its scope to kids with particular issues. Instead, it identifies the broadest segment of the population that it serves.

✔ **Where your organization operates (when applicable):** Sometimes organizations are local or regional in their missions or operations. If this is the case with your organization, your mission statement should expressly state the geographical area that it targets or in which it operates, so that the public knows who's served.

Picking up ideas from some model mission statements

The most effective mission statements tend to be those that resonate the spirit and purpose of the organization. Here are some existing examples of effective mission statements:

✔ **American Cancer Society:** *The American Cancer Society's international mission concentrates on capacity building in developing cancer societies and on collaboration with other cancer-related organizations throughout the world in carrying out shared strategic directions.*

✔ **Northumberland Big Sisters Big Brothers:** *Northumberland Big Sisters Big Brothers is a non-profit, volunteer-based organization dedicated to meeting the needs of children ages 6–18, by fostering self-worth, positive growth and a sense of belonging primarily through one-to-one friendships with mature and caring mentors.*

✔ **Alliance for Children & Families:** *Our mission is to fuse intellectual capital with superior membership services in order to strengthen the capacities of North America's nonprofit child and family serving organizations to serve and to advocate for children, families and communities so that together we may pursue our vision of a healthy society and strong communities for all children and families.*

Drafting the mission statement

Although mission statements are generally almost always approved by an entire board, they aren't always written by the board. Groups may be great for brainstorming, but they're usually not terrific at reaching a consensus on a succinctly worded written product. Instead, it's best if your organization's mission statement is drafted by one person. This one person can draft the mission statement alone or after group input.

Some boards actually go on retreats to brainstorm the mission statement. It's also not uncommon for the board members of the largest organizations to hire high-priced consultants and public relations people to help them draft the right mission statement.

After your draft is finished, you need to circulate it among the directors. You may also want to give staff members and stakeholders a chance to review the evolving statement. Eventually, board members must all agree on a statement they feel they can support, based on the input of key staff and stakeholders.

Circulate the mission statement to people outside the immediate organization to assess how easily outsiders perceive and understand it.

Getting Tax-Exempt Status

It's a common misperception that all nonprofits are automatically *tax exempt* (not required to pay taxes on their income). But it's just that, a misperception. Instead, nonprofit organizations must apply and be granted tax-exempt status from the Internal Revenue Service (IRS).

The purpose of your nonprofit organization determines whether or not it can operate with or without tax-exempt status. If your organization relies on contributions, tax-exempt status is highly desirable because your organization will be better able to attract donors who are motivated, in part, by the availability of a tax deduction. Conversely, if your primary source of revenue comes from membership dues and the provision of services, a tax exemption may be less desirable because taxpayers can often deduct dues as a business expense.

To obtain tax-exempt status, a nonprofit organization must meet a complicated set of criteria set forth under the U.S Internal Revenue Code. Section 501(c) of the Internal Revenue Code identifies the types of organizations that qualify for tax-exempt status, while Section 170 dictates how and when taxpayers who contribute to them may take their deductions.

Classifying your organization: Section 501(c)

Most tax-exempt nonprofit organizations are listed under Internal Revenue Code Section 501(c). This code contains an extensive list of different types of organizations that the IRS deems worthy of tax-exempt status based on their mission statements (see the section "Making the Mission Matter" earlier in this chapter for details on mission statements). Generally, unless your organization qualifies as a 501(c) organization, it isn't eligible for tax-exempt status as a nonprofit.

The following is a list of the most common types of organizations that qualify as Section 501(c) organizations:

- **501(c)(3) – Public benefit organizations:** These organizations include religious, educational, charitable, scientific, literary, public safety, and amateur sporting organizations and organizations for the prevention of cruelty to children and animals.

- **501(c)(4) – Mutual benefit organizations:** These organizations include civic leagues, welfare organizations, and employee associations. These organizations have a mission to benefit their members or some other group that they represent or are formed to serve.

- **501(c)(5) – Labor, agricultural, and horticultural organizations:** This particular section of the Internal Revenue Code reflects a policy of supporting these groups since the Great Depression.

- **501(c)(6) – Business leagues, chambers of commerce, and real estate boards (such as condominium associations):** These organizations have a quasi-commercial purpose, but Congress decided that their objective isn't really making money for the clubs, and so they aren't taxed. (The objective of these clubs is really making money for their members.)

- **501(c)(7) – Social and recreational clubs:** Congress at some point decided that fun should not be taxed.

- **501(c)(8) – Fraternal beneficiary societies and associations:** This category includes groups like the Shriners of North America.

- **501(c)(9) – Voluntary employees' beneficiary associations:** This group includes organizations such as your health insurance group or people in particular professions who join together for the purpose of obtaining group benefits for their members.

- **501(c)(12) – Benevolent life insurance associations, mutual ditch or irrigation companies, and mutual or cooperative telephone companies:** These organizations engage in some sort of activity that's mutually beneficial, but not in and of itself engaged in making a profit.

- ✔ **501(c)(13) – Cemetery companies:** Here's one section of the law that allows you to avoid taxes, but not death.

- ✔ **501(c)(14) – State chartered credit unions and mutual reserve funds:** These are organizations that provide banking and other services to their members without themselves earning a profit.

- ✔ **501(c)(15) – Mutual insurance companies or associations:** This is another form of a cooperative organization unique to the insurance industry.

- ✔ **501(c)(20) – Group legal service plans:** Here's the category that the lawyers managed to sneak into.

- ✔ **501(c)(26) – State-sponsored organizations providing health coverage for high-risk individuals:** Many states have special programs to cover individuals with health insurance that otherwise might not be able to get insurance because of their health status. It makes sense that these programs, since they don't turn a profit, are tax exempt. (The Wisconsin High Risk Health Insurance Program is an example of one such state sponsored service.)

"Tax exempt" doesn't mean contributions are "tax deductible"

"Tax exempt" doesn't always mean the same thing as "tax deductible." For example, tax-exempt organizations don't have to pay income taxes as long as their activities remain tax exempt. However, no matter what the company's tax-exempt status is, contributions to the organization aren't always deductible on the donor's federal income tax return.

Even though Section 501(c) and other sections of the Internal Revenue Code define nearly two dozen different categories of tax-exempt organizations, contributions to only a handful of these are actually tax deductible. This is because organizations must meet the requirements in Section 170 of the Internal Revenue Code if they want their donors to be able to deduct their contributions. These requirements must be met in addition to the organization qualifying for tax-exempt status so that its own income isn't taxed.

Public charities versus private foundations

A *public charity,* which is defined under Section 170 of the Internal Revenue Code, is a nonprofit organization that qualifies as tax exempt and receives more than one-third of its support from gifts, grants, membership fees, or certain investment income. These charities are organized and operated (or controlled by an organization that's organized and operated) exclusively for the benefit of religious, educational, medical, or other public purposes.

Under the Internal Revenue Code, the following types of organizations are classified as public charities:

- **Organizations that perform charitable service missions:** These organizations include churches, hospitals, qualified medical research organizations affiliated with hospitals, schools, colleges, and universities.

- **Organizations that raise funds for charitable goals:** These are organizations that raise funds to support public charities by conducting fund-raising activities and acting in a supporting relationship to one or more existing public charities.

Private foundations, on the other hand, are charitable organizations that depend on a small number of donors and are generally controlled by those donors. These organizations are subject to special rules as discussed in Chapter 11 and typically have a single major source of funding. The funds usually come from gifts from one family or corporation rather than from many sources, such as public donations. A private foundation's primary activity is usually providing grants to other charitable organizations and individuals (rather than direct operation of those charitable programs and individuals).

In addition to being a 501(c)(3) organization, your nonprofit organization must fit the definition of a private charity under Section 170 of the Internal Revenue Code in order for your donors to deduct their contributions.

Calculating the deduction: Public charities versus private foundations

Individuals can take charitable deductions only if they itemize deductions on their tax returns. Individuals may deduct up to 50 percent of their income to public charities, and up to 30 percent to private foundations.

Corporations can take a deduction of up to 10 percent of their income, regardless of whether the organization they're donating to is a public charity or private foundation.

Check out *Taxes For Dummies* by Eric Tyson for more info on deductions.

Documenting your tax-exempt status

At some point, your organization may be asked to document its tax-exempt status. For example, many donors will not make contributions to charities that don't qualify for deductibility under Section 170, and they will request something called a Letter of Determination.

A *Letter of Determination* is a formal notification that the IRS sends your organization once its tax-exempt status has been approved. Donors can also verify your tax-exempt status by checking IRS Publication 78, which is titled the *Cumulative List of Organizations*. This publication is an annual listing of thousands of tax-exempt organizations to which contributions are deductible as charitable donations.

Filling out the forms

Organizations differ dramatically in their functions, purposes, and roles in the community. Some organizations provide needed public services, others allow groups to associate for a common good, and others raise funds for important causes. However, all nonprofits have something in common: They must comply with IRS requirements.

Nonprofit organizations generally have to file the following forms with the IRS (or determine that they qualify for a specific exemption):

- ✔ **Form 1023 or 1024,** which is called *Application for Recognition of Exemption.* This form is used by the IRS to determine whether your organization qualifies for tax-exempt status, and you'll file one or the other depending on whether your organization is seeking exemption.

  Tax-exempt status isn't free! The law requires the payment of a user fee to process the application for tax-exempt status. The amount of the user fee depends on the type of application submitted and the anticipated level of your organization's revenues, but it usually ranges from $300 to $900 under 501(c)(3) or 501(a) of the Internal Revenue Code.

Your tax dollars at work: Government publications

The Department of Treasury and the IRS provide the public with several free publications, which you can get online at www.irs.gov. These publications explain the process of applying for tax-exempt status for your organization and are each assigned a specific number.

IRS Publication 557, titled *Tax Exempt Status for Your Organization,* is the primary guide. It discusses the rules and procedures for organizations that want an exemption from federal income tax. This publication provides general information about the procedures for receiving tax-exempt status and contains information about annual filing requirements and other

matters that may affect your organization's tax-exempt status. Publication 557 also has information about filing the initial paperwork to qualify your organization as a nonprofit, about options for organizing nonprofits, and about ongoing reporting requirements for nonprofits. (This publication can be found at www.irs.gov/pub/irs-pdf/p557.pdf.)

IRS Publication 78, *Cumulative List of Organizations,* lists thousands of tax-exempt organizations to which contributions are deductible as charitable donations (as defined in section 170 of the Internal Revenue Code).

✔ **Form 8718,** which is called *User for Exempt Organization Determination Letter Request.* This is a form used to request a specific letter from the IRS that your organization has been given tax-exempt status.

✔ **Form 990,** which is the annual information return. Any tax-exempt organization with more than $25,000 in annual gross revenues must file a Form 990 with the IRS. (Refer to Chapter 7 for more details on the Form 990.)

✔ **Form SS-4,** which is called *Application for Employer Identification Number.* Every exempt organization must have an *employee identification number* (EIN), whether or not it has any employees, and this is the form you use to get that number.

These forms are available online at www.irs.gov, under the Forms and Publications link. After you find the link, all of the forms are listed in numerical order. Some forms can be filed online, but others need to be printed. In any event, you can't save your typed forms unless you have special software such as a version of Adobe Acrobat, which allows you to save changes to PDF forms.

If you don't have online access (or you're a traditionalist who likes hard copies), you can obtain any of these forms by contacting your local IRS office. To find out where your local IRS office is located, call this national IRS toll-free number: 800-829-1040.

Gathering the right documents

The IRS is a tough tax master. To apply for tax-exempt status, not only are you required to fill out the appropriate forms (see the previous section), but you also need to submit a whole stack of documents along with them. These documents include the following:

✔ **Bylaws:** You need to include a current copy of your organization's articles of incorporation, trust indenture, or other enabling documents. Sadly, if you don't have these documents, your organization doesn't qualify for tax-exempt status. Bylaws are covered later in this chapter.

A documents submitted with the application must be a *conformed copy,* meaning that it agrees with the original and all amendments. However, don't submit original documents! All documents submitted become part of the IRS file and can't be returned. Also, all attachments should show the organization's name, address, and EIN.

✔ **A description of purpose:** This document is exactly what it sounds like — a full description of the purpose and activity of the organization. You should include any standards, procedures, or other criteria that the organization adopted for carrying out its purposes.

✔ **Financial statements:** You need to include financial statements showing receipts and expenditures for the current year and the three previous years (or the number of years you've been in existence, if less than four). You also need to include a balance sheet for the current year. If your organization is less than 1 year old or you haven't yet begun operations, a proposed budget for two full accounting periods and a current statement of assets and liabilities needs to be submitted.

✔ **Miscellaneous documents:** The IRS may also require additional information, such as copies of advertising, publications, written materials, leases, contracts, or agreements that your organization may have.

An incomplete application may be returned without being considered. If your application is sent back because it's incomplete, the IRS will tell you what additional information is required with the application and the period of time you have to resubmit it. In this case, the IRS will tell you that if the application is sent back within the deadlines they specify to you, it will be considered received on the original submission date.

Receiving acknowledgment

What happens after the application is submitted? After you submit a complete application, the IRS sends you a letter acknowledging its receipt (unless of course the application was incomplete). If the IRS decides that your application warrants special review, it will be forwarded to IRS headquarters. If it's forwarded to headquarters for consideration, you will be notified.

Withdrawing your application

If you realize after sending your application and attached documents that you've made a fatal error (or have a change of heart), you may withdraw your application anytime before the IRS issues a ruling or a determination letter. To do this, you simply write to the address identified on the correspondence confirming receipt of your application. But, remember, your withdrawal doesn't prevent any of the information in your application from being used by the IRS in any examination of your organization's returns. Also, any information you submit with an application will generally not be returned, and any user fee you paid the IRS will not be refunded.

Opening up to public inspection

Your organization's application forms and annual information returns are available for public inspection. The law also requires that the IRS allow public inspection of your approved application, including any papers you may have submitted in support of it.

If any information submitted with your application relates to any patent, trade secret, or other intellectual property, you can request that the information be withheld from the public. In other words, you can request that the IRS determine that disclosure of this information would aversely affect your organization.

If you want to withhold information, your application should include the request, and should specifically identify the material to be withheld. This material needs to be marked "Not Subject to Public Inspection" and needs to include any reasons that the information should be withheld. The correspondence requesting non-publication should be filed with the documents containing the material requested to be withheld.

Seeing your exempt status request through the review process

After it arrives at the IRS offices, your application package will be reviewed by a manager in the Exempt Organizations Determinations division. The manager can do one of three things:

- ✔ **Issue a favorable determination letter on your exemption:** This is what you are, of course, hoping for.

- ✔ **Issue an adverse determination letter denying the exemption:** This generally means that your organization needs to go back to square one. Or you can at least have your attorney make a phone call to the agent who's identified on the correspondence you received from the agency denying your application.

- ✔ **Refer the case to the headquarters of the IRS for a ruling:** Generally this is done when issues on qualification for exemption have no precedent or the case is so unusual or complex that headquarters consideration is justified. This can substantially delay the issuance of any determination on your application.

After the IRS thoroughly reviews your application and makes a determination, it'll send you a ruling or determination letter.

The ruling is effective as of the date of the formation of your organization, which means that its exempt status is effectively *backdated.* If the IRS requires your organization to alter its activities or amend its charter in order to qualify for a tax exemption, the ruling or determination letter will usually be effective as of the date specified in the letter.

You can't rely on a ruling or determination letter if there's a material change in the character, purpose, or method of operation of your organization. You may need to contact the IRS to obtain a new determination letter. So, be sure to consult with your attorney if your nonprofit changes its mission or organizational structure. He or she will tell you whether your existing determination letter is still valid or whether you need to apply for another one.

Keeping your tax-exempt status once you get it

Keeping your tax-exempt status is easy if you follow your own rules. Basically, your organization must operate within the parameters you set forth in your application to the IRS.

Your status can be revoked for the following reasons:

- ✔ Omitting or misstating a material fact.
- ✔ Operating in a manner that's materially different from that which is represented in your application.
- ✔ Engaging in prohibitive transactions or certain political activities that are inconsistent with the tax laws and your organization's purpose.

Other less likely ways to lose your status include a law being enacted that prohibits your organization's purpose or a decision of the United States Supreme Court that changes the status of current law.

Responding to a revocation notice

Generally a revocation of tax-exempt status is effective as of the date a material change takes place or the law is changed. If the determination letter or ruling was issued in error or you omitted or misstated facts in your application, the revocation may be retroactive.

If your tax-exempt status is to be revoked, you'll be advised in writing of that action and the reasons for the revocation. You can then appeal the decision within 30 days of the adverse determination letter and can have an attorney represent you.

Filing a protest

A protest of tax-exempt revocation must clearly identify the organization, its address, and its EIN. The protest must contain a statement that the organization wants to protest the determination. It must also include a statement of facts supporting the organization's position in any contested factual issue, and what law you're relying on for your position. You can request a conference with the agent ultimately assigned to review your protest, if desired. Specific appeals procedure rules are set forth in IRS Publication 557, titled *Tax Exempt Status for Your Organization.* You can find this publication online at www.irs.gov/pub/irs-pdf/p557.pdf.

Choosing an Entity Type

Nonprofit organizations generally fall within five types. These include corporations, limited liability companies, unincorporated associations, trusts, and cooperatives. Corporations are the most common type of organization.

Corporations

A *corporation* is a creature of state law, and is generally created under, and limited by, statutory law. Corporations have a separate legal existence, and they can buy and sell property, sue or be sued, and enter into contracts. However, a corporation can't act by itself. Instead, it acts through its officers and agents. A nonprofit corporation is formed without the intent of generating profit.

By law, a corporation can do the following:

- ✔ Buy, hold, or sell property
- ✔ Own and manage interests in other corporations
- ✔ Establish compensation for its employees
- ✔ Make donations
- ✔ Set conditions for admissions
- ✔ Carry on a business and carry on all such activities that aren't prohibited by law to advance the corporation's mission and activity

Limited liability companies

Limited liabilities companies, or LLCs, are entities that have become popular over the past few decades. The concept was to limit the liability to one or a few members of the LLC. These types of organizations have a wider range of choices regarding organization and governance when compared to corporations.

LLCs, which are governed by *operating agreements,* are generally formed by filing *articles of organization.* They can be controlled either by their members or through management appointed by the members.

LLCs can elect tax treatment either as a partnership or a corporation. The IRS has so far limited its recognition of tax-exempt status of LLCs to those that only have other tax-exempt organizations as their members. So, this form of entity may have limited application for organizations whose membership doesn't meet this requirement.

Some states don't allow LLCs to be used for nonprofit purposes, but that doesn't prohibit an LLC from qualifying to do business in these states if it's formed in another jurisdiction.

Unincorporated associations

An *unincorporated association* is less formal than a corporation, but it's still recognized as a separate legal entity in many states. States that have recognized unincorporated associations have adopted the Uniform Unincorporated Nonprofit Association Act (UUNAA), which is a model act that states can cut and paste into their own statutes. (Model acts are discussed in more detail in Chapter 2.) Unincorporated associations that function according to the rules of UUNAA have some of the characteristics of corporations. They can buy, hold, and sell property and sue or be sued, for example.

Typical organizations that choose not to incorporate include neighborhood associations, campaign committees, and other associations and groups. Unincorporated associations, in many cases, are adopted by happenstance. They generally start as a group of people (a club, for instance) that gets together to perform some function. The group may have some sort of guiding document that creates a structure or even officers and members. Even though none of the formalities of forming a corporation have been followed, and the association isn't registered with any particular government agency, the association still exists.

For small organizations with few wants and needs, the unincorporated association often works just fine. It has the advantage of informality, and can still qualify for tax-exempt status in many cases.

Trusts

A *trust* is generally defined as a property interest held by one person (called the *trustee*) at the request of another person (called the *settlor*) for the benefit of a third party (called the *beneficiary*). Trusts are mostly used in instances where the activities of a nonprofit revolve around the management and distribution of assets. This is because trusts are generally simpler to administer than corporations and have fewer reporting requirements.

Nonprofit organizations commonly use trusts in situations where money is collected, invested, or passively managed. For example, scholarship funds and grants for charitable purposes are generally administered through trusts. Employee benefits arrangements, such as tax-qualified retirement plans — 401(k)s — and welfare benefit plans — 419(e)s — also generally use trusts.

Because the trust is a separate entity, it can own and manage property in its own name and can distribute such property according to its terms (which are noted in the legal document that creates it). Trusts can be tax exempt, but only if they meet the 501(c)(3) requirements discussed in the section "Classifying your organization: Section 501(c)" earlier in this chapter.

Cooperatives

A *cooperative* is generally a business that distributes its income to its members, but doesn't earn any income on its own. This is a feature that distinguishes a cooperative from a partnership or a corporation.

The primary function of cooperatives is to allocate the economic benefits to its members based on the quantity of business done with the members. Cooperatives usually are formed as corporations under state cooperative laws and have bylaws and other organizational documents similar to corporations. Cooperatives are discussed in more detail in Chapter 12.

The Internal Revenue Code provides exemptions to cooperatives for income generated from business done with their members or patrons that forward the purpose of the cooperative.

Incorporating as a Nonprofit

Assume that you've evaluated all of the various forms of nonprofit operation (see the section "Choosing an Entity Type" earlier in the chapter for a list of the forms), and you've decided to form a nonprofit corporation. With this corporation, you may be starting a new venture, or maybe your informal association or club has grown to the point where you would like to bring more formality to the organization. At this point, to incorporate, you need to prepare articles of incorporation, write bylaws, and identify your officers and directors. The following sections show you how.

Drafting articles of incorporation

In order to incorporate, your organization must file *articles of incorporation*. This document, which actually creates the organization, must be filed with the Secretary of State in the state that the corporation is to be organized. If the corporation operates in other states as well, it must file as a *foreign corporation* in those states.

Here's the info that's required to be in the articles of incorporation:

- ✔ **The name of the corporation:** Your corporation's name needs to be carefully chosen. Names can be descriptive, imply a purpose, or have no direct connection with the purpose at all. (For example, Microsoft Corporation doesn't reflect that the corporation sells software, and the United Way Corporation doesn't describe the services of the organization.)

  The name of your corporation must contain the following words or abbreviations (or comparable words or abbreviations from another language):

  - Corporation, or corp.

  - Incorporated, or inc.

  - Company, or co.

  - Limited, or ltd.

- ✔ **Addresses:** You need to include the following addresses: The address of the nonprofit organization at the time of the initial registration, the address of the initial principal office of the organization at the time of the registration, and the names and addresses of each incorporator.

- ✔ **The organization's purpose:** The purpose of the organization is known as the *purpose clause*. Even though the purpose clause generally doesn't need to specify how your organization will carry out its objectives, it does need to be written narrowly enough to distinguish it from other nonprofit organizations.

✔ **The agent:** The name of the initial *registered agent* (the person who receives all of the correspondence concerning the corporation) needs to be specifically identified. The agent can either be an individual or another corporation, and the agent is generally designated to accept any legal documents in the event that a lawsuit is filed against the organization.

✔ **The organization's activities:** If your organization is hoping to gain tax-exempt status under Internal Revenue Code Section 501(c)(3), your articles of incorporation need to include provisions that limit its activities to those permitted by such organizations. You also need to note that the organization's assets will be used to further the exempt purpose of the organization.

✔ **The presence or absence of members:** You must note whether the corporation will have people named in its documents as *members*. Usually, these are the people who initially help organize the corporation.

✔ **A dissolution provision:** This provision generally states that when the organization dissolves, another tax-exempt organization will receive any assets of the dissolving corporation.

Depending on the state of incorporation, other state-specific provisions may be required. For example, directors and the length of time that the organization will exist may both need to be identified.

After the articles have been drafted and executed, they need to be filed with the Secretary of State, along with any required fee. Most states provide an acknowledgment or certified copy of the articles upon filing.

Your corporation is considered to be up and running after the articles of incorporation have been filed and the proper fee paid. States usually require a corporation to file an annual report and to pay an annual registration fee. These duties are generally completed by the registered agent.

Writing the bylaws

The *bylaws* of an organization are the day-to-day rules that the organization adopts to fulfill its mission. As operations change, so do the bylaws. A nonprofit corporation's bylaws look similar to those of a for-profit corporation in many respects.

Bylaws address the rules relating to the board of directors, including the number of directors, the election and nomination processes, the powers of the directors, and the directors' terms and duties.

Officers and agents can also be covered in the bylaws, including their titles, responsibilities, duties, elections, and terms. Other sections found in bylaws relate to committees of the board, insurance and indemnification provisions, conflicts of interest, the fiscal year of the organization, how the books of the organization are to be handled and who maintains them, how the bylaws are to be amended, how the organization should be dissolved, and if the organization is hoping to gain tax-exempt status, a prohibition against private benefit (so that all the assets of the organization will be transferred to another tax-exempt organization upon its dissolution).

The Internet has lots of examples of bylaws for nonprofit organizations, and a quick search can get you started on how your organization's bylaws should look and feel. For example, you can find the bylaws of the American Red Cross at `www.redcross.org/images/pdfs/bylaws.pdf`. Also, you can find the bylaws for the International Trademark Association at `www.inta.org/index.php?option=com_content&task=view&id=1230&Itemid=84&getcontent=4`.

Getting Leaders on the Board

Ideally, an organization would be able to assemble a group of hardworking, cooperative, and enthusiastic directors who would be dedicated to the organization's mission and wouldn't expect to be paid (or they would expect a salary far below what the private sector would pay.)

In reality, however, board members have all sorts of backgrounds and different experiences with the organization's mission. Sometimes the board members are recruited for their experience in the community, sometimes for their business background, and sometimes just because they're well-connected and can raise a lot of money. The task of any organization, then, is to meld the backgrounds and strengths of the board members to create a cohesive group that's capable of successfully leading the organization in fulfilling its mission.

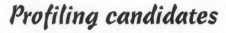

Profiling candidates

Prior to forming your board, it's a good idea to come up with a profile of the "ideal" board candidate so you know what type of person and skill set you're searching for. Here are some common considerations:

- ✔ **Personal information:** For example, certain backgrounds, ages, cultural and gender qualifications, or financial status may be desirable characteristics for your organization.

- ✔ **Expertise in running organizations:** Nonprofit and for-profit organizations don't differ in their need for effective management — they only differ in their missions. So, it doesn't matter if your candidate only has experience in one or the other.

- ✔ **Fundraising ability:** Funding is the lifeblood of virtually every nonprofit organization, which means that fundraising experience is a must for any candidate.

Persuading candidates

Because many nonprofit board members serve as volunteers or for only a nominal fee, some persuasion may be necessary in order to recruit board members. At a minimum, persuading candidates to join your board may require the following:

- ✔ **Educating the candidates on your nonprofit's mission:** Board members who don't buy into the mission at the outset can bog the board down with indecision later.

- ✔ **Convincing the candidates that the other members of the board will be effective:** Board members are increasingly aware of liability considerations and public perceptions, and they will likely be unwilling to serve on a board that's populated with underqualified members.

- ✔ **Competing with other nonprofits for talent:** Particularly when it comes to fundraising and managerial expertise, recruiting candidates for your board may be difficult because there's simply not enough talent to go around in the nonprofit sector. You may find that your organization needs to do some aggressive recruiting as you compete with many other worthy organizations.

Conducting meaningful meetings

After you've finally chosen your board members, it's time to get down to business. And, of course, that means you'll be holding plenty of meetings. A perfect meeting in the world of nonprofits should move directors smoothly through a well-prioritized agenda, while at the same time fostering creative input. In reality, however, many meetings tend to ramble, which leaves attendees frustrated or feeling as if key issues have been glossed over.

Nonprofits generally hold two types of meetings:

- *Regular meetings,* which are generally held on a set schedule (for example, the first Monday of each month)
- *Special meetings,* which can be called in accordance with bylaws and state statutes (which spell out how and when urgent matters need to be addressed by the board)

To help you make sure that you're holding ideal meetings, this section contains some rules of the road and some pointers for keeping your board members on track.

Giving proper notice of meetings

A *notice* is a formal invitation to the directors to attend a meeting. Generally, proper notice needs to be given for all special meetings. (The purpose of the meeting may be stated, but this isn't always required under state law.)

The time period to give notice is set in your bylaws or in other statutes that your state may have. For example, a common provision says that notice must be provided no less than 10, but no more than 30, days prior to the meeting. Your bylaws (or another statute) may also specify the acceptable form of the notice. Some bylaws, for instance, specify that e-mail notice is acceptable. On the other hand, some bylaws specify that certified mail is required.

Even though notice is generally required, most states allow directors to waive notice of a meeting in emergency circumstances, such as the death or illness of an executive director or in the event that the organization must deal with a natural disaster. This waiver is used when a director has little or no time to give proper notice. The director usually has to obtain the waiver in writing either before, during, or after the meeting, and the waiver is required only from those directors who aren't able to attend the meeting (because attendance constitutes a waiver of notice).

In order to hold a meeting, however, your directors must have a *quorum,* which is the minimum number of members that must be present to conduct an official meeting. Your organization's bylaws or other state statutes dictate what constitutes a quorum, but generally it's a majority. Many bylaws and state statutes allow directors to attend a meeting by telephone or even online.

Acting with an agenda in mind

Although agendas vary in style, most follow a set format. Here's a common setup:

1. **Get the meeting started with a *call to order.***

2. **Approve the minutes from your previous meeting (see the section "Taking minutes" later in the chapter for details on minutes).**

3. **Give necessary reports (financial reports, for example).**

4. **Take care of any remaining items that are dictated by the purpose of the meeting, which may include substantive matters, as well as routine issues.**

5. **Address any old business from prior meetings.**

6. **Make a call for discussion of any new business.**

    If an item of new business is raised during a meeting and is expected to require more thought and consideration than the time for the meeting will allow, it can be moved to the agenda for an upcoming meeting.

7. **Call for *adjournment,* which officially closes the meeting.**

It's a good idea to circulate the agenda ahead of time so attendees can come prepared to discuss the issues being covered. If you anticipate that resolutions may be adopted at the meeting, you may want to circulate those to the directors beforehand as well. Before a meeting, most organizations send packets to directors that include the notice, agenda, and resolutions. If you make changes to the agenda after mailing your packets, you can notify the directors of these changes ahead of time or you can announce them at the beginning of the meeting or even during the course of the meeting.

Taking minutes

The chances that anyone will remember what happened at the last meeting (which may be a month from now) are slim. So, it's essential to capture the substance of each meeting through *minutes.* Basically, anyone present can be assigned to prepare the minutes.

The form of your minutes will determine what level of information you include. For example, minutes can either be in long form or short form. A long form of minutes usually contains detailed descriptions of discussions and actions, whereas the shorter form only reports on the actions that were taken with short descriptions of deliberations. As a general rule, the more important the issue, the more detailed the description of the deliberations and actions should be.

It's a good idea to circulate a copy of the minutes of the prior meeting so that board members can read them and verify their accuracy. Depending on your organization's bylaws, your board or committee may even be required to vote to approve the written draft of the prior meeting's minutes.

Chapter 5

Getting Tax-Exempt Status

• •

In This Chapter

▶ Determining the tax-exempt status section your organization falls under

▶ Understanding the application process

▶ Following through with an appeal if your organization is turned down

• •

*Y*our organization isn't required to apply for tax-exempt status from the Internal Revenue Service (IRS). However, it should seriously consider pursuing this option because then the organization isn't required to pay federal taxes on most types of income (certain notable exceptions are discussed in this chapter).

As an added bonus, most states also allow tax-exempt nonprofits to be exempt from certain types of income, sales, and property taxes. All this talk of taxes may seem confusing and overwhelming, but don't worry: This chapter covers the federal requirements. To find out which state taxes your organization can legally bypass, contact your local attorney general's office. (Flip to Appendix C for a list of state contacts.)

Checking Out the "Eligible" List for Tax-Exempt Status

A tax exemption is basically a statement by the federal government that says that an organization is operating for the public good and that the taxpayers should subsidize its activities as a matter of policy. Organizations that are exempt from taxes are specifically identified in Section 501(c) of the Internal Revenue Code. In the nonprofit world, you often hear people refer to nonprofit organizations as "501(c) organizations" because of their location in the Code.

Skimming Internal Revenue Code Section 501(c)

Because the majority of tax-exempt organizations are listed under Internal Revenue Code 501(c), it's useful to look at each section briefly for a description of the exemptions provided to see where your organization fits in the grand scheme of the tax code.

501(c)(1): Federally organized corporations

Section 501(c)(1) applies to corporations that are organized under an act of Congress. Common examples of this type of entity are federal credit unions, federal reserve banks, and the Reconstruction Finance Corporation.

501(c)(2): Title holding companies

Title holding companies are entities that provide a tax-free method of managing and holding title to real estate and other property for their tax-exempt parent organizations.

501(c)(3): Religious, educational, and charitable organizations

Section 501(c)(3) of the Code applies to organizations that are formed for religious, educational, charitable, scientific, and literary purposes. Also under this category are those organizations that test for public safety, foster amateur sports competitions, or prevent cruelty to children or animals. Examples of 501(c)(3) organizations include the American Red Cross, Goodwill Industries, the Salvation Army, Planned Parenthood, and the American Civil Liberties Union.

501(c)(4): Civic leagues, social welfare organizations, and local associations of employees

Section 501(c)(4) exempts civic leagues and other organizations that are operated primarily for the common good and promotion of social welfare or for local associations of employees. Examples include the AARP and the League of Women Voters.

Local associations of employees are required to meet two conditions in order to obtain an exemption:

- ✔ Membership must be limited to employees of a designated corporation or organization in an identified municipality.
- ✔ The association's net earnings must be devoted solely and exclusively to educational, charitable, or recreational purposes.

501(c)(5): Labor, agriculture, and horticultural organizations

Section 501(c)(5) of the Code reflects Congress's long history of listening to lobbyists in the agricultural industry. The principal purpose of these organizations must be the improvement of conditions of those engaged in the exempt activities. They must also improve the quality of their products and develop increased efficiency in the respective professions or jobs.

Labor organizations refer to labor unions, counsels, or committees that are organized to protect the interests of workers. Such organizations must function or directly support efforts of the labor group or improve employment conditions.

Agricultural and horticultural organizations are related to those organizations whose activities concern livestock, forestry, plant cultivation, harvesting crops or aquatic resources, and other similar activities. An example of a 501(c)(5) organization is the AFL-CIO.

501(c)(6): Business leagues and chambers

Section 501(c)(6) nonprofit organizations are established to further the interests of their members and include business leagues, chambers of commerce, real estate boards, boards of trade, and professional football leagues. In addition to these organizations, other organizations that qualify under this section include professional associations and healthcare organizations. These organizations can't be organized for profit, and no part of their net earnings can benefit any private shareholder or individual.

Business leagues, which are also referred to as trade or professional organizations, are associations of people having some common business interest, the primary purpose of which promotes that interest. The primary activity of business leagues can't be the performing of services for its members, but rather the improvement of the business conditions to which the business relates.

Professional or trade associations are those organizations that operate for the benefit of a profession rather than a business. These types of organizations engage in public relations activities, work as watchdogs for a particular profession, or strive to improve the condition of its members.

Chambers of commerce or *boards of trade* are organizations that strive to promote the common economic interests of all organizations in a given trade activity or community. A chamber of commerce relates to all businesses in a particular geographic location, while a board of trade may refer to only one or more lines of business in that area. Membership in these organizations is voluntary and open to all community businesses and professionals.

Contributions to these organizations aren't deductible. Dues, assessments, and member fees also aren't deductible as charitable contributions. But they may be deductible as trade or business expenses by the members themselves (for example, a businessperson may be able to deduct her dues to a board of trade as an ordinary and necessary business expense).

501(c)(7): Social and recreational clubs

Everyone needs to have fun. So Congress decided that social and recreational clubs are organizations that operate for the public good and are therefore worthy of exemptions. Congress recognized that individuals who band together to provide recreational facilities on a mutual basis aren't attempting to profit from having their members use of the facilities. This recognition helped Congress decide to give these organizations tax-exempt status.

The prerequisite of an exemption for a social club under Section 501(c)(7) is the providing of pleasure or recreation to its members. In order to qualify for an exemption, substantially all of the social club's activities must further the club's recreational and social purposes. They must also meet both the *organizational test* and the *operational test*. In other words, the club must be both organized for the tax-exempt purpose of providing pleasure, recreation, or other permissible purposes, and it must operate on a not-for-profit basis. Examples of these types of clubs include golf clubs, tennis clubs, country clubs, dinner clubs, and swimming clubs.

501(c)(8): Fraternal beneficiary societies

Section 501(c)(8) provides for the tax exemption of *fraternal beneficiary societies*. These are organizations that are operating under the lodge system or for the exclusive benefit of members of a fraternity that itself operates under the lodge system. These organizations also provide life, accident, or other benefits to the members of the society or their dependents. "Operating under the lodge system" means that the organization is carrying on its activities under a form of organization that's made up of local branches called *lodges* or *chapters*. These local branches are chartered by a parent organization and are largely self-governing.

So, under this definition, if an organization doesn't have a parent organization or branches underneath and doesn't operate under the lodge system, it won't qualify as a fraternal beneficiary association. A popular example of a 501(c)(8) organization is the Knights of Columbus.

501(c)(9): Voluntary employee beneficiary associations

Section 501(c)(9) provides an exemption for *voluntary employee beneficiary associations,* which are also known as VEBAs. This type of association provides for the payment of life, health, accident, or other benefits to the members of the association or their dependents or designated beneficiaries.

A VEBA must be organized for an association of employees, generally employed by a common employer or affiliated employers. In a typical VEBA arrangement, an employer will establish a VEBA as a trust for the purpose of funding health benefits or a self-insured health plan. The employee members must have a commonality of interest and membership must be voluntary.

501(c)(10): Fraternal societies

Section 501(c)(10) provides the exemption for *domestic fraternal societies.* Fraternal beneficiary societies are addressed in Section 501(c)(8) as fraternal organizations that provide for the payment of certain benefits to the organization's members or dependents. A domestic fraternal society, on the other hand, is a fraternal organization that operates under a lodge system that devotes its net earnings exclusively to religious, charitable, scientific, literary, educational, and fraternal purposes. In other words, it doesn't provide benefits to its members. However, it may procure insurance from various companies to provide optional benefits to its members. In order to qualify as a fraternal organization, there must be a common objective, profession, or other link between the members. A popular example of a 501(c)(10) organization is the Ancient Order of the Nobles of the Mystic Shrine, which is the fundraising arm for the Shriners Hospital for Children.

501(c)(11): Teachers' retirement associations

Section 501(c)(11) provides an exemption for *teachers' retirement fund associations.* These organizations are operated to protect the financial stability of retirement systems for teachers and to administer contributions and distributions of retirement to association members.

501(c)(12): Insurance associations

Section 501(c)(12) provides the exemption for organizations like benevolent life insurance associations, mutual ditch or irrigation companies, and mutual or cooperative electric, water, or telephone companies. Eighty-five percent or more of the income that these organizations generate consists of income from members. Common to all of these entities is the conduct of an activity of a mutually beneficial nature.

A *benevolent life insurance association* is one that's operated to provide life insurance coverage to members at cost. However, the hitch is that they're confined to a particular community, place, or district. *Mutual ditch or irrigation companies* are those that operate irrigation systems for the use and benefit of their members.

501(c)(13): Cemeteries

Section 501(c)(13) allows a tax exemption for cemetery companies. These companies must be owned and operated exclusively for the benefit of their members on a not-for-profit basis. The members of the cemetery companies are those who own the lots and hold them for burial purposes, not for resale. A tax exemption under this section also applies to corporations that are organized solely for the purpose of the disposal of bodies by burial or cremation (as long as the organizations don't engage in business that's not necessarily incident to that purpose).

Earnings of these organizations may only be used to pay expenses of operating, maintaining, and improving the cemetery or crematorium, to purchase cemetery property, or to create a fund to provide income for the care of a cemetery.

501(c)(14): Credit unions

Section 501(c)(14) allows an exemption for state-chartered credit unions and mutual reserve funds. This exemption applies to credit unions without capital stock that are organized and operated for a mutual purpose on a nonprofit basis. Mutual organizations formed before September 1, 1957, that provide insurance for shares or deposits are also exempt under this section. Your local credit union is most likely a 501(c)(14) organization.

501(c)(15): Mutual insurance companies

Section 501(c)(15) provides the exemption for mutual insurance companies that provide insurance to members substantially at cost. In order to be a *mutual organization,* the insurance company's policyholders must be members having a common equitable interest in the organization and they have to control the company. Many smaller insurance companies are organized as 501(c)(15) nonprofits.

501(c)(16): Crop cooperatives

Section 501(c)(16) provides the exemption for cooperative organizations that finance crop operations. These corporations are organized by an exempt farmers' cooperative or its members to finance their ordinary crop operations. These organizations may issue *capital stock* (stock that evidences ownership) under certain conditions, and may also accumulate a reasonable reserve for future operations. It may also own all the stock of another business corporation.

501(c)(17): Unemployment trusts

Section 501(c)(17) provides the exemption for *unemployment trusts.* These trusts are generally intended to provide benefits to employees who have been laid off or who have become ill.

501(c)(18): Pension trusts

Section 501(c)(18) provides the exemption for employee-funded pension trusts created before June 25, 1959. This provision has limited application, and applies to the payment of benefits under a pension plan that's funded by employees or trusts that are created before June 25, 1959.

501(c)(19): Armed Forces

Section 501(c)(19) provides the exemption for a post or organization of past or present members of the U.S. Armed Forces. These organizations are typically referred to as *veterans' organizations,* which must be operated exclusively to do the following:

- ✔ Promote the social welfare of the community

- ✔ Assist disabled veterans and members of the Armed Forces and their dependents or widows (and the orphans of deceased veterans)

- ✔ Provide care and assistance to hospitalized veterans or U.S. Armed Forces members

- ✔ Carry on programs to perpetuate the memory of deceased veterans

- ✔ Conduct religious, charitable, scientific, literary, or other educational programs

- ✔ Sponsor or participate in patriotic activities

- ✔ Provide insurance benefits for members and their dependents

- ✔ Provide social and recreational activities for their members

501(c)(20): Group legal service plans

Section 501(c)(20) allows an exemption to an organization or trust that forms part of a qualified *group legal services plan.* Basically, a group legal services plan is sponsored by an employer for the exclusive benefit of its employees, spouses, or their dependents, and it provides certain prepaid personal legal services.

501(c)(21): Black lung benefit trusts

Section 501(c)(21) provides the exemption for *black lung benefit trusts,* which are self-insurance programs for coal mine operators. These programs provide adequate worker's compensation coverage for liability that may be incurred as a result of disability or death due to *black lung diseases* (those diseases caused by the inhalation of coal dust).

501(c)(22): Employer withdrawal liability payment funds

Section 501(c)(22) allows an exemption for trusts that are formed to administer withdrawal liability payment funds. These trusts provide funds to meet the liability that an employer may incur from withdrawing from a multi-employer pension fund.

501(c)(23): Pre-1880 veterans' organizations

Section 501(c)(23) provides an exemption for veterans' organizations created before 1880. This exemption was established by Congress in 1982. To be eligible for this exemption, an organization has to have been formed before 1880, and more than 75 percent of its members must be present or past members of the Armed Forces. The organization must also provide insurance or other benefits to such veterans or their dependents. An example of a 501(c)(23) organization is the Navy Mutual Aid Association.

501(c)(24): Employee benefit plans

Section 501(c)(24) provides an exemption for trusts established for certain *employee benefit plans* under the Employee Retirement Income Security Act of 1974, such as 401(k)s, profit sharing plans, or other retirement plans.

501(c)(25): Title holding corporations

Section 501(c)(25) allows an exemption for *title holding corporations*. A title holding corporation is organized exclusively to hold title to property, collect income from that property, and turn that income over to one or more tax-exempt organizations. To be eligible, the corporation can have not more than 35 shareholders or beneficiaries and only one class of stock or beneficial interest.

501(c)(26): High-risk insurance coverage

Section 501(c)(26) provides the exemption for state-sponsored organizations providing healthcare coverage for high-risk individuals. These organizations provide medical care coverage on a nonprofit basis to its members through insurance or an HMO. The individuals receiving the care must be residents of the state sponsoring the organizations, and the state specifies the composition of membership.

501(c)(27): Worker's compensation

Section 501(c)(27) provides the exemption for state-sponsored worker's compensation reinsurance organizations. These organizations are formed to reimburse members for losses arising under worker's compensation acts. Membership in these organizations generally consists of all persons who issue insurance covering workers compensation lawsuits, as well as governmental entities who self-insure against such losses.

501 (c) (28): Railroad retirement

Section 501(c)(28) provides the exemption for the National Railroad Retirement and Investment Trust as established by the Railroad Retirement Act of 1974.

Exemptions in other parts of the Code

Even though Internal Revenue Code 501(c) provides the most commonly recognized tax exemptions, other subsections of the Internal Revenue Code provide that the income of certain organizations can be tax exempt.

Section 501 (d): Relief for religious and apostolic associations

Section 501(d) of the Internal Revenue Code provides an exemption for religious and apostolic associations that have a *common treasury* or *community treasury,* even if they're engaged in business for the common benefit of the members. If this is the case, however, the members must include in their gross income their pro rata shares of taxable income of the association for the year.

The concept of a common treasury or community treasury refers to the property of such organizations as not being held by members individually, but rather in a community capacity with all members having equal interests in the property. This requirement is satisfied when all the income generated by the community-operated business and from the property owned by the business is placed into a community fund maintained by the organization and used for the maintenance and support of its members.

This separate exemption exists because apostolic organizations weren't found to qualify for tax-exempt status under the general religious organizations exemption (primarily because of the presence of community activities and private benefits). This exemption is rarely used by organizations.

Section 501 (e): Hospitals

Section 501(e) provides an exemption for organizations that perform cooperative services for hospitals. These organizations are required to be organized and operated solely for two or more exempt hospitals and must be organized and operated on a cooperative basis (meaning one member, one vote and sharing in profits based on the amount of business done with the cooperative, rather than on ownership interest). They generally perform services, such as processing, billing, laboratory services, printing, and similar services, for their members. (See Chapter 12 for more on cooperatives.)

Section 501(f): Education

Section 501(f) provides the exemption for cooperative service organizations that are operating educational organizations. These cooperative organizations are regarded as charitable organizations, which are organized and controlled solely by members that are private or public educational institutions. These organizations are organized and operated solely to hold, commingle, and collectively invest and reinvest in stocks and securities contributed by each member of the organization and to collect the income from these investments and turn it over to the members.

Section 501(k): Child care

Section 501(k) provides the exemption for child care organizations. The exemption applies where substantially all of the care provided by the organization is for the purpose of enabling individuals to be gainfully employed. The services provided by the organization must be available to the general public. In other words, if a child care facility provides preference for the children of employees of a specific employer, it doesn't qualify for the exemption.

Section 501(n): Charitable risk pools

Section 501(n) provides an exemption for *charitable risk pools,* which are entities organized and operated solely to pool insurance risks of its members (other than risks related to medical malpractice) and to provide its members with information concerning loss control and risk management. All members must be tax-exempt charitable organizations.

Section 521(a): Farmers' co-ops

Section 521(a) provides an exemption to *farmers' cooperative associations.* Farmers' cooperatives are associations of individuals that give their members a place to market their products. These organizations are organized and operated on a cooperative basis for the purpose of marketing the products of members. They return the proceeds of sales less operating expenses to their members on the basis of either the quantity or the value of the products furnished by them, or for purchasing supplies for the use of members and turning over the supplies and equipment to the members at actual cost plus expenses.

Section 527: Exempt political organizations

Internal Revenue Code Section 527 gives political organizations tax-exempt status. A *political organization* is a party, committee, fund, or other organization that's organized and operated primarily to directly earn and directly accept contributions or spend money for an exempt function. An *exempt function* is an activity that influences or attempts to influence the selection, nomination, election, or appointment of any individual to any public office or office in a political organization.

The *political action committee,* or PAC, is the most recognized form of the political organization.

Applying for Tax-Exempt Status

The application for tax-exempt status, which has to go to the IRS, is an arduous process. Unfortunately, no fast-track process exists to expedite the review of your application. The best way to ensure that your application will be processed quickly is to complete it as thoroughly as possible prior to mailing it.

For example, all questions and line items to the application should be completed as clearly and fully as possible. Any attachments to the application (such as bylaws or articles of organization) should be clearly marked and identified and should show the organization's name, address, and employer identification number, along with a brief statement that it's an attachment to your application form. In the brief statement, you need to identify the part and line number of the application form to which the attachment applies.

Even though there's no fast track, there is a slow track, and you'll be put on it if your application is incomplete, missing attachments, incorrectly filed, or requesting an exemption for which the application needs to be referred to the exempt organizations' examinations headquarters.

In the event that your application is incomplete, it will be returned to you, and you'll be notified that you can resubmit within a specific period of time — as long as the proper information is provided.

If your organization appears to qualify for exemption under a section of 501(c) that's different from the one for which it originally applied, a different application form may be required. The IRS will advise you if this is the case, and it will provide you with the appropriate form. At that point, you must provide any additional necessary information required to complete the application, and if a reply isn't received within the time specified on the IRS's communications to you, your application will be processed only under the section under which you originally applied.

Filling out the forms

In order to apply for tax-exempt status, most organizations use one of the specific application forms provided by the IRS. These forms include the following:

> ✔ **Form 1023,** which is titled *Application for Recognition of Exemption under Section 501(c)(3) of the Internal Revenue Code*
>
> ✔ **Form 1024,** which is titled *Application for Recognition of Exemption under Section 501(a)*

These forms are available online (www.irs.gov), and they contain instructions and checklists to help you provide the information necessary for the IRS to process the application.

If the form is properly completed and the IRS recognizes your organization's tax-exempt status, it will issue a *determination letter,* which is an official letter from the IRS addressed to the applicant organization which specifically states that the organization has (or has not) met the requirements for a tax exemption under the specific section of 501(c) the applicant applied for. Determination letters won't normally be given if an issue involving the organization's exempt status is in litigation or is under consideration within the IRS.

Paying the fees

You know the common saying "Nothing in life is free," right? Well, it applies to the nonprofit world too. In other words, the application process for receiving tax-exempt status isn't free of charge. The law requires the payment of a *user fee* to process the application. The fees are paid using IRS Form 8718. The amount of the user fee depends on the type of application submitted, but in 2006 the fee ranged from $300 to $900.

Providing additional documents

In general, no matter what type of tax exemption is being applied for, certain documents need to be submitted with the application. For example, every exempt organization must have an employee identification number, whether or not it has any employees. (Your organization can obtain its number by submitting IRS Form SS-4, which is titled *Application for Employer Identification Number.*)

You also need to include a copy of your organization's articles of incorporation, trust indenture, or another enabling document. If no such document exists, the organization won't qualify for exempt status. If the organization has bylaws, a current copy should also be included. (Check out Chapter 4 for more on these documents.)

The application for exempt status should also contain a full description of the purpose and activity of your organization, including any standards, procedures, or other criteria that the organization has adopted for carrying out its purposes. The IRS also wants to know about the organization's finances. So you need to include financial statements showing receipts and expenditures for the current year and the three previous years and a balance sheet for the current year. If your organization is less than 1 year old or if it has not yet begun operations, a proposed budget for two full accounting periods and a current statement of assets and liabilities needs to be submitted. Beyond these documents, the IRS may require additional information, such as copies of advertising, publications, written materials, leases, contracts, or agreements.

The documents submitted with the application must be *conformed copies,* meaning that the copies agree with the original documents and all amendments. However, remember that original documents shouldn't be submitted because all documents submitted become part of the IRS's file and can't be returned. Any attachments to a document must show the organization's name, address, and employee identification number.

An incomplete application may be returned without being considered. If sent back, the IRS will state what additional information is required with the application and the period of time you have to resubmit it. If you send the application back in a timely fashion, it will be considered received on the original submission date.

Understanding the approval process

If you're still wondering what happens after your organization's application is submitted, you've come to the right place. This section explains just that.

Once a complete application is submitted, the application package will be reviewed by an IRS manager in a department called Exempt Organizations Determinations. This manager will either issue a favorable determination on the organization's exemption, issue an adverse determination denying the exemption, or refer the case to the headquarters of the IRS for a ruling. Referrals to headquarters are made when issues on qualification for exemption have no precedent or the issue is so unusual or complex that headquarters consideration is justified. Although not widely publicized, a referral to IRS headquarters will most likely substantially delay the issuance of any determination.

After the IRS thoroughly reviews an application and makes a determination, a ruling or determination letter is sent to the applicant. A ruling or a determination letter is usually effective as of the date of the formation of the organization. If the IRS requires an organization to alter its activities or amend its charter in order to qualify for a tax exemption, the ruling or determination letter is usually effective as of the date specified in the letter.

If an applicant has a change of heart, it may withdraw its application at any time before the IRS issues a ruling or a determination letter, but the withdrawal doesn't prevent any of the information in the application from being used by the IRS in any examination of the organization's returns. Any information an applicant submits with its application will not be returned, and any user fee paid to the IRS will not be refunded.

After a completed application goes through and the applicant receives a determination letter, an organization's application forms and annual information returns are, by law, available for public inspection. The same law also requires that the IRS allow public inspection of an approved application, including any documents that the applicant may have submitted in support of it.

However, an applicant can make a request for withholding of information from the public if any information submitted with its application relates to a patent, a trade secret, or any other intellectual property (if the IRS determines that disclosure of the information would aversely affect the organization). Such requests must specifically identify the material to be withheld (which should be marked "Not Subject to Public Inspection"), must include the reasons that the information should be withheld, and must be filed with the documents containing the material requested to be withheld.

As a final note, any ruling or determination letter recognizing a tax exemption can't be relied on if there's a material change in the character, purpose, or method of operation of your organization that's inconsistent with the exemption initially provided.

Applying if your organization hasn't begun operating

If you want to apply for tax-exempt status even though your organization isn't up and running yet, you just have to be sure and describe your organization's proposed operations in enough detail to permit the IRS to conclude that your organization clearly meets the particular requirements of the section of the Internal Revenue Code under which you're claiming an exemption (see the section "Skimming Internal Revenue Code Section 501(c)" earlier in this chapter for a list of the most common exemption sections).

In other words, a statement of your organization's purpose isn't enough to satisfy this requirement. You must be able to describe the following in detail:

✔ The procedures, standards, or other activities adopted or planned for carrying out your organization's activities

✔ The expected sources of funds

✔ The anticipated expenses

If you fail to furnish a sufficiently detailed description of proposed activities and financing, the IRS may turn you down by issuing an adverse ruling or determination letter. You have a right to appeal this decision. (Flip to the section "Appealing an Adverse Determination with the IRS" later in this chapter for more.)

Getting a determination

If you get approved for tax-exempt status, the status will likely be legally effective as of the date of the formation of your organization. Assuming that your organization has filed and paid taxes prior to receiving the recognition, you may file for a refund of any taxes paid for the period for which the exempt status is recognized.

Suppose the IRS contacts you and says prior to issuing a determination letter or ruling recognizing your organization's exempt status, you will be required to alter your activities or substantially amend your charter. In that case, the ruling or determination letter ultimately issued to recognize your tax exemption will become effective as of the date specified in the letter or ruling.

Appealing an Adverse Determination with the IRS

If the IRS turns down your organization for tax-exempt status, you'll get a letter that includes information about your right to protest this determination by requesting an Appeals Office consideration. To follow up on the appeal, you must send your protest to the manager of the office that issued the adverse letter. You must do this within 30 days from the date of the adverse letter, and you must state that you want to have an Appeals Office conference.

Your organization can be represented by a principal officer or trustee at any level of appeal within the IRS, or it may be represented by an attorney, a certified public accountant (CPA), or any other individual enrolled to practice before the IRS.

In order to represent an organization, a representative needs to have a power of attorney authorizing such representation on file with the IRS.

Doing the paperwork

In filing a protest to the local Appeals Office, you must include the following information:

- **Identifying information:** The organization's name, address, and employer identification number.

- **Statement of protest:** A statement that the organization wants to protest the determination.

- **Date of denial:** The date and any code that the IRS asks you to include with correspondence (which will be noted on the determination letter).

- **The facts:** A statement of the facts that support your organization's position, and any contested factual issues.

- **Legal position:** A statement that outlines the law of authority that you'll be relying on.

- **Request for a conference:** A statement acknowledging that you want to have a conference at the Appeals Office.

After considering the organization's protest and any information presented in the conference, the Appeals Office will notify your organization of its decision and will issue an appropriate determination letter. You may then appeal any adverse decision to the courts (this process is explained in the following section).

Taking it to court: An exhausting process

Before an unfavorable ruling or determination letter from the IRS can be appealed to the courts, your organization needs to exhaust its administrative remedies to ensure that all possible steps have been taken before resorting to court action. These remedies include:

✔ A filing of the substantially completed application form (in the event that any information was missing)

✔ In the case of a later filed application, a request for extension of time for making an election or application for relief from tax

✔ The timely submission of all additional information requested

✔ The exhaustion of all administrative appeals to the IRS

After you've exhausted the administrative remedies, you can appeal to a U.S. District Court or the U.S. Court of Federal Claims if your organization was forced to pay taxes because of the unfavorable determination (but it otherwise met all other statutory prerequisites). You can also file a suit for redetermination of tax deficiencies in the U.S. Tax Court. Deciding which court to appeal to is complicated, and you'll need to talk to a good tax lawyer before deciding what to do at this point.

If your organization received an adverse determination, or if the IRS failed to make a timely determination on your qualification as an exempt organization under Section 501(c)(3), you can file suit for a declaratory judgment in the U.S. District Court for the District of Columbia, the U.S. District Court of Federal Claims, or the U.S. Tax Court.

A court determination can take years to complete, and your organization is well-advised to continue filing the proper tax forms during the suit.

If a suit results in a final determination that recognizes the tax-exempt status of your organization, the IRS will issue a favorable ruling or determination letter, provided that your organization has filed an application for exemption and submitted a statement that the facts and law are the same as in the period considered by the court.

Chapter 6

Paying Nonprofit Directors, Officers, Staff, and Volunteers

....

In This Chapter

▶ Forming a compensation committee

▶ Understanding the IRS guidelines

▶ Determining reasonable compensation packages

▶ Accounting properly for payments made to volunteers

....

*O*ne of the most sensitive issues for any nonprofit organization is how much to pay its officers, directors, and staff. If salaries aren't in line with the marketplace, it's difficult to attract competent, talented people to serve in key positions. However, if salaries for officers and directors are set to be competitive with for-profit companies, these amounts run the risk of appearing excessive to the constituency who wants to see more funds spent on programs. Setting salaries is far from an exact science, and in recent years the Internal Revenue Service (IRS) has found it necessary to add its opinion into the mix as to what should be considered "reasonable."

In this chapter, we take a close look at how nonprofits set income for their top officers, what limits the IRS imposes on setting income, and what benefits it considers to be counted as income.

Convening a Compensation Committee

When a board finds a particular task to be sticky, time-consuming, or controversial, it may opt to delegate the matter to a committee (see Chapter 9 for more details on committees). Compensation committees are a case in point. Generally boards try to put board members on the compensation committees who have some sort of relevant expertise in evaluating skills sets and setting compensation.

When they establish compensation committees, many nonprofits assign the following duties to it:

✔ **Researching appropriate initial salaries for new positions:** These determinations may be based on market surveys and on analysis of the nonprofit organization's recruiting needs.

✔ **Evaluating the performance of senior management and staff:** This is an ancillary duty to setting compensation. The committee's role may be simply to compile performance evaluation data from other board members and staff, and then link it to a compensation recommendation in some meaningful way.

✔ **Recommending salary levels and adjustments, usually on an annual basis:** Recommendations should include the research and analysis that the committee used in making its decision, such as salary surveys and advice from trained consultants with backgrounds in personnel and human resources management. These people are sometimes referred to as *compensation consultants*.

Setting the officers' salaries

It's rare to find someone who thinks that he or she is overpaid, and in the nonprofit arena, salaries of top executives are constantly under scrutiny. Every nonprofit needs to strive toward balance and fairness when setting executive compensation.

A nonprofit organization can have a number of different officer positions, including a chief executive officer or president, an executive director, a vice-president, a secretary, and a treasurer. Generally, an officer is any person who has a position of trust or authority within an organization. Determining their compensation raises sensitive issues because of their assumed position of influence within the organization. Accordingly, officers of a nonprofit organization shouldn't serve on the compensation committee.

Although corporate officers are generally employees, not all are. Officers who don't perform any services or receive salaries aren't considered employees for insurance and other purposes.

With support staff, such as secretaries and receptionists, it's pretty easy to set salaries based on the market rate. That's because the going rates for these types of services within a specific geographic area can easily be assessed by looking at what others are paying. However, setting the salary for top-level officers poses more of a challenge for the following reasons:

✔ **Difficulty in getting comparable data:** Because an organization generally has only one president, and every organization is different, there may not be a lot of comparable data available.

✔ **Uniqueness of each organization:** The type of individual it takes to run a nonprofit differs from organization to organization. Some nonprofits may need a leader with fundraising skills, while others require someone with political savvy, administrative skills, technical expertise, industry reputation, or some other characteristic that the board considers essential to the future success of the organization.

✔ **Concerns about competitive recruiting:** For-profit corporations generally look for people with similar skill sets, and they often compete for the person who may be considered a qualified candidate by either a nonprofit or a for-profit entity. However, nonprofits have the advantage of attracting candidates with altruistic motives who aren't influenced by salary alone, but who are motivated by humanitarian or other reasons.

✔ **The organization's ability to pay:** Overriding nearly every other consideration is setting compensation in line with the organization's ability to pay. The resources of a nonprofit organization can vary dramatically from year to year, and some organizations operate on a shoestring budget over the long term. So, the realities of the organization's financial resources must be considered. In addition, because an officer's pay is made public through the filing of Form 990 (which lists compensation information), the amount must be supportable by the nonprofit's constituency.

Comparing salaries paid at other nonprofits

Compensation committees are constantly faced with the problem of trying to make apples-to-apples–type comparisons. Nonprofits vary widely in their sizes and missions, and due to this variety, they often don't have objective measurable standards of comparison (like earnings, as would be the cases with their for-profit counterparts). Because of the specialized nature of nonprofit compensation, committees are more likely to be stuck with an apples-to-oranges–type of comparison. Some of the factors that nonprofits might look at to determine whether other organizations are comparable to theirs for purposes of determining salaries may include the following:

✔ **Similar size of budgets:** The overall budget of an organization is a good indicator of its complexity to manage and administer.

✔ **Organizational revenue:** How much revenue an organization generates in the form of donations or earned income is an objective yardstick for comparing organizations.

- ✔ **Number of employees:** Arguably, the more people an organization has, the more personnel issues there are to manage. So, higher salaries are justified for those who do the managing.

- ✔ **Similarity of mission:** This is a more subjective standard, but it can be useful. For example, if your organization is a preschool, you could compare it to other early childhood programs (as opposed to chambers of commerce or rotary clubs).

- ✔ **Geographic location:** Wages differ dramatically by geographical region, and this is a comparative standard that shouldn't be overlooked. Wages are (and rightfully should be) higher in New York City than in Arkansas, no matter what the position is.

A lot of information about comparable nonprofits can be found in their most recent Form 990 (see Chapter 7). Form 990s are publicly available for review by going to www.guidestar.org, which is discussed in more detail in Chapter 7. If it's clear that such data isn't available or is nonexistent, for-profit comparables can be used. But remember that they may be subject to adjustment because of their for-profit nature.

The buck stops with the board

A nonprofit board is ultimately responsible for major financial decisions, but it can delegate the task of setting salaries to a compensation committee. It can also delegate decisions about the hiring of an executive, about evaluating performance, and about formulating the executive's compensation packages. However, this doesn't insulate the organization from liability. Ultimately, the responsibility for all decisions always remains with the entire board. Delegation doesn't absolve them from their responsibility for oversight of compensation decisions.

For example, a common trap that compensation committees can fall into is to accept recommendations from the executive as to what his or her compensation should be, or hire a compensation consultant referred by the executive. These considerations may seem harmless enough, but they nonetheless have the potential to directly or indirectly slant the view of the board and taint the entire compensation decision-making process.

After the compensation committee formulates its recommendations, the entire board must participate in the decision-making process, have a command of the full details of the compensation package, and have the opportunity to discuss and approve the package.

Following IRS Guidelines

One may wonder why the IRS would want to be involved in determining what nonprofits pay their workers. The simple answer is that the IRS has an interest in making sure that nonprofit organizations aren't used to the advantage of private individuals. In other words, it wants to make sure that nonprofits aren't abused. For example, siphoning off large salaries to cronies who perform no real services for the organization is one way nonprofits could be used to further private interests.

The IRS offers guidelines on what's considered reasonable compensation, and it has the authority to revoke the exempt status of tax-exempt organizations that ignore them. According to the IRS, if a nonprofit organization meets the following requirements, its officers' compensation arrangement is presumed to be reasonable:

- **Advance approval:** The IRS frowns on arrangements that are made without full disclosure to the board of directors. The compensation arrangement must be approved by the full board (not just the compensation committee or a compensation consultant) in advance of paying it.

- **Authorization by independent individuals:** The compensation arrangement must be authorized and approved by individuals who are independent and who don't have a conflict of interest concerning the pay. For example, a compensation committee consisting of some members of the board is considered independent as long as none of the members has a substantial relationship with the individual whose compensation is being set.

  Independence minimizes the possibility of undue influence or consideration of factors that wouldn't normally carry weight with persons who are independent from the organization and the person being considered.

- **Documented data:** The IRS doesn't want nonprofit organizations pulling numbers out of a hat, even if the compensation arrangements are preapproved completely by independent individuals. The nonprofit must be ready to show that the compensation amount is based on actual data of comparable salaries.

Determining what's "reasonable"

Reasonable compensation is a term that can be difficult to pin down. In fact, it can be pretty subjective, and compensation committees can vary widely in what they view as reasonable. The IRS defines reasonable compensation as the amount that would ordinarily be paid for like services by like enterprises (whether taxable or tax exempt) under like circumstances. Some of the factors that the IRS looks at in determining what's reasonable include the following:

- ✔ **Amounts paid for similar services:** This can include amounts paid in both the nonprofit and for-profit sectors, because the focus is on the actual services and skill set of the organization.

- ✔ **Similarity of organizations:** The work of some organizations may be more challenging than others. The IRS figures that it's helpful to look at the type of organization when deciding how much to pay the people who work for it.

- ✔ **Actual duties and responsibilities of the executives:** This involves comparing duties and responsibilities, not titles. For example, the salary of an executive who's involved in major decisions and formulating long-term business plans isn't comparable to that of an executive with the same title who's charged with administrative duties and implements strategies designed by others.

- ✔ **Similar for-profits:** Where no appropriate nonprofits are available, for-profit comparables can be used. IRS regulations do allow comparisons to nonprofit or for-profit entities, or both. Ideally comparisons are made against entities of similar size, budget, revenue, number of employees, industry, and geographic location. However, comparing against a for-profit organization doesn't allow a rebuttable presumption of reasonableness, and it will likely draw increased scrutiny from the IRS.

Documenting the decision process in the minutes

All compensation committees should "paper its trails to cover its tail." In other words, document everything carefully. Detailed minutes of what's discussed at compensation committee meetings and how all the issues are resolved can go a long way in avoiding future charges of favoritism or arbitrariness. This is true for both large nonprofits, as well as smaller community-based organizations, because salaries are often a significant portion of an organization's budget.

In fact, IRS regulations specify that a compensation committee must adequately and in a timely manner document the basis for its determination concurrently while making its determination. You want to avoid having to reconstruct what a committee did weeks, months, or even years later. One way to make sure your organization meets this requirement is to have the compensation committee keep minutes of its meetings. The minutes should include the following items:

- **Attendees:** The minutes should include a list of attendees, their titles or roles, and how they voted on the issues that were discussed.

- **Consideration of conflicts:** Potential conflicts of interest of any members of the compensation committee should be completely aired and fully discussed, and these discussions should be documented in detail.

- **The date the compensation package was approved:** Dates of approval are important because the IRS guidelines require preapproval, not post-approval, of compensation packages.

- **Due diligence:** Minutes should also reflect that the committee took the time and trouble to obtain and review the necessary data about comparable salaries. The comparability data that was obtained and relied on should either be referenced and available for later review, or included with the minutes themselves.

- **Terms of the compensation package:** It's important to document that all of the costs of the compensation package were considered and specifically approved.

A compensation committee that follows these guidelines will be presumed to have acted reasonably in setting an officer's compensation. The IRS can refute this presumption of reasonableness only by developing sufficient contrary evidence to rebut the data that the committee relied on.

If the committee doesn't satisfy the previous IRS guidelines, the IRS will look at the particular facts and circumstances to determine whether the compensation is reasonable.

Cooking Up a Compensation Package

What's included in a compensation package? The IRS stresses the importance of including all forms of compensation. In other words, IRS regulations are very specific about what items can and can't be excluded from income. Problem areas that frequently crop up include the following:

- Expense reimbursements
- Gifts and gift certificates
- Personal use of employer-owned property

✔ Spousal travel expenses

✔ Club memberships

✔ Personal components of business travel

Unless a specific exemption applies, each of these components needs to be added into any employee's income whether or not they're treated as income for income tax purposes.

Identifying the additional ingredients of a compensation package

The following types of compensation are acceptable for organizations to pay, but they must be reported as compensation:

✔ **Non-cash items:** Any and all forms of cash and non-cash compensation, including salaries, bonuses, severance payments, and deferred compensation.

✔ **Insurance premiums:** Payments for liability insurance premiums, or the payment of taxes or certain expenses.

✔ **Other benefits:** All other benefits that are meant as compensation, whether or not they might be included in gross income for income tax purposes.

✔ **Fringe benefits:** Most taxable and nontaxable fringe benefits.

✔ **Interest-free loans:** Foregone loan interest.

Putting the compensation recipe in writing

A financial benefit to an officer won't be considered part of his paycheck unless the organization providing the benefit clearly indicates that it intends to treat the payment as part of the compensation package. For example, the organization has a choice as to whether to treat expenses like mileage, professional education, laptop computers, and frequent flyer miles as compensation.

Generally, an organization will treat the items that seem to elude classification as compensation. It does this to avoid having a situation with the IRS where the officer or employee ends up owing unexpected income taxes. This practice helps protect the IRS from later coming in and reclassifying the item as income and requiring the officer to amend his or her tax return, as well as assess penalties on the nonprofit.

Your organization can easily document in writing which perks it intends to include as compensation, and which are reimbursed expenses that don't count as earnings. A few ways you can do this include the following:

- **Having a written agreement:** Having a signed contract (usually an employment contract) is a simple way to clear up any confusion.

- **Reporting the item as wages:** Let the officer know that it's compensation by reporting the benefit as compensation on his or her Form W-2.

- **Using IRS Form 1099:** When the person being compensated isn't considered an employee, but he or she serves the organization in some other capacity (such as an independent contractor or a consultant), the report can be made on a Form 1099 (as opposed to a W-2, which is generally used for employees).

- **Reporting IRS Form 990:** Listing the officers' compensation on the organization's annual Form 990 tax return informs the IRS of what the compensation level is.

- **Telling the officer or employee to report it:** Having the officer report the benefit as income on his or her individual income tax return (in cases where it isn't already listed on a W-2 or 1099) is another way to document how the item is to be treated. Of course, it may be difficult for your organization to know if this has been done, because it isn't privy to the tax returns of the people working for the organization.

Looking at the consequences of paying unreasonable compensation

Up to this point in the chapter, we've discussed how reasonable compensation is established. But what happens when the IRS determines that compensation is unreasonable because it doesn't meet the foregoing standards? Bad things. Really bad things.

The IRS imposes severe sanctions on persons of influence (officers and directors) who receive excessive economic benefits from a nonprofit organization. The person is the target here; the nonprofit organization itself isn't usually punished — unless of course, the indiscretion is so flagrant that a revocation of the organization's tax-exempt status is warranted.

Okay, so what's unreasonable? The IRS has determined that under certain circumstances, the following items can be considered unreasonable compensation:

The sting of the Pension Protection Act

The Pension Protection Act of 2006 (PPA) not only doubles the excise tax on excess benefit transactions, but it also creates new rules that apply to situations where no abuse may be present. One such situation applies to nonprofit organizations that are classified as *donor-advised funds.* Where a nonprofit donor-advised fund pays compensation to a donor or someone related to the donor who advises the fund, that payment is automatically considered an excess benefit transaction. The entire amount of compensation will be treated as an excess benefit, regardless of the value of the service rendered.

For example, under this *automatic excess benefit transaction rule,* even though a donor's family member may provide reasonable necessary personal services that are necessary to accomplish the nonprofit's mission to a donor-advised fund, the entire amount of compensation paid to the donor's family member can still be considered an excess benefit transaction. This subjects the unsuspecting family member to excise taxes.

Similarly, expense reimbursements to any family member of a donor (even if related to the benefit of the nonprofit) will be considered an automatic excess benefit transaction. The PPA's penalty provisions impose much stricter rules on donor-advised funds than on private foundations. Of particular importance, however, is that a donor, as well as his or her family members and related parties, are now subject to the excise tax penalties.

- Leasing of property owned by an executive to the nonprofit in return for excessive rent

- Loans made by a nonprofit to an executive

- Payment by the nonprofit of expenses for a for-profit corporation owned by the executive

- Payment by the nonprofit of personal expenses of members of an executive's family

- Personal use of vehicles (for example, airplanes)

- Receipt of royalties from a book published by the nonprofit organization

- Reimbursements of personal expenses

The IRS labels all of these transactions as *excess benefit transactions.* An excess benefit transaction is one where an economic benefit is provided by a nonprofit to an executive, where the value of that benefit exceeds the value received by the nonprofit for the benefit from the executive. Or, to be blunt, an excess benefit transaction is when the IRS believes that the executive's effort is being substantially overvalued.

The IRS makes sure that excess benefit transactions are costly and something to be avoided by imposing the following penalties:

- ✔ **Initial 25-percent penalty:** The IRS will send the executive a bill equal to 25 percent of the excess benefit for each excess benefit transaction.

- ✔ **A 200-percent penalty for those who persist:** If the excess benefit transaction isn't corrected within a given time period, an additional excise tax equal to a 200-percent penalty may be imposed. Ouch!

- ✔ **Doubling the pain under the Pension Protection Act of 2006:** To make matters even more serious, the Pension Protection Act of 2006 doubles (yes, doubles) the penalties applicable to excess benefit transactions. For more on the Pension Protection Act, see the sidebar, "The sting of the Pension Protection Act."

Governance Issues and Compensation

In this day and age, issues of executive compensation and governance are closely intertwined. We have a Sarbanes-Oxley mindset to thank for this. (Sarbanes-Oxley and its relationship to nonprofit organizations is discussed in Chapter 13.)

IRS compliance checks

The IRS has a special division for reviewing issues relating to executive compensation. This division is known as the Exempt Organizations branch of the Tax Exempt/Government Entities Division, or TE/GE Division (as discussed in Chapter 15).

The TE/GE Division has taken an active role in the past when it comes to executive compensation of exempt organizations. In 2004, it announced a new enforcement effort to curb abuses by exempt organizations. The agency contacted over 1,800 public charities and private foundations to request compensation practice information. The TE/GE announced that the goal of the contacts was to learn how exempt organizations determine and report compensation, and to raise awareness of compensation-related tax issues and questionable practices.

About 1,200 of the initial 1,800 contacts were considered *compliance checks.* A compliance check is an IRS review to determine whether an organization is following proper record-keeping and reporting procedures; it isn't an audit. Compliance checks are intended to alert an organization to potential errors. The 2004 compliance checks were mostly triggered by some sort of error on the organization's Form 990s, such as a question being incorrectly answered or omitted entirely. The most common types of information omitted included information related to loans, deferred compensation, and fringe benefits.

The IRS is always concerned as to whether governing boards of nonprofit organizations exercise a sufficient degree of due diligence in setting the compensation for leaders of their organizations. The media seems to delight in reporting on executives of both private foundations and public charities who are receiving what many consider to be unreasonably large compensation packages.

Identifying best practices

When talking compensation, the IRS believes that exempt organizations should focus on four key governance areas:

- **Creating legal structures:** Every board should strive to set compensation in advance by disinterested board members on the basis of appropriate comparability data.

- **Reporting all the benefits:** This means timely reporting of all economic benefits to officers, directors, and key employees on IRS Form 990 (check out Chapter 7 for more info on this form).

- **Being timely:** Organizations should take care to report the benefits in the time period that they're paid.

- **Staying accountable:** Boards that delegate compensation issues to committees still have the ultimate responsibility over the compensation decision.

- **Avoiding payments to private individuals:** The Internal Revenue Code says that the assets of an organization can't be diverted for the benefit of private individuals. If an organization pays or distributes assets to insiders in excess of the fair market value of the services rendered, it's running afoul of this rule, and the organization can lose its tax-exempt status.

Steering clear of excise taxes

Insiders of public charities and of private foundations are subject to excise taxes on any overpayments that they receive from the entities.

Although an overpayment to an insider of a public charity could result in a revocation of tax-exempt status, the Internal Revenue Code provides an *intermediate sanction* that ameliorates that result in many cases. Under the intermediate sanction rules, an excise tax can be imposed on the insider who received the overpayment and on certain managers who knowingly approved the overpayment.

Exempt organizations are generally safe if they develop and follow procedures for setting compensation and if they make honest, responsible efforts in line with their size and revenues to determine what the appropriate level of compensation is.

Weighing all the factors

At the risk of beating a dead horse, it bears repeating that neither a public charity nor a private foundation can pay more than reasonable compensation without running afoul of IRS issues. And reasonable compensation is determined by weighing all facts and circumstances, considering the market value of the services performed. Generally speaking, reasonable compensation is measured with reference to the amount that would ordinarily be paid for comparable services by comparable enterprises under comparable circumstances.

Avoiding Tax for Volunteers

Volunteers are the lifeblood of many organizations. They come in all shapes and sizes, and serve in all manner of capacities.

Many nonprofits have volunteer officers who aren't paid for their services. However, these officers can get reimbursed or receive an allowance for the out-of-pocket expenses that are incurred in connection with their volunteer service. These reimbursements can have tax consequences. For example, if an officer is required to attend a conference to represent the nonprofit, the organization may foot the bill for the trip. Just how an officer's reimbursement or allowance is paid and accounted for will determine how it will be treated for employment tax purposes.

Generally, reimbursement payments to volunteers are made in two ways: accountable plans and non-accountable plans, both of which are described the following sections.

Keeping track with an accountable plan

An *accountable plan* is one where all the funds are tracked and business expenses don't have to be reported on the volunteer's income tax return. An accountable plan has the following characteristics:

✔ **Relationship:** There's a "business" connection between the expense paid and the mission or operations of the organization.

✔ **Accounting:** The volunteer adequately accounts for the expenses within a reasonable period of time.

✔ **Return of funds not used for expenses:** Under an accountable plan, a volunteer must return any excess expenses to the organization within a reasonable period of time.

If any one of the above three conditions isn't met, the plan will be considered a non-accountable plan (see the section "Opting for a non-accountable plan" for more).

Payments made under an accountable plan don't need to be reported on a Form W-2.

Opting for a non-accountable plan

Under a *non-accountable plan,* reimbursements are includable as gross income, and they're required to be reported on a Form W-2. They're also subject to *employment taxes.* Because employment taxes must be paid, W-2's must be issued. This option requires a nonprofit organization to keep careful records. Employment taxes are a liability imposed on an employer by both state and federal law, and failure to report and pay them can result in fines and penalties to the organization.

Part III
Structuring a Nonprofit to Meet Its Mission

The 5th Wave   By Rich Tennant

THE MILLBURY POETRY ASSOCIATION

"Concerning the bylaws, Mr. Morganstern's group firmly believes they should be written in iambic pentameter quatrain form, whereas Ms. Ahern's group prefers the couplet form..."

In this part . . .

This part gives you the lowdown on filing the dreaded Form 990, including who has to file, what information is required, and what the penalties are for not filing. You also can find out what duties you'll assume if you agree to become part of a nonprofit board of directors. Finally, we also delve into the area of creating effective committees, with an entire chapter devoted to audit committees.

Chapter 7

Filing the Dreaded Form 990

● ●

In This Chapter

▶ Understanding who has to file the Form 990

▶ Deciding which form to use

▶ Filing with your state

▶ Avoiding filing problems

▶ Using the Internet to research a nonprofit's 990s

▶ Viewing some sample forms

● ●

*A*fter getting tax-exempt status from the Internal Revenue Service (IRS), did you think that your organization was home free and would never have to file another revenue form? Well, no such luck. The IRS may not want a tax payment from your organization every year, but it does want information — and lots of it. And it all has to be painfully extracted and meticulously organized on the IRS's very own Form 990.

To get you acquainted with this important form, this chapter explains which organizations are required to file Form 990, what kinds of information the IRS is after, and what happens to negligent nonprofits that attempt to skirt their obligations. This chapter also offers tips for legally snooping into other nonprofits' affairs by accessing their Form 990s.

Introducing Form 990: What It Is and Who Has to File It

Not every tax form requires a payment of tax. Sometimes information is what the IRS is after. For example, Forms 990, 990-EZ, and 990-PF (the three, um, forms of Form 990) are considered *information returns* or *reporting forms*. The public uses the information on these returns to evaluate nonprofits and how they operate. On these forms, you can see what a nonprofit's income and expenses are, how much it pays its key people, and other useful information that can help you assess what a nonprofit does.

Form 990 is a fairly critical form for the public disclosure of information, because the law doesn't require typical annual reports from nonprofit organizations. Even financial audits by independent accountants aren't required by law (except in special circumstances).

The organizations that must file the Form 990s don't have to pay federal income tax on income that's related to their exempt purposes and programs. However, many private foundations do have to pay an excise tax that's based on their investment income.

After an organization files its completed Form 990 or Form 990-EZ, it's available for the world to see. This public access is required under Section 6104 of the Internal Revenue Code. (See the section "Researching Form 990s Online" later in the chapter for details on the best ways to snoop around in other nonprofit organizations' forms.) Form 990-PF (for private foundations) must also be made available for public inspection by the private foundation, but that usually requires an appointment and a trip down to the foundation's main office.

Some nonprofits have income that isn't related to their exempt purpose. This so-called *unrelated business income* is reported on Form 990-T, which is discussed in more detail in the section "Monitoring unrelated business income with the Form 990-T" later in the chapter. (Check out Chapter 14 for more on unrelated business income.)

Organizations that must file a 990 without fail

The IRS wants to know about some groups every year. These groups include the following:

- ✔ **Private foundations:** Every private foundation must file a Form 990-PF, regardless of its size.

- ✔ **Larger nonprofits:** Most nonprofits that have incomes of more than $25,000 generally have to file either Form 990 or 990-EZ.

- ✔ **Everyone else:** Organizations that are tax-exempt under Sections 501(c), 527, or 4947(a)(1) of the U.S. tax code and that don't fall into the exemptions listed in the next section ("Organizations that don't have to file a 990") must file a 990 or 990-EZ every year without fail.

Organizations that don't have to file a 990

Some organizations are exempt from filing any of the Form 990s. If your organization is fortunate enough to be exempt from filing these forms, after glancing through this section, you can safely skip the rest of this chapter — unless, of course, you want to find out how to snoop into the affairs of other organizations using these forms. If that's the case, skip to the section "Researching Form 990s Online" later in this chapter.

To be sure that your organization is exempt, check out the following list of exempt entities:

- **Small nonprofits:** Organizations with annual incomes of $25,000 or less get a free ride, probably because the IRS itself has staffing and cost constraints.

- **Faith-based organizations:** Just about all faith-based organizations get to skip filing Form 990, regardless of size. Hallelujah!

- **Subsidiaries of other nonprofits:** The IRS believes in nepotism! Any subsidiary organization whose parent organization or national headquarters filed a 990 for the entire organization gets to skip the formalities.

- **Nonprofits that aren't in the system yet:** Nonprofits that haven't applied to the IRS for exemption from federal income tax don't have to file a Form 990 because the IRS wouldn't even know who the form is from.

- **Religious schools:** A school below college level that's affiliated with a church or operated by a religious order doesn't have any Form 990 homework.

- **Missions and missionary organizations:** This category includes a mission society sponsored by or affiliated with one or more churches or church organizations, if more than half of the society's activities are conducted in or directed at persons in foreign countries.

- **State institutions:** A state institution that gets a free tax ride because it provides essential government services (a university for example) doesn't have to file a Form 990.

- **Government corporations:** A corporation organized under an act of Congress that's an "instrumentality of the United States" doesn't have to file a Form 990 because it's an arm of the government and is exempt from federal income taxes under 501(c)(1).

Filing deadlines and extensions

The filing deadline for Form 990, 990-EZ, or 990-PF is "the 15th day of the 5th month after [an] organization's accounting period ends," according to the IRS. So, if a nonprofit's fiscal year ends on December 31, its 990 will be due on May 15 of the following year.

A nonprofit can get an automatic three-month extension by submitting Form 8868 to the IRS. The organization often can get another three-month extension by submitting a second Form 8868 — if it has an acceptable reason (known as *good cause*) for requesting the extension. (Examples of good cause would be an illness or a hurricane.)

Figuring Out Which Form to File

Form 990 comes in many flavors, including the 990, 990-EZ, 990-PF, and 990-T. Each is discussed in the following sections. Generally, the type of form you file depends on the type of organization for which you're filing.

Form 990 versus 990-EZ

Because the public relies on Form 990 and Form 990-EZ as the primary or sole source of information, the IRS is a stickler for the specific details required on the forms (see the section "Researching Form 990s Online" later in this chapter for more info on how the public uses the information from 990s).

Both Form 990 and Form 990-EZ are used by tax-exempt organizations, nonexempt charitable trusts, and certain types of exempt political organizations to provide the IRS with annual reports of their activities and income.

Organizations with gross receipts of less than $100,000 and total assets of less than $250,000 at the end of the year can file a 990-EZ, which is the short form. However, if an organization that meets these earnings *wants* to file the long Form 990, the IRS is more than happy to let it do so.

In fact, some organizations that aren't required to file anything with the IRS may actually want to file a Form 990-EZ. (Check out the section "Organizations that don't have to file a 990" earlier in the chapter for details on those organizations that are exempt from filing the forms.)

So why would these organizations go to all the work and bother of filing a form that the feds don't even require? One likely answer is that they may want to use it to satisfy state reporting requirements, as discussed in the section "Satisfying the States with Form 990" later in this chapter.

If an organization chooses to file a Form 990 or 990-EZ even though it isn't required to file one, it still must attach all the schedules and statements that are required to be filed with the form. Otherwise, the return may not be accepted by the IRS.

A private matter: The 990-PF

All private foundations file Form 990-PF annually, regardless of whether they have any assets or annual receipts. These private organizations include the following:

- ✔ Exempt private foundations
- ✔ Taxable private foundations
- ✔ Organizations whose applications for exempt status are pending on the due date for filing the Form 990-PF
- ✔ Organizations that are qualified for basic research
- ✔ Organizations that are terminating their private foundation status
- ✔ Certain nonexempt charitable trusts that are treated as private foundations

As with Forms 990 and 990-EZ, some states will accept a copy of Form 990-PF and its required attachments instead of all or part of their own financial report forms. The discussion in the later section "Satisfying the States with Form 990" applies equally to Form 990-PF.

Monitoring unrelated business income with the Form 990-T

If an organization earns income that's unrelated to its nonprofit missions, the government imposes taxes on that income. This income is called *unrelated business income* (see Chapter 14). If Congress didn't levy this tax, commercial businesses would be at a huge competitive disadvantage with nonprofit organizations because the nonprofits would get to compete tax-free. To remove the competitive disadvantage, the government says that if an organization has enough unrelated trade or business income, the organization could lose its tax-exempt status altogether.

So, if a nonprofit has unrelated business income of $1,000 or more, it's required to file IRS Form 990-T. This form is in addition to the Form 990, 990-EZ, or 990-PF. The filing date for the form varies depending on the type of organization.

In order for income to be considered unrelated, which is a classification that would require a Form 990-T, the following three factors must be present:

✔ The nonprofit organization conducts a trade or business

✔ The trade or business isn't substantially related to the nonprofit purpose of the organization

✔ The trade or business is *regularly* carried on by the nonprofit organization (in other words, the IRS won't come down too hard on the isolated sale of a plate of cookies or the sale of an old church organ)

Satisfying the States with Form 990

Prior to the 1980s, most states required a separate report (separate from the IRS's Form 990) to be filed with state charities regulation offices. Unfortunately, these states all used different forms with wildly different formats to obtain similar information. This inconsistency meant an awful lot of work for charities operating in several states.

State charities regulators and representatives from the nonprofits all advocated for changes to IRS Form 990 so that states would accept it in lieu of their own information returns.

Today, some states graciously accept a copy of the IRS's Form 990 or Form 990-EZ in place of their own version of the form, which serves as the basic annual report to over 35 state charities offices.

Scoping out state statutes

To figure out if a Form 990 or a Form 990-EZ is required in a particular state, you need to check its laws. This check is easily accomplished by reviewing the Web site for the state's department of revenue. Generally, your organization is required to meet the reporting requirements of any state in which it does the following:

- ✔ **Solicits contributions:** If your organization solicits grants or contributions from individuals, businesses, or other charitable organizations, it generally must meet the reporting requirements of that state.

- ✔ **Conducts programs:** If your organization has employees in a state, it generally must file with that jurisdiction.

- ✔ **Parks its property in the state:** If your organization maintains a checking account or owns or rents property in any jurisdiction, it generally is subject to the local filing requirements.

Avoiding some sticky state issues

It's important to remember that because of the variation of state laws, you may come across some unexpected trouble spots when filing Form 990s in states other than your own. For example:

- ✔ Many states have dollar limits for triggering filing requirements that are much lower than the general IRS dollar limitation of having a minimum of $25,000 in gross receipts.

- ✔ Even if a state jurisdiction accepts the Form 990 or Form 990-EZ as filed with the IRS, this alone may not be enough to provide all the required information a state may ask for.

  For instance, the state may require additional financial statements, notes to financial statements, additional financial schedules, reports on financial statements by an independent accountant, and answers to additional questions.

Each jurisdiction has its own rules, so in order to sidestep the sticky issues, carefully review a state's laws prior to filing.

Avoiding Common 990 Nightmares

Filing Form 990s is tedious enough without making common (avoidable) mistakes that require corrective action and delay processing. Making these mistakes may cause the IRS to send the return back to you, or require you to provide additional information. In some cases, missing information can even trigger an audit.

Here are a few things to remember forever (okay, at least until after your filing date):

✔ **Get the return signed by the right person.** To make a return complete, an authorized officer of the nonprofit organization must sign the tax return in the space provided. The officer may be a president, vice-president, treasurer, assistant treasurer, chief accounting officer, or other corporate or association officer who's authorized to sign. If the return is filed for a trust, it must be signed by an authorized trustee.

✔ **Check the correct boxes.** Several sections of Form 990 and 990-EZ ask you to check boxes or answer "yes" or "no" to specific questions about your organization's operations and activities. Make sure your organization discusses these questions with the preparer or firm responsible for completing the return. In particular, make sure that the information submitted is current and verified each year instead of being blindly copied off of a prior year's return.

✔ **Leave the right spaces blank.** For example, if an officer or employee of the organization prepares the return, leave the paid preparer's space blank. Only someone who's paid to prepare the tax return should sign the return and fill in his or her name as the paid preparer.

✔ **Keep your records for at least three years.** You need to keep your nonprofit organization's records for three years from the date that the return is due or filed, whichever is later. However, keep records that verify what the organization paid for property much longer — generally until the property is sold or otherwise disposed of. Keep the returns themselves indefinitely.

✔ **Assemble accurately.** Form 990 or Form 990-EZ must be assembled with supporting documents in the following order: Form 990 or Form 990-EZ; Schedule A; Schedule B; attachments to Form 990 or 990-EZ; attachments to Schedule A; and attachments to Schedule B. The instructions for each type of Form 990 lists the order of attachments.

✔ **Label attachments.** If attachments are filed with your form, they must be labeled appropriately with the form number and tax year, the organization's name, and the employer identification number.

Researching Form 990s Online

IRS Form 990 is a major source of nonprofit research in the United States. Private foundations, government entities, and individual donors all routinely research the information contained on Form 990s and 990-PFs.

For the public, Form 990 or 990-EZ may be the primary (or even sole) sources of information about a particular organization. The public can use these forms to find out all sorts of information, such as how the organization is accomplishing its mission or how its grants are paid to support other organizations.

Getting Form 990 directly from a nonprofit

Any organization filing Form 990, 990-EZ, or 990-PF must make the annual return available to the public for inspection. A nonprofit must also provide copies of its annual returns or exemption application to anyone who requests a copy in person or in writing (unless these documents are otherwise widely available, such as being posted on the organization's Web site).

Nonprofits are required to make their annual returns and exemption application available for public inspection (without charge) at their regional and district offices during regular business hours. Generally if the office has employees who are paid for 120 hours or more a week, the open-door policy requirement applies. However, if a site doesn't serve as an office for management staff other than managers who are involved only in managing the exempt function activities at that site, the doors need not be opened for the inspection of Form 990. If the nonprofit doesn't maintain a permanent office at all, it can comply with the inspection rules by making the documents available at a reasonable location of its choice within a reasonable amount of time after receiving request for inspection (about two weeks) and setting a reasonable time of day for the inspection.

However, this mandatory open-door policy does have some limits. For example, the nonprofit can require that an employee be present to monitor an inspection. Also, the nonprofit must allow the "inspectors" to take notes and make photocopies, but only if the individual brings photocopying equipment to the place of inspection.

A nonprofit can also opt to mail a copy of the requested forms instead of allowing an inspection. A nonprofit must mail the copy within two weeks of receipt of the request. The organization can charge for photocopying and postage only if the person requesting the documents consents to the charge.

Finally, a nonprofit may also disregard any harassment-intended requests for copies of any document beyond the first two requests received within any 30-day period, or the first four requests received within any one-year period from the same individual or the same address.

The Form 990s can be viewed on the Internet at www.guidestar.org. Guidestar is itself a nonprofit organization. Its mission is to provide information to the public about other organizations.

Guidestar offers several paid services that allow you to view sophisticated reports and comparative data for nonprofits. Its services allow you to access the three most recent Form 990s for any organization that has filed them. Studying Form 990s on Guidestar for organizations that are similar to yours can give you insight as to how those organizations handled certain issues, such as compensation levels for execs.

Before you can do anything on Guidestar, you need to register by clicking the registration link on the homepage. The next time you return to this Web site, you can simply log in. After you're registered and logged in, you can use the keyword search function that appears in the upper right-hand corner to search for an organization by name or to look for organizations that have a particular keyword in their name. For example, if I enter the word "animals," the search function pulls up charities that donate causes furthering the interests of nonhuman creatures. By clicking the hypertext links, I can access a sample profile for the organization, and by scrolling down, I can see the three most recently filed Form 990s.

Sampling Some Form 990s

Any IRS form looks daunting at first glance. But once you know what you're looking for, it can be empowering to know that such extensive data about any nonprofit organization is available to you. In fact, it's reassuring that every organization must report the same information on identical lines and in a format that varies relatively little. This standardization is the very reason that many states have been accepting Form 990 in lieu of their own filing requirements. (Check out the section "Satisfying the States with Form 990" earlier in the chapter for more details.) If you're still concerned about the daunting nature of Form 990s, don't worry — this section guides you through all the important information on the 990 and 990-EZ.

Finding answers on the Form 990

Each organization's Form 990 holds a wealth of important information, as the following sections explain. This goes for any size or type of nonprofit entity.

How much income did the organization receive and from where?

Part I of Form 990 (shown in Figure 7-1) is divided into three subparts: Revenue, Expenses, and Net Assets. The Revenue subpart is the focus here. It reports all of the organization's income broken down over more than a dozen sources, including contributions, program service revenue, membership dues, and so on. The total of all the revenue sources is shown on Line 12 (which is labeled "Total revenue") at the bottom of the Revenue subpart.

How did the nonprofit organization spend its money?

Lines 13-17 on a Form 990 show where the money goes. Line 17 reports total expenses, which include program expenses, management expenses, and fundraising expenses.

Form **990**	**Return of Organization Exempt From Income Tax**	OMB No. 1545-0047
	Under section 501(c), 527, or 4947(a)(1) of the Internal Revenue Code (except black lung benefit trust or private foundation)	**2006**
Department of the Treasury Internal Revenue Service	The organization may have to use a copy of this return to satisfy state reporting requirements.	**Open to Public Inspection**

A For the 2006 calendar year, or tax year beginning _____ , 2006, and ending _____ , 20 ____

B Check if applicable:	Please use IRS label or print or type. See Specific Instructions.	**C** Name of organization			**D** Employer identification number
☐ Address change		Number and street (or P.O. box if mail is not delivered to street address)		Room/suite	**E** Telephone number ( )
☐ Name change					
☐ Initial return					
☐ Final return		City or town, state or country, and ZIP + 4			**F** Accounting method: ☐ Cash ☐ Accrual ☐ Other (specify)
☐ Amended return					

☐ Application pending

● **Section 501(c)(3) organizations and 4947(a)(1) nonexempt charitable trusts must attach a completed Schedule A (Form 990 or 990-EZ).**

G Website:

J **Organization type** (check only one) ☐ 501(c) ( ) ◀ (insert no.) ☐ 4947(a)(1) or ☐ 527

K Check here ☐ if the organization is not a 509(a)(3) supporting organization **and** its gross receipts are normally **not** more than $25,000. A return is not required, but if the organization chooses to file a return, be sure to file a complete return.

H and I *are not applicable to section 527 organizations.*
H(a) Is this a group return for affiliates? ☐ Yes ☐ No
H(b) If "Yes," enter number of affiliates _____
H(c) Are all affiliates included? ☐ Yes ☐ No
(If "No," attach a list. See instructions.)
H(d) Is this a separate return filed by an organization covered by a group ruling? ☐ Yes ☐ No
I Group Exemption Number
M Check ☐ if the organization is **not** required to attach Sch. B (Form 990, 990-EZ, or 990-PF).

L Gross receipts: Add lines 6b, 8b, 9b, and 10b to line 12

Part I **Revenue, Expenses, and Changes in Net Assets or Fund Balances** *(See the instructions.)*

Revenue		
1 Contributions, gifts, grants, and similar amounts received:		
a Contributions to donor advised funds	1a	
b Direct public support (not included on line 1a)	1b	
c Indirect public support (not included on line 1a)	1c	
d Government contributions (grants) (not included on line 1a)	1d	
e **Total** (add lines 1a through 1d) (cash $_____ noncash $_____)		1e
2 Program service revenue including government fees and contracts (from Part VII, line 93)		2
3 Membership dues and assessments		3
4 Interest on savings and temporary cash investments		4
5 Dividends and interest from securities		5
6a Gross rents	6a	
b Less: rental expenses	6b	
c Net rental income or (loss). Subtract line 6b from line 6a		6c
7 Other investment income (describe _____)		7
8a Gross amount from sales of assets other than inventory	(A) Securities 8a / (B) Other	
b Less: cost or other basis and sales expenses	8b	
c Gain or (loss) (attach schedule)	8c	
d Net gain or (loss). Combine line 8c, columns (A) and (B)		8d
9 Special events and activities (attach schedule). If any amount is from **gaming**, check here ☐		
a Gross revenue (not including $_____ of contributions reported on line 1b)	9a	
b Less: direct expenses other than fundraising expenses	9b	
c Net income or (loss) from special events. Subtract line 9b from line 9a		9c
10a Gross sales of inventory, less returns and allowances	10a	
b Less: cost of goods sold	10b	
c Gross profit or (loss) from sales of inventory (attach schedule). Subtract line 10b from line 10a		10c
11 Other revenue (from Part VII, line 103)		11
12 **Total revenue.** Add lines 1e, 2, 3, 4, 5, 6c, 7, 8d, 9c, 10c, and 11		12

Expenses		
13 Program services (from line 44, column (B))		13
14 Management and general (from line 44, column (C))		14
15 Fundraising (from line 44, column (D))		15
16 Payments to affiliates (attach schedule)		16
17 **Total expenses.** Add lines 16 and 44, column (A)		17

Net Assets		
18 Excess or (deficit) for the year. Subtract line 17 from line 12		18
19 Net assets or fund balances at beginning of year (from line 73, column (A))		19
20 Other changes in net assets or fund balances (attach explanation)		20
21 Net assets or fund balances at end of year. Combine lines 18, 19, and 20		21

Figure 7-1: The first page of Form 990.

For Privacy Act and Paperwork Reduction Act Notice, see the separate instructions.   Cat. No. 11282Y   Form **990** (2006)

What are the assets of the organization?

The net assets of the organization are broken down in lines 18–21. Line 18 tells whether the organization operated at a surplus or deficit for the year. Line 19 tells you the organization's net assets at the beginning of the year. Line 20 shows any other changes in net assets or fund balances, and Line 21 reveals what the net assets or fund balances are at the end of the year.

What programs does the organization conduct?

Part III of Form 990 reveals a lot about what the nonprofit organization actually does. For example, the form states the organization's primary purpose on a short line near the top. For each program the organization conducts, it must describe the program's purpose, and it must include other important information, such as the number of clients served or the service units issued. To the right of this information, the nonprofit lists the expenses for each program. This helps the public assess the activities of the nonprofit.

Who are the filer's board members and how much does its top staff get paid?

Part V-A of Form 990 lists the names of current officers, directors, trustees, and key employees. It also shows whether any board member receives any compensation for the duties he or she performs, and if so, how much.

Did the nonprofit board members engage in any "self-dealing" transactions during the year?

Line 2 of Schedule A asks a series of questions about transactions among the nonprofit organization, directors, and key employees. For example, Line 2a asks whether any sale, exchange, or leasing of property occurred between the filer and any board member or key employee. If the answer is "yes" to any of the questions in this part of the form, the nonprofit is required to attach a detailed statement explaining the transactions.

Did the organization do any lobbying?

Many nonprofit groups advocate for changes in public policy as part of their mission. The term *lobbying* refers to legal attempts to influence legislators, for example, to propose and vote for specific laws, or to support or oppose proposals made by others.

You can tell if an organization has engaged in lobbying by looking at Line 1 of Schedule A's Part III (Statement of Activities). This line asks whether the filer attempted to influence national, state, or local legislation. If the filer answers "yes," it must report its expenses and lobbying activities.

Breezing through Form 990-EZ

Form 990-EZ is much shorter than Form 990, but it can be just as enlightening in many respects. The first page of Form 990-EZ is shown in Figure 7-2. The following sections go over a few things that you can find out from this form.

How does the organization derive its revenue?

To find out about an organization's revenue, take a look at Part I, Lines 1–8. This part of the form tells you about activities, donations, and grants.

How does the organization spend its money?

Part I, Lines 10–16, of the Form 990-EZ reports expenses by object, not function. Accordingly, the form doesn't really tell you if the organization is spending money in a way that meets its mission. However, program services expenses for the current year are identified on Line 32, which means that you can identify the portion of the total expenses that's devoted to program services. Also, Part II describes the organization's major activities and the total expenses for each.

Is the organization in debt?

Line 27 shows the balance of assets over liabilities, which is referred to as the *balance of funds* or *net assets*. Nonprofits need to accumulate sufficient resources to carry out operations in the face of routine fluctuations in revenue. For this reason, all healthy nonprofit organizations should show a positive balance of funds on the tax return.

Is the organization paying its board members appropriately?

Part IV lists officers, directors, trustees, and key employees and their salaries. Board members of nonprofits generally serve on a voluntary basis, but the CEO is usually compensated. In some organizations, however, board members also work for the organization in some capacity. If you come across this, don't worry — it's generally permissible. Key employees, such as officers, directors, and trustees, may receive compensation. So, if you want to find out their salaries, just take a look at Part IV.

			OMB No. 1545-1150

Form **990-EZ**

Department of the Treasury
Internal Revenue Service

Short Form
Return of Organization Exempt From Income Tax
Under section 501(c), 527, or 4947(a)(1) of the Internal Revenue Code
(except black lung benefit trust or private foundation)
Sponsoring organizations, and controlling organizations as defined in section 512(b)(13) must file Form 990. All other organizations with gross receipts less than $100,000 and total assets less than $250,000 at the end of the year may use this form.
The organization may have to use a copy of this return to satisfy state reporting requirements.

2006

Open to Public Inspection

A For the 2006 calendar year, or tax year beginning _____ , 2006, and ending _____ , 20 ____

B Check if applicable:
☐ Address change
☐ Name change
☐ Initial return
☐ Final return
☐ Amended return
☐ Application pending

Please use IRS label or print or type. See Specific Instructions.

C Name of organization

Number and street (or P.O. box, if mail is not delivered to street address)   Room/suite

City or town, state or country, and ZIP + 4

D Employer identification number

E Telephone number
( )

F Group Exemption Number .

● **Section 501(c)(3) organizations and 4947(a)(1) nonexempt charitable trusts must attach a completed Schedule A (Form 990 or 990-EZ).**

G Accounting method: ☐ Cash ☐ Accrual
Other (specify) ►

I Website: _____

J Organization type (check only one)— ☐ 501(c) ( ) ◄ (insert no.) ☐ 4947(a)(1) or ☐ 527

H Check ☐ if the organization is **not** required to attach Schedule B (Form 990, 990-EZ, or 990-PF).

K Check ☐ if the organization is not a section 509(a)(3) supporting organization **and** its gross receipts are normally **not** more than $25,000. A return is not required, but if the organization chooses to file a return, be sure to file a complete return.

L Add lines 5b, 6b, and 7b, to line 9 to determine gross receipts; if $100,000 or more, file Form 990 instead of Form 990-EZ . ► $ _____

Part I Revenue, Expenses, and Changes in Net Assets or Fund Balances (See page 47 of the instructions.)

Revenue	1	Contributions, gifts, grants, and similar amounts received.	**1**
	2	Program service revenue including government fees and contracts	**2**
	3	Membership dues and assessments	**3**
	4	Investment income	**4**
	5a	Gross amount from sale of assets other than inventory · · · · **5a**	
	b	Less: cost or other basis and sales expenses **5b**	
	c	Gain or (loss) from sale of assets other than inventory (line 5a less line 5b) (attach schedule)	**5c**
	6	Special events and activities (attach schedule). If any amount is from **gaming,** check here ☐	
	a	Gross revenue (not including $ _____ of contributions reported on line 1) **6a**	
	b	Less: direct expenses other than fundraising expenses · · · **6b**	
	c	Net income or (loss) from special events and activities (line 6a less line 6b) · · · ·	**6c**
	7a	Gross sales of inventory, less returns and allowances **7a**	
	b	Less: cost of goods sold · · · · · · · · · **7b**	
	c	Gross profit or (loss) from sales of inventory (line 7a less line 7b) ·	**7c**
	8	Other revenue (describe ► _____)	**8**
	9	**Total revenue** (add lines 1, 2, 3, 4, 5c, 6c, 7c, and 8). · · · · ·	**9**
Expenses	10	Grants and similar amounts paid (attach schedule) · · · ·	**10**
	11	Benefits paid to or for members · · · · · · · · ·	**11**
	12	Salaries, other compensation, and employee benefits · · · ·	**12**
	13	Professional fees and other payments to independent contractors · ·	**13**
	14	Occupancy, rent, utilities, and maintenance · · · · · ·	**14**
	15	Printing, publications, postage, and shipping · · · · · ·	**15**
	16	Other expenses (describe ► _____)	**16**
	17	**Total expenses** (add lines 10 through 16) · · · · · ·	**17**
Net Assets	18	Excess or (deficit) for the year (line 9 less line 17) · · · · ·	**18**
	19	Net assets or fund balances at beginning of year (from line 27, column (A)) (must agree with end-of-year figure reported on prior year's return) · · · · · ·	**19**
	20	Other changes in net assets or fund balances (attach explanation) · ·	**20**
	21	Net assets or fund balances at end of year (combine lines 18 through 20) ·	**21**

Part II Balance Sheets—If Total assets on line 25, column (B) are $250,000 or more, file Form 990 instead of Form 990-EZ.

(See page 51 of the instructions.)

		(A) Beginning of year		**(B)** End of year
22	Cash, savings, and investments		**22**	
23	Land and buildings · · · · · ·		**23**	
24	Other assets (describe ► _____)		**24**	
25	**Total assets** · · · · · · · ·		**25**	
26	**Total liabilities** (describe ► _____)		**26**	
27	**Net assets or fund balances** (line 27 of column (B) **must** agree with line 21) ·		**27**	

For Privacy Act and Paperwork Reduction Act Notice, see the separate instructions.   Cat. No. 10642I   Form **990-EZ** (2006)

Figure 7-2:
The first page of Form 990-EZ.

Chapter 8

The Responsibilities of the Board

In This Chapter

▶ Discovering what directors do

▶ Identifying the director's duties

▶ Understanding your rights as a director

▶ Looking to SOX when adopting practices for your board

*I*n 2004, the U.S. Senate Finance Committee proposed a number of regulations and reforms to correct perceived problems with how the nation's nonprofits were governing themselves. The Committee found that many nonprofits (even some of the largest ones, such as the Red Cross) didn't have basic accounting procedures in place for running programs. The Committee concluded that the nonprofit boards weren't doing a good job of overseeing their organizations.

To improve this situation, many nonprofits are voluntarily adopting basic organizational and management policies that are based on the requirements of the Sarbanes-Oxley Act, which was passed for for-profit organizations in 2002.

This chapter takes a look at the evolving role of boards of directors in the world of nonprofit organizations, including their powers and duties under current law. (Check out Chapter 4 for some hands-on info about creating your own board of directors.)

Introducing the Basics of the Board of Directors

Directors, as their name implies, direct the course of an organization. They sit at the strategic and financial helm of the organization. At that helm are usually several additional directors that collectively make up what is called the *board of directors.* The experience and backgrounds of the board members varies widely in each nonprofit, as does the process of selecting the board.

As far as duties are concerned, in nonprofit corporations, directors are guardians of assets and resources. Their focus is on accomplishing the mission statement of the organization, and ensuring that sufficient resources flow into the nonprofit entity.

In some organizations, directors have worn more than one hat. For example, they have been employed by the nonprofit corporation, or they have acted as officers or agents in other capacities. This multi-hat practice is now discouraged because of the passage of the Sarbanes-Oxley Act (SOX). (See the later section "SOX Policies and Nonprofit Boards.") Instead, most nonprofits are encouraged to have a majority of independent board members who have little or no connection with the organization other than serving on the board.

Striking a balance: Strategic boards versus meddlesome ones

It's generally accepted that boards are responsible for the direction of the organization and charged with seeing that the organization fulfills its mission. However, it isn't the role of the board (whose members don't work full time) to become involved in the day-to-day operations of the organization. For example, boards shouldn't worry about tasks such as ordering office supplies, evaluating administrative staff, or deciding whether the copy machine breaks down too often.

Instead, boards should strive to define the organization's objectives and both the short- and long-term strategies for achieving them. Boards should address issues that are similar to the following:

- Whether the public is aware of the organization's mission
- Whether the nonprofit's programs are reaching the intended beneficiaries
- How well the purposes for which the organization was set up are being served

The board should also set up effective procedures for evaluating management and verifying the information that it receives from management. These tasks ensure that the day-to-day operations of the organization and the controls and procedures that are in place are working.

But what if the board (or one of its members) smells a rat? Or senses inefficiency? It should never hide behind its mandate to do strategic planning to ignore a looming crisis. As a board member, it's your duty to bring the issues to the forefront, address them as a board, obtain the necessary information from management, and resolve the issue so that the goals of your organization may be met.

Electing the board of directors

Directors of nonprofit corporations can be selected, appointed, or recruited in any way that the organization's *bylaws* specify (see Chapter 4 for more on bylaws). A corporation's bylaws also usually specify how many people will sit on the board. Typically, the number is no less than seven and no more than ten. However, there may be more or fewer directors depending on the specific provisions of the bylaws or applicable state laws. Bylaws also specify the powers and duties of the directors (see the section "Understanding a Director's Responsibilities" later in the chapter for more).

If something isn't covered under the bylaws, the law of the state in which the nonprofit is incorporated or located will apply. For example, if election requirements aren't specified in the bylaws and you're in Wisconsin, you can look to the Wisconsin statutes that cover these issues for nonprofits.

Typically directors are elected for a term of one or more years. Often the terms are *staggered,* which means that each director's term is set up to expire in a different year so that the nonprofit is never confronted with a board completely filled with novices in a single year. Many organizations, such as religious ones, have boards that are *self-perpetuating,* meaning that the current board elects the new members.

You may hear the following common terms in connection with boards:

- ✔ **Ex officio status:** An ex officio member is automatically given a seat on the board because that person holds some other related position. For example, an officer of the corporation or of a related nonprofit entity may be an ex officio board member.

- ✔ **Honorary, life, or emeritus status:** These are honorary designations, and are purely symbolic in that the people who hold these titles generally don't have the right to vote on issues. Usually, these titles are awarded to people who have served on the board for a long time in the past, have given a lot of money to the organization, or have raised a lot of money for it.

Governing as a body

Individual directors sitting on boards can't do much on their own; a board of directors governs as a body. The board, as a whole, may have considerable power, but the individual directors must come to a level of consensus specified in the bylaws (check out Chapter 4 for more on bylaws) in order to act.

Despite the fact that an individual director has virtually no power, he or she can still be held liable for corporate actions in certain circumstances, particularly when the board takes actions outside of its legal scope of authority (as discussed in the later section "Understanding a Director's Responsibilities").

The key functions of a board

Congress and a number of costly studies have looked at what makes nonprofit boards tick. In particular, they examined the key functions that directors must perform. According to a 2005 study by Johns Hopkins University, the most important key functions of a nonprofit board of directors include the following:

- ✔ **Setting mission statements:** The *mission statement* of an organization defines its reason for existence (check out Chapter 4 for more on creating a mission statement). An organization's statement may evolve over time, so the board is always busy. A whopping 93 percent of the respondents surveyed in the Johns Hopkins study said that they look to their board of directors to establish the organization's mission.

- ✔ **Selecting the chief executive and financial officers and deciding how much to pay him or her:** A board of directors doesn't get involved in the day-to-day operations of an organization, but it does hire and fire management, such as the chief executive officer. Eighty-eight percent of the nonprofits surveyed said that they rely on their boards to do this.

- ✔ **Reviewing auditing practices and polices:** Many of the nonprofits surveyed said that they had independent audits. Even if these nonprofits didn't have audits, they indicated that they relied on their boards to evaluate financial data and communicate with accounting professionals.

- ✔ **Approving significant financial transactions:** Most of the nonprofits surveyed (81 percent) said that they relied on their boards to review and approve major financial transactions proposed by management.

- ✔ **Establishing the budgets:** Most nonprofits leave the budgeting process to the board, probably because this is a function so closely related to achieving the organization's objectives.

The legal obligations of directors

Many state laws provide immunity for directors of nonprofit organizations that are acting within the legal bounds of their authority. But, even if your state doesn't provide immunity, there are limitations on when various groups can and can't sue directors. For example, the following groups can't sue a board or its individual directors:

✔ **Donors:** No matter how much money they put up, donors to nonprofit organizations can't sue the board of directors. However, some exceptions do exist. For example, if a donor gives funds that are earmarked for a certain purpose to an organization and the nonprofit spends the money on another purpose, a particularly effective lawyer may take the case.

✔ **Beneficiaries and people who receive services from the nonprofit:** Generally, the intended beneficiaries of a nonprofit can't sue the directors either. For example, an animal welfare advocate couldn't sue a nonprofit with a mission of enforcing animal rights. And a battered woman couldn't sue a sheltering organization.

This isn't the vacuum in accountability it seems to be at first glance. In most states, the attorney general is an aggressive advocate for the beneficiaries of nonprofits, with broad powers to investigate, sue, and otherwise publicly embarrass corrupt and negligent directors.

✔ **The members who elect them:** To the extent that directors are elected, they may lose their office via the elective process, or may be removed under specific circumstances specified in the bylaws.

Understanding a Director's Responsibilities

A director's duties stem from several sources, with the most important being the mission or purpose of the organization, the bylaws of the organization, and laws of the state in which the nonprofit organization is located.

The first task that should be on the list of any director who wants to avoid becoming embroiled in controversy and legal liability, is to thoroughly understand the purpose of the organization. The purpose of the organization is usually embodied in its mission statement (flip to Chapter 4 for more details on mission statements).

Directors' common-law duties

Even though nonprofits are creatures of state law and have unique missions, all of their directors are generally subject to a few common duties. (*Common law* is a culmination of court decisions and precedents that are relied on to establish legal principles.) The duties discussed in this section are taken from a myriad of state cases and statutes, and are general guidelines to which directors must adhere if they want to be able to defend their organization against a lawsuit.

Many states offer directors of both incorporated and unincorporated nonprofit organizations immunity as long as they're acting on behalf of the corporation and within the scope of authority authorized by the corporation.

The duty of care

The *duty of care* is a two-part test. First, a director must be informed about matters within the scope of the board's authority and discretion. Second, the director must exercise reasonable care in making decisions. (This second part is sometimes called the *business judgment* rule.)

This two-part test seems so obvious that you probably wonder why it has to be legally mandated. Nevertheless, countless court cases have centered on whether directors have acted with due care in approving financial transactions, rubber stamping budgets, and so on.

The following are some duties that directors can perform to establish that they have acted as careful and informed directors:

- ✔ **Show up for meetings:** It's difficult to argue in the course of a lawsuit that you cared passionately about the organization when you never took the time to go to the meetings during which the issues that are the subject of the litigation or investigation were being discussed. In some states and organizations, missing meetings is cause for removing a director.

    Directors usually have to attend meetings to vote and can't vote by proxy, like shareholders are permitted to do. However, some states allow directors to "attend" via telephone.

- ✔ **Exercise independent judgment:** Make up your own mind on issues that are before the board, and if something doesn't make sense, ask questions. Don't just go along with it. No director should cast a vote based on what another director thinks.

- ✔ **Read the reports:** Directors are entitled to rely on information provided in reports by management and subcommittees (such as an audit committee). They can also rely on opinions by outside advisors, such as their legal counsel. However, the rules that permit directors to rely on information never apply if the director has personal knowledge that would make reliance on the information implausible or unreasonable.

    For example, if a director *knows* that a particular company is about to go bankrupt and allowed the nonprofit to approve a contract with the company because management recommended the contract, he or she wouldn't be shielded by the business judgment rule.

- ✔ **Adopt some meeting and control procedures:** Directors aren't responsible for performing the day-to-day operations of the corporation. But, they are responsible for monitoring them. In order to monitor effectively, board members should have some procedures in place to help them take the pulse of the organization.

For example, the boards may review revenue reports for specific programs, or they may have a standard list of transactions that they must be specifically informed of.

✓ **Document your actions:** Some states allow directors to take action without a specific vote or even a formal meeting. In these situations, it's a good idea for the board to document the actions it has taken and its reasons for doing so.

For example, if your community youth group decides not to allow kids to skateboard in the parking lot of the community center, this action should be formally documented as well as communicated to the kids. This documentation can be useful when a parent later sues for a broken arm or cracked skull.

✓ **Keep minutes:** All boards and committees should keep minutes of what they discuss and the actions that they opt to take and opt *not* to take. If possible, document the concerns raised and information relied on in addressing the issue.

Chapter 17 gives you some more guidance as to the things you need to know to fulfill the duty of care.

The duty of loyalty

Directors of nonprofit organizations aren't supposed to use their positions as springboards for personal gain. This is known in legalese as the *duty of loyalty*.

The duty of loyalty requires directors to act in the interests of the corporation — not on their own behalf. For example, if you're on the board of a public museum, you'll probably be questioned if you steer a lucrative public relations contract to your spouse (as recently happened in one major city.)

So, if you're a director of a nonprofit, you not only want to avoid actual conflicts of interest, but situations that simply look like conflicts to those who have nothing better to do than drum up a scandal. Sending a contract to someone you know personally because they do good work, or urging the organization to employ them, is a recipe for having to defend yourself. If you really want the board to consider an issue that could potentially be perceived as an action in your personal interest as a board member, ask the Board to vote on the action while you step out of the room. Better yet, have the minutes reflect that you didn't participate in the vote.

Here are a few examples of transactions that seem like great ideas at the time, but that can come back to haunt a well-intentioned director later:

✓ Making acquisitions of artwork, inventory, or equipment, or purchasing services from companies in which a director or someone related to the director has a financial interest

✔ Asking the nonprofit organization to take a political position (for example, on a specific tax or public works project) in which a director stands to benefit financially

✔ Requesting that an organization expand its mission or programming objectives to create an awareness or use products, services, or facilities in which the director has an interest

 Because many nonprofit organizations are community-based, and board members are volunteers from the community, it's easy for one thing to lead to another, which creates a conflict of interest scandal that no one has ever dreamed of. That's why it's a good idea for every nonprofit organization — large or small — to have a written conflict of interest policy.

Here are some items that your organization may want to include in its conflict of interest policy:

✔ A statement about how matters in which a board member is potentially "interested" will be handled

✔ A provision requiring that transactions be approved by a majority of directors who have no financial interest in the transaction

✔ A requirement of disclosure of relationships between directors and organizations with which the nonprofit organization does business

✔ A record of conflict issues that arise and how they're resolved

Confidentiality

As you can probably imagine, board members aren't free to blurt out information to the public, especially when sensitive issues like medical or mental health information of program recipients are involved. Unfortunately, though, it isn't usually that easy to ignore a reporter who shoves a microphone in your face or calls unexpectedly demanding to know about some action (or alleged inaction) by your organization. But, you have to remember that individual directors aren't spokespersons for the corporation and that they can create infinite problems by thinking or acting like they are.

However, some meetings are open to the public, and board members, as advocates for the organization, may need to talk about its activities to the media and potential donors.

 The general rule of thumb, however, is that directors shouldn't disclose information about the nonprofit's finances or activities unless this information is already known to the public through other sources.

Disclosure of illegal activities

As with several of the other duties discussed in this section, the one I focus on here should be a no-brainer. But, unfortunately, it's never that simple.

If, as a director of a nonprofit organization, you discover illegal activity, you have a duty to tell the rest of the board. Don't just hope it will go away, or that management will resolve it. Not only is the integrity and stability of your organization at stake, but you can also end up with some sticky personal liability issues yourself if you're indicted. You could also potentially end up with a legal bill for advice on how to respond to inquiries made of you down the road if you don't dump the issue in the board's lap early on.

If by some unfortunate chance you're deemed as being complicit in the wrong-doing by failing to report it to the board (state attorney generals love this sort of thing), you may really be out in the cold. Depending on your organization's bylaws, you may not be *indemnified* (paid back) for the legal fees you incur defending your decision to keep mum.

If it's the board itself that appears to be taking illegal action, excuse yourself from the vote, and contact your personal attorney.

In some states, if registration with the state isn't completed properly, is expired, or is suspended, the directors may be personally liable for the actions and obligations of the nonprofit because laws granting legal immunity to directors of validly registered nonprofits may not apply to criminal activities.

Other important board of director duties

Not every duty of a director is spelled out in bylaws and state statutes. This is because a board's responsibilities often evolve in response to the realities of carrying out the organization's mission.

Some of the duties and typical tasks of a board's directors may include the following:

- ✔ **Defining the mission and long-term goals of the entity:** Missions often evolve over time, and an organization is usually evaluated by its success in meeting its mission (as discussed in Chapter 4).

- ✔ **Hiring and firing management and other key employees:** Even though board members often serve in a voluntary capacity, and many organizations function primarily using services provided by volunteers, most nonprofits of any size have key managerial employees that must be hired and fired by the board.

✔ **Receiving and reviewing reports from management:** Board members are usually provided with detailed information that allows them to assess how the organization is doing financially and whether its programs are effectively meeting its mission. The ability of the board to understand and intelligently act as a cohesive group on the information it is receiving is essential to the health of any nonprofit.

✔ **Authorizing major projects:** Even though boards don't become embroiled in the day-to-day minutiae of running the organization, they should be fully informed about major projects and program initiatives.

✔ **Handling lawsuits and litigation:** Ideally, nonprofits avoid becoming involved in lawsuits, litigation, and the threat of such. However, when liability issues rear their ugly head, the board must deal with them.

✔ **Managing the media:** It's a basic fact of fundraising that most nonprofit organizations can't afford a hint of scandal. Negative press can mean negative cash flow. For this reason, boards need to be kept in the loop on public relations issues, and must respond to inquiries and challenges on behalf of the organization. (Check out Chapter 19 for tips on handling the media.)

Going above and beyond the scope of authority

To make an organization run smoothly, directors often perform advisory and fundraising functions that aren't specifically spelled out under bylaws and state statutes. These functions, although not always mandated, can be critical to the well-being and positive public perception of the nonprofit entity. Sometimes the functions are delegated to individual board members.

When carrying out these extra duties, directors must make sure that they're acting within the *scope of authority* granted to them under state law and the bylaws. Scope of authority basically means that directors have the authority necessary to carry out their legal and designated duties, and to further the nonprofit organization's mission. If a director acts beyond the scope of his or her authority, the director may forgo some of the legal protections that nonprofit directors normally have.

For example, assume that a director of a nonprofit community recreational facility wants to open a hot dog stand in front of the facility. Assume that the directors go by the book procedurally in voting on this action and approve the food stand. Now, imagine that there's an outbreak of salmonella from food sold at the stand, and a lawsuit is brought against the directors of the organization. This stand may be well beyond the mission and hence the scope of authority of the community facility. On the other hand, if this is deemed a fundraising activity that's within the scope of the nonprofit mission, the board of directors would enjoy immunity in many states for their actions.

Extra obligations for directors who are trustees

If your nonprofit organization operates a trust, the directors who sit on the board may be deemed *trustees* of the funds. A trustee is a person legally in charge of managing property for a third party. If you're one of these directors who falls into the special legal classification of "trustee," you'll have stricter duties than the ones outlined in the previous few sections. While there's little leeway for directors in conflict situations, someone who acts as a trustee on behalf of a trust is given absolutely no wiggle room whatsoever.

A day in the life of a nonprofit executive director

The following was contributed by Judith Steininger, who is both a serial volunteer and nonprofit board member.

Generally speaking, an executive director or CEO of a nonprofit organization is the person in the visible leadership position of the organization. His or her professional reputation is tied to the organization's success.

If an employee of the organization absconds with tens of thousand of dollars, he or she may go to jail, but the CEO will also share blame in the eyes of the organization's members and the public at large.

Regardless of the size of the organization, the CEO sets the moral tone. It's usually his or her job to model the values of the organization, ensure adherence to the organization's mission on a daily basis, and report to the board.

The CEO is also the public face and spokesperson for the organization. If there's trouble at a rehab center, a homeless person from a shelter dies outside the front door on a cold night, a donor doesn't like a textbook being used in a particular class at a small private university, or a season ticket holder-donor thinks there is just too much Shostakovich being played this year, he wants a call from the CEO ASAP.

A typical day for a CEO might include a morning meeting with the grant-writing department or the marketing department, and everything is on deadline. There may be a meeting with the developer of a new wing of one of the organization's facilities.

For lunch, the CEO may be expected meet with and thank a group of volunteers. The day may be interrupted with frantic calls from program managers, volunteers, and administrators. The balance of the day may be taken up with meetings on issues such as the ever-increasing healthcare costs for the nonprofit's employees. Should they raise premiums or cut benefits knowing that the salaries of everyone at a nonprofit are usually several percentage points below those in profit-making institutions? Will two or three key people leave as a result?

Evening may be filled with events and award dinners for those who contribute to and support the organization, including events sponsored by other nonprofit organizations. The CEO will, by the end of the day, have thanked many people for supporting the organization, and hopefully, have been thanked at least once by a board member or stakeholder.

If you're in the unenviable position of serving as a trustee, here are a few critical rules to remember regarding conflicts of interest:

- ✔ If a gift is made to the nonprofit corporation with specific conditions attached to it (called a *restricted gift*), adhere strictly to the terms. The organization is deemed a trustee of these gifted funds.

- ✔ If the nonprofit corporation is deemed a trustee of funds in an employee benefit plan, don't dip into these funds to meet other organizational needs.

- ✔ If *prior gifts* were made based on the nonprofit's mission, and the mission then changes, the nonprofit may be in the position of acting as a trustee to ensure that the prior gifts are matched up with programs that fulfill the prior mission.

Funds held by the corporation in trust should be held in segregated accounts and clearly identified on the organization's financial statements.

Your Rights as a Director

It's a sad fact of life that volunteer directors run the risk of being sued in the course of carrying out duties for which they aren't paid. Fortunately, many state laws realize the importance of philanthropy and volunteerism and have adopted laws to protect directors from lawsuits when they're acting on behalf of the organization and within the scope of their authority.

This section covers several principles gleaned from court cases and other legal precedents. It's a summary of legal doctrines that support directors in doing good work.

Protection under the business judgment rule

The *business judgment rule* is a legal doctrine that protects directors of for-profit corporations from having to second-guess their actions — as long as they're acting in a reasonable, informed manner that they believe to be in the best interests of their corporation. Many courts have applied this rule to the nonprofit context discussed here.

If a corporate director undertakes an action in good faith, exercises independent judgment, and has taken steps to be reasonably informed, courts have ruled that litigants shouldn't be permitted to second-guess their decisions. Hindsight is 20/20, the courts figure.

By the same token, directors don't have to pass an IQ test. A bad business decision won't be the basis for a winning lawsuit, unless the decision was made for bad motives (such as the director's financial self-interest).

Access to corporate books and records

Directors of both for-profit and nonprofit corporations have an absolute right to view the corporate books and records. If they can't look at them, who can? If you serve on a board, you can also usually permit your attorney or accountant to see the data so that he or she can advise you personally.

Access to the minutes

Directors have a right to receive a copy of the minutes from every meeting. Even though you may be tempted to toss them aside after hashing out an issue for hours — don't. Those minutes can come back to haunt you years later when the board needs to review them to see why an action was or wasn't taken.

Minutes are the only record memorializing what took place at a meeting, and they can have unanticipated legal significance. So, even though you can't change time, do make sure the minutes are complete, and that the reasons for any controversial actions and votes taken are fully (and accurately) reflected.

Communication with management

If you're a director of a nonprofit, you have the right to communicate (reasonably) with management. If something doesn't make sense on the financial front, you can call up the chief executive officer or chief financial officer and ask questions.

You don't have the right to restrict or interfere with these individuals in carrying out their own duties. You also can't make demands on staff or organizational resources without approval from the board as a whole.

The right to dissention from board actions

There isn't always rationality in numbers. It's amazing how opinions fall like dominos in some settings, with each person adopting another's viewpoint.

Not only do you have a right to vote as a board member, in many states you can also go on record as having *dissented* (disagreed) with the majority.

SOX Policies and Nonprofit Boards

"Board governance" has been a buzz phrase in corporate America since Enron, the world's largest energy corporation, suddenly filed for bankruptcy in 2001. Now the term is becoming part of the vernacular of just about every nonprofit organization in America.

Sarbanes-Oxley (SOX) is a complicated law that was passed in 2002, in the wake of the Enron bankruptcy. It ushers in new principles of independence and accountability for boards of directors of public corporations, and it's likely to impact the outcome of future lawsuits brought against nonprofit corporations and boards — even though, technically, the law doesn't apply to them. Nevertheless, the law is regarded as the "gold standard" for governance and accountability.

In fact, it's actually a myth that SOX doesn't affect nonprofit organizations. Even though nonpublic corporations aren't currently subject to Sarbanes-Oxley, they are accountable to their stakeholders (for example, donors, members, and granting authorities). Accordingly, most lawyers agree (to the extent that lawyers ever agree on anything) that nonprofit organizations should move toward voluntarily adopting some of the governance standards provided in SOX. These protective measures include adopting whistle-blower and document-retention policies, installing independent board members, establishing audit and compensation committees, evaluating board members, and other measures, all of which are discussed in this section.

Policies that nonprofit boards are required to adopt after SOX

Two provisions of SOX do actually apply to nonprofits as mandatory legal requirements (rather than optional best practices). These two provisions of the law include adopting the following:

✔ **Whistle-blower policies:** Because of SOX, boards of nonprofit organizations are required to develop formal procedures for handling complaints about financial misdeeds within the organization. They're also required to prevent retaliation against those who come forward to report these misdeeds. (Whistle-blower policy requirements are discussed in more detail in Chapter 13.) Under the law, nonprofits are also required to make sure that complaints are investigated. They must document that corrective actions have been taken.

✔ **Document retention and destruction policies:** SOX requires nonprofit organizations to have written, mandatory document-retention and periodic-destruction policies that include guidelines for electronic files and voicemail. The policies must specify that if official investigation is contemplated, those who destroy documents that are relevant to the investigation will be subject to stringent criminal penalties. If you even suspect any illegal activity, stop the document shredders immediately in order to avoid criminal obstruction.

Following the trend toward independent boards

When Congress held hearings after the bankruptcy of the energy giant, Enron, it found a definite historical correlation between corporate fraud and boards of directors dominated by insiders who had financial ties to the company. So, Congress took a hard line, in the private sector context, on the issue of board independence. This same thinking found its way into the nonprofit sector as well.

However, nonprofits boards find this change difficult to adapt to because most nonprofit board members serve as volunteers and likely have a prior connection or commitment to the organization. For example, members are often recruited from the ranks of dedicated volunteers and philanthropists who are savvier at raising funds than managing them on behalf of an organization. Often board members are intimately familiar and even passionate about the needs of organizational stakeholders, yet ill-equipped to deal with the complicated overlay of bylaws, state laws, and federal tax-exemption regulations imposed on their organizations.

But, it's impractical for most organizations to scrap the dedicated board members they have in favor of independent outsiders who may not understand the delicate balance between the mission, financial constraints, and community image of the organization. It is, however, important that organizations recruit and retain as many independent board members as possible — particularly to serve on sensitive committees, such as the audit committee (flip to Chapter 10 for more on audit committees).

The criteria for independent directors

This section shows you what makes a director "independent" according to the standards set forth under SOX. Even though this law applies primarily to for-profit corporations, it's increasingly being viewed as a source of the best practices for nonprofit organizations.

According to SOX, an independent director can't serve "directly or indirectly as a partner, shareholder, or officer of an organization that has a relationship with the company." This provision is intended to apply to the company's affiliates as well as the company itself. For example, the CEO of a company wouldn't be considered an independent director if he or she served on the board of a subsidiary company.

This provision is intended to stop directors of nonprofit boards from conveniently steering lucrative contracts to their own companies. SOX-related standards also require companies to know what directors have done in the three years prior to joining the board. A director's independence may be deemed compromised if the director was an employee or executive officer of a related company in the three years prior to joining the board of directors.

Loss of independent classification due to prohibited payments

Prior to SOX, many directors received large payments, personal loans, and bonuses that they were unable to justify to the Securities and Exchange Commission (SEC) and company shareholders. Criminal proceedings ensued in many cases, and irreversible damage was done to the companies that directors had treated as their personal trust funds. SOX prohibits personal loans to directors, and so should your nonprofit organization.

Some bad, bad board moves

Even the largest, most well-established nonprofits have found themselves under the glare of unwelcome public scrutiny in recent years. Consider the following examples:

✔ The board of the American Red Cross was forced to answer for a $200 million ill-advised action in which it used funds earmarked for surviving family members and victims of the September 11 terrorist attacks for blood distribution programs instead.

✔ A high-profile scandal in California led to the collapse of a prominent nonprofit organization that defrauded esteemed contributors by using donations intended for other charities to cover its own costs.

✔ In 2003, the United Way became embroiled in a scandal that paraded excessive salaries and the misuse of funds.

✔ In the late 1990s, Attorney General Eliot Spitzer spearheaded an investigation involving the Hale House, a highly respected Harlem charity with a 30-year history of caring for homeless infants and toddlers. The controversy began when the investigation revealed that Dr. Lorraine Hale, a director, may have permitted the organization to divert hundreds of thousands of dollars toward self-serving projects that were unrelated to the organization's mission.

Other savvy SOX moves for directors

In addition to providing standards for independence, SOX contains some other provisions that board members may want to consider having their organizations adopt as the "gold standard" of nonprofit governance.

Holding meetings without management being present

After SOX, more boards began holding meetings outside of the earshot of management. These boards took this move because excluding the top dogs from meetings enables the boards to more easily evaluate the performance and independence of management.

Forming committees for nominating directors

Many organizations are adopting specific procedures for recruiting and nominating qualified directors, and they're also publicly disclosing these policies.

Forming compensation committees

With all the compensation scandals in both the profit and nonprofit sectors, many boards are adopting *compensation committees* made up of independent members. These committees help to closely study the issue and make well-considered recommendations. (Flip to Chapter 6 for more details on convening a compensation committee.)

Establishing independent audit committees

Even though it may be impractical to form an entirely independent board of directors, the board members that sit on the *audit committee* (discussed in Chapter 10) should be independent. Audit committees deal with the outside accountants and auditors, and they address issues relating to the accuracy of the organization's financial statement.

Making governance guidelines public

Similar to the SOX requirements of for-profit corporations, many nonprofit organizations are opting to post their *corporate governance guidelines* on their Web sites. The following is a checklist of issues that your board may want to address in creating its own guidelines for governing the organization:

- ✔ Director qualification standards, including procedures for training and continuing education
- ✔ Responsibilities of directors, including obligations to attend meetings
- ✔ Policies for director access to management and independent advisors

   ✔ Procedures for determining director compensation

   ✔ Management succession policies

   ✔ A procedure for the board to conduct an annual self-evaluation

Evaluating the board's performance

An important component of board self-governance can be the board's own self-evaluation, which is a mandated exercise for all for-profit corporations subject to SOX. It's only a best practice for nonprofits.

Many boards tackle the self-evaluation requirement by giving board members a questionnaire that asks them to rate how well the board has performed its designated tasks. This approach can have unintended consequences: If the board doesn't address problems disclosed by negative feedback on a questionnaire, a perception may arise that the board isn't diligent about fulfilling its responsibility. Thus, the board may feel compelled to follow up on each less-than-perfect rating it receives on the questionnaires.

If your organization uses questionnaires for self-evaluation, make sure the questionnaires are preserved so that you can produce them in the unfortunate event of a future lawsuit or investigation.

For most companies, a more practical approach to self-evaluation is to hold regular meetings for purposes of board discussion and self-evaluation. During such meetings, the board can determine what further action, if any, is necessary as a result of the self-evaluation process. The issues raised in the meetings and the details about how the issues were handled should be carefully documented.

Chapter 9

Creating the Right Committee Structure

In This Chapter

▶ Understanding the basic committee structures

▶ Discovering the common committees nonprofits create

*B*oards have limited amounts of time, and addressing every issue in depth could easily turn meetings into retreats. As an alternative to sequestering their members, many boards create *committees* to delegate key issues to. A committee is generally made up of a subset of board members that reports to the full board. The committee may or may not have authority to act on its own.

Creating committees allows your board to delegate specific tasks and functions to the board members who have the skill sets to best accomplish them. This chapter identifies the different types of committees that your organization may consider creating, and the types of functions typically delegated to them.

Basic Committee Structures

Some boards create committees in response to special tasks that arise (such as hiring a CEO), and then they terminate the committee as the tasks are accomplished. Other boards, however, set up committees and rules for them well before issues arise.

The following are two types of committee structures that your board may create (these terms refer to the duration that the committee's authority is in effect):

✔ **Special committees:** This type of committee (sometimes referred to as an *ad hoc committee*) is a committee created by the board to resolve or research a specific issue, such as the viability of a new project or the handling of a litigation matter. This type of committee is generally created by board *resolution,* which means that the board documents (and perhaps votes) that it is taking this action.

Examples of special committees would include an executive search committee formed to select and recruit a chief executive officer, or a policy committee formed to write and recommend policies for certain operations (such as branch operations).

✔ **Standing committees:** These committees are permanent committees that may be provided for in the corporation's bylaws or board resolutions. The most common example of a standing committee is the audit committee, which functions on an ongoing basis to review and evaluate the organization's financial matters (see Chapter 10 for more on audit committees).

The powers of these committees depend on the bylaws or resolutions that created them. A typical standing committee, for instance, may have considerable power to recommend action to the board or to decide which information is relevant to a board's decision. For example, a nominating committee may decide which management candidates are actually considered by the board (see the section "Types of Committees" later in the chapter for more on nominating committees).

Special committees may also have broad power. One reason a special committee may be formed is to protect the remaining board members from having to assume responsibility or involvement with a particular decision. Occasionally non-board members may be asked to serve on special committees (in a consultant capacity) because they may offer a particular perspective or expertise not found within the composition of board itself.

Forming a Committee

An organization's board of directors is responsible for forming committees when necessary. Committee members must be drawn from the current members of the board itself, so having a talented and diverse board is an extremely important ingredient to the success of an organization. The board's power to form committees is usually addressed in the organization's bylaws. A typical bylaw provision on this subject usually allows the board to form any type of committee it deems appropriate, and also allows the board to delegate certain powers to a committee.

It's important to note that although a board can delegate certain powers to a committee, it's the board at large that's ultimately responsible for the decisions it makes based on the work of a committee.

When committees are formed

Standing committees are generally formed at the onset of an organization's existence — usually at the first or second meeting of a newly formed board. Special committees, on the other hand, usually evolve from a board discussion of a pressing matter or issue that needs attention. At this time, the board asks volunteer directors to sit on the committee in order to study the issue and make a recommendation to the full board. The formation of a special committee is noted in the minutes of the board meeting, along with what the committee's mission is, who will serve on it, who will chair it, and what time frame it is on to accomplish its mission.

Who sits on a committee

The function of a committee drives who will serve on it. The board of directors looks at its roster and decides who would fulfill the functions of a particular committee — this is especially important with standing committees that require special expertise (see the earlier section "Basic Committee Structures" for details on standing committees). An organization's audit committee generally requires that at least one committee member is well-versed in financial matters. Where a committee is formed to accomplish a specific task, special expertise may not be as important as other considerations, such as which committee members have the time to devote themselves to the task.

What a committee's process looks like

After a committee is appointed, it usually schedules its own meetings. Unless face-to-face communications are required, many committees conduct some meetings by teleconference. The first point of order at an initial committee meeting is to decide what the scope of the task is, what form the committee's work product will take (for example, a report, a recommendation, an evaluation, and so on), and who will do what to accomplish the committee's goal. A timetable with milestones is generally set and at the conclusion of the meeting, the committee sets a date to reconvene so that each member can report on the progress of an assigned task.

Minutes of committee meetings may be taken, depending on the formality of the meetings, the type of committee, and the tasks assigned. However, where a committee needs to report to the board on a periodic or ongoing basis, minutes are usually required.

When a committee concludes its task, the committee chair reports the findings and recommendations to the full board of directors. Discussion of the committee's conclusion generally follows, and individual committee members may supplement the conclusion and answer questions from the board at large. If the committee's conclusion requires some form of action from the board, a vote usually follows the committee's report and is made part of the board minutes.

Types of Committees

Committees can vary widely depending on the mission and organizational requirements of an organization. This section discusses some examples of common types of committees that your board may opt to form.

Establishing an executive committee

Because many boards meet monthly (or even less often), some organizations create *executive committees* to deal with issues that come up between meetings. Most executive committees are made up of a few directors within the organization, and sometimes management (such as the CEO and CFO).

Executive committees can be an efficient solution for dealing with issues that arise when it would be impractical or even impossible to convene the entire board.

Executive committees must be delegated sufficient authority to act, which means that the executive committee members may have considerable power within the organization. So, the board should make sure its actions are properly documented and reported at regular meetings in case legal issues related to their actions arise in the future.

Appointing a nominating committee

As the name suggests, the purpose of a *nominating committee* is to nominate people who would make good board members. This type of committee is almost always a standing committee (see the section "Basic Committee Structures" earlier in the chapter for details on standing committees).

The skill set of the prospective candidate is a starting point for identifying quality candidates, but the committee's responsibility generally doesn't stop there. Today, most nominating committees also have to consider issues such as diversity, financial expertise, and fundraising ability.

Adding an audit committee

After the passage of Sarbanes-Oxley (SOX), *audit committees* have been receiving a lot of attention in both for-profit and nonprofit organizations (check out Chapter 13 for more on SOX and how it affects nonprofits). In the nonprofit world, these committees are responsible for reviewing an organization's accounting and audit practices.

One specific function of the audit committee is to create a buffer between the people that manage the nonprofit and the auditors and accountants who verify the activities of management. So, most experts agree that the committee should consist entirely of directors who aren't involved in the management of the nonprofit.

Other typical functions of a nonprofit audit committee include the following:

- ✔ **Hiring the audit or accounting firm:** The audit committee should make sure that the firm it hires is free of any conflicts. And, if appropriate, the committee needs to confirm that the audit firm isn't reviewing its own accounting work (which would of course be a conflict of interests).

- ✔ **Reviewing the audit and accounting policies of the organization:** Many reporting issues can arise. These issues can affect the accuracy and presentation of the financial statements. It's the audit committee's role, then, to thoroughly vet these issues.

- ✔ **Resolving issues that arise between the organization's management and the auditors:** Because part of the auditors' task is to verify the actions of management and identify the presence of any possible error or fraud, management and auditors should be independent from each other. This means that the board may have to step in to resolve any issues that arise instead of allowing management to negotiate with the auditors (thus compromising the auditors' independence).

- ✔ **Reviewing the organization's internal controls:** The audit committee must resolve issues relating to the controls within a nonprofit organization. If these types of issues aren't resolved, the reliability and integrity of the information that appears on its financial statements can be affected.

Creating a compensation committee

Compensation can be a politically charged issue for nonprofits. On one hand, most organizations must pay sufficient salaries to attract competent and qualified people. On the other hand, however, there's always a sentiment that every dollar spent on executive salaries is a dollar that's subtracted from intended nonprofit program beneficiaries. Luckily, *compensation committees* can help bridge the gap.

The role of a compensation committee typically includes the following duties:

- ✔ **Researching what similar organizations pay:** This research includes identifying similar organizations and positions involving similar skill sets.

- ✔ **Documenting how the committee makes compensation decisions:** This documentation is important because if salaries are questioned, the committee needs to be able to explain how it decided on the salary it ultimately awarded.

- ✔ **Awarding raises:** Typically compensation committees are charged with evaluating staff, documenting the results of performance reviews, and deciding the level of raises and bonuses to award.

Initiating an investment committee

Nonprofit organizations that have significant fund balances and cash reserves must decide how to invest those funds. This function is usually delegated to an *investment committee.* This committee may be required to obtain the approval of the entire board for certain types of investments.

Because many states have regulations in effect that govern the levels of acceptable risk and other issues that affect investment decisions, the investment committees must do their homework. (The Uniform Management of Institutional Funds Act and other model acts are discussed in Chapter 2.)

Chapter 10

All About Audit Committees

In This Chapter

▶ Exploring the world of audit committees

▶ Understanding audit committee requirements

▶ Determining your duties when serving on an audit committee

Do you want to send a message from the get-go that your nonprofit organization is serious about maintaining its financial integrity and showing that it's squeaky clean when it comes to governance issues? If so, consider forming an *audit committee.*

An audit committee is a subcommittee of the nonprofit's board of directors. The purpose of an audit committee is to review and direct the accounting and audit practices of your organization. As such, the committee needs to be solely made up of independent directors who aren't employed by or involved in the day-to-day management of the nonprofit organization.

The Sarbanes-Oxley Act (referred to as SOX), which passed in 2002, ensures that the audit committees of publicly traded companies are carefully regulated. While not legally applicable to nonprofits, SOX is a really good source for developing standards that will determine the functions and responsibilities of your voluntarily created audit committee.

This chapter explores the nuts and bolts of putting together an audit committee according to the SOX standards that apply to corporations. It also explores the implementation of new standards for audit committee independence, expertise, and objectivity.

The Role of the Audit Committee

Audit committees, in a nutshell, ensure the accuracy and integrity of the financial statements of the organization upon which donors, members, and other people rely. It's the job of the audit committee to become familiar with the financial statements and reports of the nonprofit and ask tough questions of the accountants, the chief financial officer, and other individuals involved in preparing them.

Audit committees are the norm among larger nonprofits, but they're becoming increasingly common in smaller organizations as well. A 2005 survey by the National Urban Institute found that 20 percent of all nonprofits surveyed had a separate audit committee. Not surprisingly, larger organizations were more likely to have audit committees than smaller ones. Fifty-eight percent of the larger organizations (who have revenues with more than $40 million in annual expenses) had audit committees. In smaller organizations with annual expenses of less than $100,000, only 20 percent reported having an audit committee.

Most experts agree that an audit committee is a good practice. It sends the message to your constituency and the public at large that the activities of your nonprofit will always be honest and legal.

Using an independent accounting firm

An *audit* is a procedure where an independent accounting firm formally certifies whether an organization's financial statements have been prepared according to Generally Accepted Accounting Principles (GAAP).

Some states have audit requirements for nonprofit organizations. However, if the nonprofit has received federal funds (including entities that receive federal funds that trickle through state or local government entities), they're required to comply with the audit requirements contained in the Office of Management and Budget Circular No. A-133. This document was issued in response to the Single Audit Act passed by Congress in 1990 to ensure that nonprofits that receive federal funds comply with certain minimal audit procedures. It's called the Single Audit Act because it's intended to provide uniform audit standards for all the entities required to comply with it (instead of a patchwork of individual state standards). You can view a copy of the Office of Management and Budget Circular No. A-133 (which explains the single audit requirements) at www.whitehouse.gov/omb/circulars/a133/a133.html.

Most larger nonprofits voluntarily have their statements audited even if states don't require them to do so or they don't receive federal funds. But, because audit opinions are expensive (they require the organizations to pay their auditors on an hourly basis to test and verify the information in the financial statements), many nonprofits choose not to have their information audited.

But, remember, if your organization doesn't have independent auditors, the role of the audit committee can be even more important, because the audit committee is charged with making sure management has done its job with respect to preparing accurate financial statements.

Developing audit committee standards

If you're looking for guidance on developing standards and practices for an audit committee, a good place to start is Section 301 of the Sarbanes-Oxley Act (SOX). Even though SOX doesn't technically apply to nonprofits, it can serve as an excellent model.

Three elements found in Section 301 of SOX are especially adaptable to and useful for your nonprofit audit committee standards:

- ✔ **Responsibility:** SOX states that the audit committee should be directly responsible for the appointment, compensation, and oversight of the work of any registered public accounting firm. This responsibility helps maintain the independence of management from the auditors who are auditing the organization (and consequently the management's actions).

- ✔ **Resolving disputes:** SOX requires audit committees to be responsible for resolving disagreements between management and the accountants. Disagreements can come up as to how various items are reflected and reported on the financial statements, particularly if management's compensation is tied in any way to that of the organization (for example, a bonus).

- ✔ **Communicating with the auditors/accountants:** SOX makes clear that the audit committee is responsible for communicating directly with the auditors or accountants and ensuring that management isn't filtering the information in an attempt to portray it as rosier than it really is.

Depending on the size and activities of your nonprofit organization, it may hire an outside accounting firm to audit or review its financial statements and books and records. A review of financial statements is a verification process that's less extensive than an audit and is undertaken when federal and state law doesn't require a formal audit.

Starting with a charter

A *charter* is a document that serves as a road map for an organization, and it may include a mission statement and description of the organization's contemplated activities and details as to how these will be carried out (for example, monthly meetings, written reports to the board, and so on). These charters define the scope of authority of the audit committee and determine who can sit on it.

Here are a few key elements to include in your audit committee's charter:

- **Purpose:** The purpose and function of the audit committee needs to be clearly spelled out. The role of the audit committee should be to ensure the integrity of the company's financial statements.

- **Monitor compliance:** The audit committee should monitor compliance with legal and regulatory requirements, such as getting the organization's tax returns and annual reports filed.

- **Ensuring that the accountants stay independent:** Part of the role of the audit committee is making sure that management and auditors don't get too chummy. A close relationship between these folks could compromise the accountant's objectivity in the event that he or she does find some sloppy accounting practices on the part of management.

- **Policies for fixing problems:** The charter must address the audit committee's policies with respect to notifying the entire board of a problem and working with management to identify known risks and problems. Example problems may include accounts that aren't being properly monitored or particular databases containing financial information that aren't secure.

Interfacing with management

Regardless of whether an organization employs independent auditors, audit committees are responsible for objectively evaluating the relationship of management with the accountants and auditors. The committee monitors the management's effectiveness in providing auditors with the information needed to determine whether the company's financial statements are prepared in accordance with Generally Accepted Accounting Principles (GAAP) and Generally Accepted Auditing Standards (GAAS), which are the professional standards to which accounting and auditing firms are subject in performing their duties.

Audit committees should *not* get involved in performing audits; rather, they should facilitate them. The internal audit committee provides an essential objective interface between a company's management and its independent (outside) auditors to ensure that, at all times, the auditors' opinions and certifications are based on full and accurate information about the company's operations.

Audit committees are responsible for ensuring that the organization maintains a work environment that

- ✔ Enables auditors to perform necessary testing
- ✔ Encourages employees to come forward with issues that may be relevant to the audit process (see the later section "Handling complaints" for more details)

Audit Committee Membership Guidelines

In order to fully comply with SOX standards, an audit committee must be established according to specific membership requirements. Members of the audit committee are drawn from the nonprofit's board of directors. These independent directors (who have no financial interest in the company) may be eligible to serve on the nonprofit's audit committee if they meet the requirements discussed in this section.

Independence is key

To ensure that audit committees are fair and objective advocates for effective audit procedures, SOX requires audit committee members to be financially independent from the company in two respects:

- ✔ **Compensation:** A committee member may not receive any type of compensation or fee from the organization other than payment for serving on the board of directors of the nonprofit. However, audit committee members *can* be paid for providing accounting, consulting, legal, investment, banking, or financial advisory services to the nonprofit or for working for companies that provide these services.

- ✔ **Affiliation:** A member can't be affiliated with the company through family or employment relationships. Unfortunately, SOX Section 302 doesn't clearly define the term "affiliated person." It merely states that if you're affiliated, you're prohibited from serving on an audit committee. However, the legislative history of SOX and past practices of the SEC make it possible to determine who will be deemed an affiliated person and thus ineligible to serve on your company's audit committee.

  For instance, the definition of the term "affiliated person" that's used in most other sections of securities laws applies to SOX as well. Under this definition, a director is considered to be an affiliated person if he or she has a direct or indirect influence over the management of the company's business or affairs other than solely by virtue of being a director.

Figure in a financial expert

At least one person on a company's audit committee should be a *financial expert.* Generally, a person is a financial expert if he or she has, through education and experience, an understanding of Generally Accepted Accounting Principles (GAAP), financial statements, and internal accounting controls.

The SEC doesn't consider former CEOs to be financial experts for companies that are required to comply with SOX.

Serving on an Audit Committee

If you serve on a nonprofit's board of directors and meet the requirements, you very likely will be asked to serve on an audit committee. Doing so involves more than simply rubber-stamping the company's financials. For starters, you'll be asked to play a fairly active role in recruiting and deciding how much to pay the company's auditors. You'll also be a go-to person within the organization when financial issues arise.

Monitoring events and policing policies

The audit committee not only must be a nonprofit's internal moral compass, but it also must monitor external publicity and events that can impact the audit process. It's responsible for making sure that the nonprofit responds appropriately.

Examples of what the audit committee is responsible for reviewing and monitoring include

- The annual audited financial statements and quarterly reports filed by the nonprofit
- Press releases and financial information provided to the public
- Policies for risk management within the nonprofit
- Problems that occur during an audit as well as management's response to such problems
- The role and performance of the nonprofit's internal auditors
- Changes in your nonprofit's accounting policies
- Issues regarding internal controls and audit adjustments
- The policies and procedures of the audit committee itself

Interfacing with the auditors

Using SOX as a model, the nonprofit's audit firm must report *solely* to the audit committee. This arrangement is a departure from pre-SOX days, when auditors in private companies also reported to management on a variety of issues. Congressional hearings on SOX revealed an inherent conflict in the interaction between management and the auditors who were, in effect, evaluating the effectiveness of management's policies.

The audit committee is expected to prevent management from influencing audit outcomes. SOX specifically states that the committee's role includes the resolution of disagreements between management and outside auditors regarding financial reporting. Using the SOX model means that the audit committee must have a full understanding of events that affect the nonprofit and the nonprofit's operations in order to properly understand and resolve these disputes.

Further, auditors are required to report the following information directly to the audit committee:

- All critical accounting policies and practices to be used

- All alternative treatments of financial information within Generally Accepted Accounting Principles that have been discussed with management, the ramifications of using alternative disclosures and treatments, and the treatment preferred by the auditor

- Any other *material* (significant) written communications between the auditor and management, such as a management letter or schedule of unadjusted differences

Preapproving nonaudit services

Private companies that are subject to SOX face strict rules about what accounting services an independent audit firm can and can't perform for a company. Basically, Congress didn't want auditors to be auditing their own work. Any functions that the audit firm can't perform under SOX must be sent to another accounting firm, performed by an outside consultant, or handled internally.

The audit committee has *sign-off authority* for audit services, which means that it must authorize every accounting service the company's audit firm provides, including confirmation letters and compliance with the financial reporting requirements of regulatory agencies.

Your nonprofit audit committee may want to take a cue from SOX and discuss under what circumstances it is okay for the audit firm to perform the following services when doing an audit or review for your organization:

- ✔ Bookkeeping or other services related to accounting records or financial statements

- ✔ Financial information systems design and implementation

- ✔ Appraisal or valuation services, fairness opinions, or contribution-in-kind reports

- ✔ Actuarial services

- ✔ Internal audit outsourcing services, management or human resources functions

- ✔ Broker or dealer, investment advisor, or investment banking services

- ✔ Legal services or expert services unrelated to the audit

If a nonaudit service isn't on this list, it's permitted under SOX as long as the audit committee approves the service before the audit firm provides it.

Handling complaints

Under SOX, private companies are required to have procedures in place for handing complaints abut the companies accounting and audit procedures. This is yet another "best practices" standard that many nonprofits are adopting voluntarily.

If you adopt theses standards, your audit committee is responsible for maintaining policies about the disposition of complaints about the nonprofit. It's also required to have procedures in place for receiving confidential and anonymous complaints by employees.

The audit committee serves as a resource for employees, management, and auditors, as well as for the nonprofit's constituency. With the complaint function, the audit committee complements whistle-blower provisions put forth by SOX (see Chapter 13).

Considering CEO and CFO certifications

Managers of nonprofit organizations aren't required to sign certifications affirming the organization's compliance with legal and regulatory requirements. However, this is a requirement of SOX, and some nonprofits are voluntarily following suit.

Under SOX, the chief executive officer and chief financial officer are required to certify in annual and quarterly reports that they have disclosed the following to the auditor and the audit committee:

✔ All significant deficiencies and material weaknesses in the design or operation of internal controls that could adversely affect the nonprofit's ability to record, process, summarize, and report financial data

✔ Any fraud, whether or not material, that involves management or other employees who have a significant role in the nonprofit's internal controls

Under SOX, an audit committee must make sure that any relevant information gleaned from the certifications is brought to the attention of the audit firm.

Ferreting out improper influence

SOX Section 303 regulates the relationship between the audit committee, the auditors, and management with a catch-all provision to discourage company management from improperly influencing audits and auditors. SOX prohibits officers and directors of public companies from fraudulently influencing, coercing, manipulating, or misleading any outside auditor engaged in an audit for the purpose of making the audited financial statements misleading. This is a good practice for nonprofits to consider voluntarily adopting.

Rotating the audit partners

SOX requires public accounting firms to rotate certain individuals every five years. This may be overkill for many nonprofit organizations, but it is one that large organizations with high-stakes audits that are constant fodder for the media attention may seriously consider.

This particular SOX standard requires rotation of the following individuals:

✔ The audit partner primarily responsible for a company's audit

✔ The audit partner responsible for reviewing the audit

The audit committee is responsible for making sure that this rotation actually happens.

Engaging advisors

Your audit committee may be involved in hiring more than just the auditors. Under SOX, the committee must also have authority to engage independent counsel and other advisors as it deems necessary to carry out its duties.

Under SOX, if a company doesn't have a separately designated audit committee, it must state that the entire board of directors is acting as the audit committee. This is a standard to which the public will likely hold larger nonprofit organizations, despite the lack of any formal legal requirements that apply specifically to nonprofits.

At a minimum, your nonprofit should plan on disclosing the following in your annual reports:

✔ Whether you have an audit committee

✔ Whether the members of the committee, if you have one, are independent under the rules of the public stock exchanges

Part IV
Some Special Types of Nonprofits

The 5th Wave   By Rich Tennant

"I'm not sure I can reconcile point 3 with the other two points."

In this part . . .

The nonprofit sector is made up of many different types of organizations, ranging from small, unincorporated associations and community groups to large private foundations and cooperatives. This part gives you a rundown of them all.

Chapter 11

Forming a Solid Foundation

● ●

In This Chapter

▶ Understanding the function of private foundations

▶ Exploring types of private foundations

▶ Satisfying the many legal requirements

▶ Choosing a board of directors to head up your foundation

● ●

*P*rivate foundations are charitable organizations that don't quite qualify as public charities. They usually get their funds from a small group of wealthy benefactors, while larger public charities get their funding from a variety of sources.

Private foundations have some legal leeway when it comes to distributing their money. They get tax-exempt status on all of their earnings, yet only have to distribute a mere 5 percent of their capital each year toward their charitable purpose. Those who establish private foundations are allowed very broad discretion as to who receives their money, and they also don't have to release much information about what they've done. Public charities, on the other hand, generally don't have this level of autonomy or privacy.

According to the most recent Internal Revenue Service data, 76,348 private foundations filed U.S. tax returns in 2003, and of these, 64,884 were *grant-making foundations*. Grant-making foundations essentially are charities that distribute money to other charities.

Although private foundations are charitable organizations, a different set of rules apply to them. This chapter explains what these rules are and sheds light on the differences between private foundations and public charities.

Why Form a Foundation?

If you're wealthy, want to champion a charitable cause, and insist on some degree of control over the charity, then a private foundation is the way for you to go.

Drawing the legal lines between private and public charities

The modern rules governing private foundations came into being way back when Congress passed the Tax Reform Act of 1969 and created special rules to establish a presumption that every tax-exempt charitable organization (think public charity) would be considered a private foundation *unless* it fell into one of the following predefined categories:

✔ It is a traditional public charity, such as a hospital, school, or medical research organization.

✔ It is a publicly supported organization, such as a youth program or a medical research facility. This type of organization receives at least one-third of its annual support from the public through gifts, donations, and membership dues.

✔ It is a supporting organization, which supports (and is significantly involved in) the activities of a specific public charity. A booster club that raises funds for a hospital or treatment nonprofit is an example of a supporting organization.

The lesson here is that if you're thinking of starting a private foundation to send your kids to college or take care of your dog after you die, forget about it. To obtain recognition as a private foundation from the IRS, you have to jump through the same hoops as if you were applying to be recognized as a public charity. So, the purpose of the foundation must fall into one of the same categories that the IRS would recognize to grant public charity status (educational, religious, scientific, and so on).

Keeping it all in the family

The overwhelming majority of private foundations are independent family foundations that are run by the person who set up the foundation (or his or her family members). They can do good things privately, and as long as they follow the rules (mostly tax rules), the foundation can go about fulfilling its mission in the manner its sees fit.

Maintaining privacy and control

Control and privacy are the two biggest reasons why rich people establish private foundations. The cost of setting up and running a private foundation is formidable, and if you're just "sort of" rich, you might just consider making an outright gift to your favorite charity (which may be an established private foundation) to accomplish your purpose. However, if you have "serious money" (think hundreds of thousands, millions, or hundreds of millions), setting up your own private foundation is a practical way to accomplish philanthropic goals.

Comparing Private Foundations to Public Charities

You may not be aware of it, but public charities are all around you: They're hospitals, schools, universities, and more. Public charities often strive for visibility and recognition that buttresses their fundraising efforts.

Some famous private foundations

The model for modern day private foundations has its roots in the Gilded Age, after John Rockefeller and Andrew Carnegie amassed large fortunes and chose to use their financial influence to improve society. Carnegie had an interest in building libraries (see the sidebar "The captivating history of the Carnegie Foundation" for more details); Rockefeller was interested in areas such as education and medical research.

The Rockefeller Foundation was established in 1913 (the same year that income tax was established) by Rockefeller himself. Prior to establishing his foundation, Rockefeller was already a widely recognized philanthropist. At the turn of the century, he gave $80 million to a small Baptist college, transforming it into the University of Chicago. He also founded the Rockefeller Institute for Medical Research in New York City (which is now known as Rockefeller University), and he established the General Education Fund in 1902 to promote nationwide education programs. The Rockefeller Foundation was funded with $250 million. The Foundation provided the endowment for the Johns Hopkins School of Hygiene and Public Health and helped build the Peking Union Medical College. It's estimated that over the course of his life, Rockefeller gave away over $550 million. Remember this though: He was one of the very wealthiest men in history. When he died in 1937, his remaining fortune was

estimated at $1.4 billion, and since that time no other American (including Bill Gates or Sam Walton) would come even near that.

Another famous foundation is the Ford family's Ford Foundation, which was established in 1936 and funded largely through bequests in the 1940s from Henry Ford and his son, Edsel. The foundation's board, chaired by Henry Ford II, commissioned a study of how the foundation should concentrate its future activities. The resulting recommendations formed the charter for the foundation's modern-day mission, which included strengthening democratic values, reducing poverty and injustice, promoting international cooperation, and advancing human achievement.

More recently, Microsoft co-founder Bill Gates and his wife Melinda (whose 2006 personal net worth was estimated at $53 billion) founded the Bill and Melinda Gates Foundation in 2000. Based on the principle that all lives have equal value, the foundation works to reduce inequality around the world. The foundation is headquartered in Seattle, Washington, and is led by co-chairs Bill Gates and Melinda Gates as well as Bill's father, William H. Gates, Sr. Billionaire Warren Buffett was so impressed by the work of the foundation and by Bill Gates personally that he announced that he would give approximately $30 billion of his fortune to the foundation.

Generally, public charities have active fundraising programs and receive contributions from a range of sources, including the general public, various governmental sources, public and private corporations, and other public charities and private foundations.

Public charities can earn income from conducting activities that further their exempt purposes. For example, a public charity established as a workshop for the blind can sell the goods it produces in furtherance of its exempt activity. (However, there are limitations on the activities public charities can perform that compete with the private sector, as discussed in Chapter 14.) Public charities also can exist to raise funds for other charities.

In contrast to public charities, private foundations generally have the following characteristics:

- ✔ **Single funding source:** Private foundations are established from a single major source of funding (such as a gift from one family or corporation).

- ✔ **Grant-making mission:** Private foundations have a primary mission in making grants to other charitable organizations and individuals (instead of operating a charity or engaging in direct charitable functions).

- ✔ **Low-key community presence:** Private foundations are far less visible in the community because they don't raise funds from the public. In fact, some private foundations make anonymous gifts to avoid constant solicitation from other nonprofits.

- ✔ **Special tax hoops to jump through:** Private foundations have extra federal tax filing and compliance requirements. Some rules apply to all types of private foundations, and some rules apply only to certain types of private foundations (and may well apply to other organizations as well).

The Types of Private Foundations

Private foundations come in different flavors, and the one you'll like best will be the one that matches your taste; that is, the one that fits your needs and is most suited to accomplish the goals that you have in mind. The two main classifications are private operating and grant-making (or non-operating) foundations. Both types of foundations are discussed in this section.

Private operating foundations

Imagine for a moment that you're eager to use some spare cash to set up a program that helps out a particular charitable program. Suppose further that

---

The David and Minnie Meyerson Foundation

The David and Minnie Meyerson Foundation is a private operating foundation focusing on children with physical disabilities. You can view the foundation's Web site at www.meyerson foundation.org. The Meyerson Foundation runs many of its own projects, which include research on disability issues, the provision of support to children with disabilities, and other endeavors.

Another example of a private operating foundation is the Synopsys Silicon Valley Science

Technology and Outreach Foundation, which offers programs for teachers and training, administrative support, and students interested in developing science projects for competition. The foundation conducts seminars and various instructional activities for teachers. Check out the foundation's Web site at www.outreach-foundation.org.

---

you don't really need any outside contributions to set up and run your program. In this case, you'd want to establish a *private operating foundation*.

Private operating foundations usually don't make grants to any outside organizations or individuals. They operate their own programs and often make direct gifts to other needy causes and individuals, which are generally funded from the income off of the return on investment from the original endowment to set up the foundation.

Your organization will be classified as a private operating foundation if it uses the majority of its resources to run its own charitable programs or to provide its own charitable services.

So how do you know if you qualify? From a technical standpoint, you need to spend at least 85 percent of your adjusted net income (that is, your gross income minus allowable deductions) directly on conducting your exempt activity.

The Internal Revenue Service calls this the *income test,* and it's one of those special hoops you must jump through in order to get recognized as a private operating foundation. In addition, you must also meet one of the following tests:

- **Asset test:** This test is met if 65 percent or more of your foundation's assets are devoted to conducting its exempt activity, and these assets consist of corporate stock that's controlled by the foundation.

- **Endowment test:** This test is satisfied if your foundation distributes at least two-thirds of its minimum investment return directly in connection with actively conducting its exempt activity.

✔ **Support test:** This test has three parts, all of which must be met:

- At least 85 percent of your foundation's support is normally received from the general public or five or more unrelated exempt organizations

- No more than 25 percent of your foundation's support is normally received from any single exempt organization

- No more than 50 percent of your foundation's support is generated through investment income

Sound confusing? It is. If you need to go anywhere near this level of detail, suffice it to say that you need to work with an accountant or attorney to make sure you don't get stuck in one of the hoops you're supposed to be jumping through.

When you file an application for tax-exempt status for a new nonprofit organization, the IRS will presume your organization to be a private foundation unless your organization meets one of the tests for non-operating private foundation status.

Grant-making foundations

Suppose you love music and want to use your money to conduct free concerts and other similar events that encourage the enjoyment and appreciation of

---

The history of the Carnegie Foundation

The Carnegie Corporation of New York is an example of a high-profile grant-making foundation. Created in 1911 by Andrew Carnegie, the Carnegie Corporation of New York promotes "the advancement and diffusion of knowledge and understanding." The foundation has an extensive Web site at www.carnegie.org, where you can read about the history and philanthropic endeavors of the organization. The site contains the biography of Andrew Carnegie, born in Scotland in 1835, who immigrated with his family to the United States in 1848 and went to work as a bobbin boy in a cotton mill at age 13. After trying his hand at a number of different occupations, he established his own business in 1865 and went on to form the Carnegie Steel Company, which began the Pittsburgh steel industry. At age 65, he sold the Carnegie Steel Company to J.P. Morgan for $480 million, and from that point forward devoted his life to philanthropic activities. One of his major accomplishments was to establish free public libraries so that everyone could have access to self-education. Under his direction, over $56 million was spent to build 2,509 libraries in English-speaking countries throughout the world.

music. The thing is, you don't have the time or inclination to develop or conduct specific programs, and there are a large number of charitable organizations actively endeavoring in these fields.

If this is your situation, you may want to consider establishing a *grant-making foundation,* which is sometimes referred to as a *private non-operating foundation.* This way, you can simply give your money to other charities that are already doing what you'd like to do.

Grant-making foundations are entities that give money to other charitable organizations instead of directly carrying out their own charitable activities. If your organization isn't a private operating foundation, it will more than likely be classified as a grant-making foundation.

Establishing a Foundation: Time to Jump Through Some Legal Hoops

When establishing a private foundation, you can either set it up as a trust or a nonprofit corporation. However, with the heightened concern over legal liability and the fact that directors and officers of nonprofit corporations may have some degree of protection from liability under state law, the corporate form is most frequently used.

As discussed in Chapter 5, for an organization to qualify for tax-exempt status as a charity, it needs to be organized for educational, scientific, religious, or other special purposes.

Federal-level compliance

The first step to set up a nonprofit corporation is to prepare its articles of incorporation or articles of organization. The IRS looks closely at these when you ask it to grant you tax-exempt status. The IRS suggests that your soon-to-be private operating foundation's articles of organization include the following provisions:

- **Distribute money every year:** You must have a clear statement that the foundation will distribute its income for each of its tax years in a time and manner so as not to be subject to any tax on undistributed income.

- **Avoid self-dealing:** Include a directive that the foundation will not engage in any *self-dealing* (see the sidebar "Self-dealing is a big no-no" for more details on this practice).

Self-dealing is a big no-no

If you're the person who established a private foundation, you are, by definition, what's called a *disqualified person*. If you're a disqualified person, you can't engage in *self-dealing*. The term self-dealing is generally used to describe deals between a private foundation and a disqualified person that involve one or more of the following types of transactions:

✔ **The sale or exchange of property:** This transaction between a private foundation and a disqualified person is automatically an act of self-dealing, even if unintentional. For example, a disqualified person who's a medical supplies salesperson can't make any sales to his hospital's private foundation, regardless of the amount of the sale.

✔ **Leases:** Any lease between a disqualified person and a private foundation is automatically considered to be self-dealing.

✔ **Extending credit or making loans:** These types of transactions between private foundations and disqualified persons are acts of self-dealing unless the loan is completely interest-free.

✔ **The provision of any goods, services, or facilities (including office space, cars, secretarial help, meals, parking, and so on):** These transactions between a private foundation and a disqualified person is automatically an act of self-dealing unless these items are provided without charge and are used exclusively for the exempt purpose of the private foundation.

✔ **The payment of any compensation or expense reimbursement:** This transaction between a private foundation and a disqualified person is considered to be self-dealing unless the payment is for personal services necessary to carry out the private foundation's mission and the payment isn't excessive.

✔ **Transferring foundation income or assets to, or for the use or benefit of, a disqualified person:** This transaction is automatically considered an act of self-dealing.

✔ **Certain agreements to make payments to government officials:** This transaction would generally be considered an act of self-dealing unless such payments are logically excluded. For example, a prize doesn't have to be included in gross income if the official receiving it is selected from the general public. Similarly, a scholarship grant would also be exempt.

If a case of self-dealing is egregious enough, the tax-exempt organization could lose its tax-exempt status. For example, if an officer of a nonprofit enters into a lease agreement for the headquarters of the organization that's in a building she owns, and the rent for the space is way above market rent, this would constitute self-dealing.

✔ **Distribute excess business holdings:** Be sure to put in a requirement that the foundation will not retain any excess business holdings (no more than 20 percent of an interest in a business enterprise).

✔ **Only make permitted investments:** Include a prohibition that the foundation will not make any investments that would jeopardize its charitable purpose.

✔ **Don't make taxable expenditures:** Include a statement that the foundation will not make any taxable expenditures, such as spending cash on prohibited political activities (for example, endorsing particular candidates).

If you choose to establish a trust rather than a nonprofit corporation for your foundation, the trust document needs to provide for substantially similar provisions to the ones shown in the previous bulleted list.

State-level compliance

Our glorious Union is comprised of 50 states, all with slightly different rules governing foundation activities. Your foundation must comply with the rules of each state in which it carries out any activities. Fortunately, all 50 states also share some certain similarities that make compliance a bit less arduous. But learning the differences is important.

Scoping out the state requirements

The go-to place for figuring out what you have to do to satisfy the requirements of each state is the Web site of the National Association of State Charity Officials at www.nasconet.org. This is the association of state offices that are charged with the oversight of charitable organizations.

If your state requires you to register, it's typically with the state's taxing authority, which generally also requires an inclusion of a copy of IRS Form 990-PF (see Chapter 7 for more on this form).

Your foundation may be required to follow the registration process of a given state if your foundation operates within that state, solicits contributions within that state's borders, or is deemed to be *doing business* within the state. "Doing business" may include soliciting contributions by mail or telephone, conducting activities or programs, having employees, keeping a checking account, or owning or renting a property in a particular state. The level of connection your organization has with a particular state will determine whether or not your private foundation is subject to that state's filing requirements.

If your private foundation solicits donations or contributions for charitable purposes, you should also know that most states require you to register and file periodic financial reports. Although many states accept a copy of your IRS Form 990-PF to satisfy this reporting requirement, the foundation should double-check the laws of each state in which it does business to ensure that it's following all the rules of each state in which it operates.

Complying with some more complicated requirements

Not all states will be satisfied simply because your foundation has filed the IRS Form 990-PF and registered with the state taxing authorities. Some states require additional items of information, which may include the following:

- ✔ **More financial statements:** They may want to know the details for the items you have reported on the other forms.

- ✔ **Explanations about notes to financial statements:** A state may ask you about the footnotes in your financials or in the auditors' reports.

- ✔ **A report by an independent accountant:** The state may not require a full-fledged audit, but it may request a report confirming what's reported on your financial information.

As if all this wasn't burdensome enough, each state may require the additional material to be presented on forms that they proscribe, or in specific formats, even though it doesn't need to be submitted with the private foundation's return as filed with the IRS.

If the required information isn't provided to a particular state, or the state determines that its form wasn't completed properly, you can expect a terse note asking you to provide the missing information or submit an amended return.

If, for some reason, your private foundation finds itself in a position where it needs to file an amended Form 990-PF with the IRS for a given year, you must also send a copy of that amended return to any state that required a copy of the original return. The deadline for filing Form 990-PF with the IRS generally differs from the time for filing any similar reports or the Form 990-PF with the various states.

Running Your Foundation

As with most businesses and nonprofit organizations, a private foundation is usually headed up by a board of directors. The board provides management and business oversight to the foundation, but it generally isn't involved in the day-to-day activities that are performed through the officers of the foundation. The board is an experienced group of advisors that the foundation relies on for long-term direction and strategy.

The foundation directors are usually selected based on their skill, experience, and ability to achieve the foundation's mission. But they may also be selected based on their relationship with the founder of the private foundation. This means that they can be family members. The foundations may compensate their directors, and many do. However, remember that the compensation must be reasonable (and what's reasonable to the IRS may not seem reasonable to the director or the foundation!)

One of the functions of the board of directors is to set the compensation for its officers. Compensation is usually set by comparing similar organizations and by looking at their salary and benefits information that's published on an annual basis by the Council on Foundations (find out more about the Council on Foundations at www.cof.org). Cost-of-living adjustments for the particular geographic region may also be appropriate.

For more information about selecting a board of directors and defining its duties, see Chapter 8.

Terminating a Private Foundation

Not all foundations are forever. Some private foundations start out with a specific goal in mind, and when that goal is accomplished, the need for the foundation ends. Other private foundations may grow in size or change directions such that the private foundation form of operation may no longer be suitable and public charity status may be desirable. Still other private foundations may run out of money or worse yet, engage in transactions that aren't suited for tax exemption. Whatever the reason may be, there are situations where private foundation status will terminate, either voluntarily or involuntarily — both of which are explained in the following sections.

Giving it away

Imagine that you established a private foundation to end world hunger and finally, after years of tireless efforts, you actually reach your goal. Now you decide that it's time to terminate your private foundation. Your private foundation has several options: It can give any remaining assets it may have to a public charity or another private foundation, or it can convert itself into a public charity. It could also choose to merge with another private foundation or split up into several private foundations.

Having it taken away

Suppose that your private foundation has failed to observe tax laws. After all it's your money, right? Right, but if you intentionally disregard the rules through flagrant violations or willful failure to act appropriately, the IRS will involuntarily terminate your private foundation. And to top it all off, you'll be socked with various sanctions and will have to pay a *termination tax* in an amount equal to the foundation's net assets. The take-away from this section is to follow the rules!

Chapter 12

Capitalizing on Cooperatives

· ·

In This Chapter

▶ Understanding how cooperatives work

▶ Discovering the many types of cooperatives

▶ Getting tax benefits

▶ Forming and running a cooperative

▶ Dealing with some day-to-day issues

· ·

Cooperatives are a completely different kind of animal when it comes to nonprofit organizations. In its simplest form, a cooperative is a group of people who get together to help each other meet a common goal. Cooperatives are jointly owned and democratically controlled entities.

Cooperatives exist in every industry in all geographic areas, and they exist for the sole purpose of meeting their members' needs. In a cooperative, any profits (or margins as they're called in the cooperative world) are returned to the co-op's members. These members, who may be individuals or businesses, participate in the functioning of the cooperative. In the affairs of a cooperative, each member of the co-op gets one and only one vote.

Co-ops are classified as nonprofit organizations because they return any margin they make on the sale of goods or services to each member of the co-op, much like a corporation pays out dividends to shareholders on its profits. These refunds, sometimes called *patronage dividends,* are paid to each member annually in proportion to each member's percentage of business done with the co-op for the year.

In this chapter, you can explore what a cooperative is, what its advantages are, and what rules it must follow to gain tax-exempt status.

Cashing In on Collaboration: How Cooperatives Work

In its simplest form, a *cooperative* is a collaboration of individuals or businesses that band together to gain a benefit through numbers. Many different types of cooperatives exist, but they all have one similar goal: to operate at lowered costs for the benefit of their members or others they do business with (called *patrons*).

A cooperative isn't a charitable organization, but it does operate on a nonprofit basis. And although cooperatives are similar in many ways to plain old corporations, there are some key differences as to how cooperatives do business. (We explain these key differences in the later section "Running a Cooperative: Is It Any Different Than a Corporation?".)

Banding together to meet business objectives

Cooperative organizations often exist to leverage their combined economic strength in order to share and reduce selling costs. For example, members of a *marketing cooperative* band together to deliver their products to the cooperative, which in turn sells the products to a particular market. Grape growers may form a cooperative to sell tons of grapes to wineries, retailer grocers, or juice companies.

Members of a *distribution cooperative* purchase services from the cooperative in order to distribute to customers. For example, a telecommunications cooperative may purchase bulk, long-distance telephone service and sell it back to members who then make it available to their customers.

Buying and selling in bulk

Purchasing in bulk provides an opportunity to get goods and services at a greater discount than may otherwise be available to individual businesses. Cooperatives operate on a nonprofit basis, so buying and selling goods and services through a cooperative assures the cooperative members that they aren't being charged a markup by a middleman.

Selling in bulk allows service providers and producers of goods and agriculture the assurance that there will be a market for their goods and services. It also ensures that a fair price will be negotiated on their behalf by their cooperative.

Tracing the concept of cooperation

The concept of running a business on a cooperative basis has been around for centuries. In fact, historians have found evidence of cooperative organizations among cultures in early Greece, Egypt, Rome, and Babylon.

Modern-day cooperatives follow a set of rules that originated with the Rochdale Society of Equitable Pioneers in Rochdale, England. The Rochdale Society was established by a group of textile weavers who had lost their jobs due to automation within the textile industry. The three primary modern-day principles of cooperatives derived from the Rochdale Society include the following:

✔ Subordination of capital (which makes funding of the cooperative unimportant as far as control is concerned)

✔ Allowing each person one vote regardless of their percentage of cooperative ownership

✔ Dividing profits among the members according to the percentage of business done with the cooperative organization for the year

Making a margin for the members

The term "profit" is frowned upon in cooperative parlance. Instead, the term *margin* is used to describe what's left over after accounting for the selling costs, operating expenses, and capital needs of the cooperative. At the close of each year, the cooperative generally distributes the margin for that year to members. How much of the annual margin each member gets is determined on a pro-rata basis, which is determined by how much business each member did with the cooperative during that year.

For example, if a member grocery store bought 50 percent of all of the dairy products sold by the Fresh Cheese Cooperative during 2007, the store would receive a distribution of 50 percent of the margin paid out by the Fresh Cheese Cooperative from its 2007 business. This is what's meant by the requirement that a cooperative must *operate at cost.*

Categorizing Cooperatives

Even though cooperative organizations are nonprofit enterprises, they differ from the traditional notion of what a nonprofit is. This is because their basic function is to provide economic utility to their members, as opposed to serving some sort of charitable, religious, or social motive. That said, the functions of a cooperative are practically limitless. This section describes a handful of cooperative types.

Consumer cooperatives

The *consumer cooperative* is one where members band together to realize economies of scale in purchasing or in competing. Some organizations follow a horizontal form of integration where cooperative stores band together to increase their ability to compete with large box retailers (for example, combined advertising campaigns by independently owned hardware stores aiming to compete with the Home Depots of the world).

Other consumer cooperatives follow a vertical method of integration so that they can benefit as a group in wholesale or even manufacturing activities. An example of this would be a large-scale grocery cooperative that purchases and warehouses food items and also produces private brand-label merchandise to compete with the name brand products.

A primary goal of consumer cooperatives is member participation and control. Ideally, the member-owners periodically meet to set policies and elect directors. Directors then hire management to run the cooperative on a day-to-day basis.

Housing and condominium cooperatives

Cooperative housing apartments came into vogue in the late 1920s as an economical way for housing ownership or proprietary leasing arrangements in urban areas where housing was an issue. The concept gained substantial popularity when federal mortgage insurance was extended to cover these arrangements. And beginning in 1960, almost every state in the United States adopted some form of law regarding condominium cooperatives.

The practical difference between condominium ownership and membership in a condominium cooperative is that a cooperative member has no direct ownership of real estate. Instead, he or she simply owns a cooperative share or membership certificate. The modern trend is to use cooperative housing law for homes and self-standing dwellings in a neighborhood development where real estate is owned, but rules are maintained for how things are done. Plus, the costs for maintaining streets, street lights, and common areas are shared.

Electric, telephone, and utility cooperatives

One of the most successful areas of cooperative development has been in the area of rural electric service. In the mid 1930s, only 10 percent of farms and

---

From cooperative to DIRECTV

In the mid 1980s, a cooperative called the *National Rural Telecommunications Cooperative* (NRTC) was formed largely through the efforts of Bob Phillips, who was a visionary lawyer from Kansas with a background in rural electric cooperatives. Phillips saw an unfilled need for the provision of television, video, and other related services to portions of rural America that cable television could or would not serve. In the early stages of the cooperative, Phillips was able to form a cooperative membership consisting primarily of rural electric and telephone cooperatives. The NRTC partnered with a little-known satellite venture to test and validate the concept of a commercially distributed satellite television service for rural American households as an alternative to cable television. That venture is today known as DIRECTV. Following on the success of that venture and in furtherance of its core mission, NRTC continues to seek out, develop, and deliver the latest available technology in the telecommunications area to its membership, who in turn acts as local distributors of these various service offerings.

---

agri-businesses were receiving electrical services from a centralized electrification system. In the 20 years that followed, more than 4 million farms were connected to lines furnished by *rural electric cooperatives.* This was largely due to financing programs made available through the *Rural Electrification Association,* or REA, which is now known as the Rural Utilities Service. In 1949, the REA began a similar financing program for *rural telephone cooperatives.* Even though telephone co-ops had been around since the 1920s, the REA established a financing program for these entities beginning in 1949, and they, too, have become extremely important in the fabric of rural America.

These utility-based cooperatives are often themselves members of larger cooperatives. For example, the National Rural Electric Cooperative Association is a cooperative organization whose members are smaller electric cooperatives throughout the United States. The National Telephone Cooperative Association is a similar organization made of rural telephone cooperative associations.

Health cooperatives: Nothing to sneeze at

Cooperatives can serve to provide better and less expensive healthcare services through value purchasing and obtaining preferred pricing on services by forming *healthcare cooperatives.* In these types of cooperatives, doctors typically furnish services on a fixed-fee basis, or by becoming employees of the cooperative. In the healthcare industry, the cooperative form of organization has been used to provide hospital and medical care, dental care, and care in other areas of specialization.

Marketing as a cooperative

Following the Great Depression, incentives abounded for the formation and development of *agricultural marketing cooperatives.* These incentives included the ability to bring products to market through a central repository at cost so that any profits would be returned to the members of the cooperative. Since those early days of development, the marketing cooperative has broadened in scope to include any type of marketing that's used to produce economic goods (for example, fishermen banding together to market their catches). This collective form of marketing provides real and immediate benefits to both the producers and the public. Such cooperatives reduce transportation and handling and merchandising costs, and they realize economies of scale in conducting advertising campaigns and avoiding middleman markups. These efficiencies in service and reduction on costs help benefit the public through lowered retail costs and increased availability of popular products.

Purchasing cooperatives

The cooperative form of purchasing has as its primary goal the reduction of member costs in the acquisition of goods and services. *Purchasing cooperatives* can be either consumer-oriented or business-oriented. Business purchasing cooperatives help their members obtain a higher profit when dealing with third parties, whereas consumer-based purchasing cooperatives strive to provide goods and services at cost to their members. Use of the term "purchasing" in the context of this type of cooperative should be broadly construed because many purchasing cooperatives don't in fact make any purchases. Instead, they simply arrange for the delivery of goods or services to their members, much like an agent might function to purchase goods for its principal. Typical industries that use purchasing cooperatives include grocery, drug, and hardware retailers.

Workers' cooperatives

Workers' cooperatives are usually composed of a group of workers who band their resources together to operate a business in which they work. In the context of workers' cooperatives, the term "worker" includes all forms of labor and professions, from plywood manufacturers to physicians. This form of cooperative organization is popular in Europe, but much less so in the United States.

Financial cooperatives

Financial institutions may also function on a cooperative basis. Credit unions, mutual savings banks, and savings and loan associations can all be forms of *financial cooperatives.* These forms of cooperatives enable patrons to borrow or save under equitable terms that may be difficult to obtain at traditional institutions.

Such organizations also may be formed to primarily serve other cooperatives. For example, the *National Cooperative Finance Corporation* is a primary facilitator of funding for rural electric cooperatives in need of capital for system maintenance and expansion.

Members Only: Who Can Be Part of a Cooperative?

In many cases, membership in a cooperative is *closed,* or restricted. These membership limitations are sometimes imposed by state or other laws, but they're also often determined by those establishing the cooperative. If a person wants to join the cooperative, he or she must meet all the necessary requirements and go through an application and approval process.

Depending on the type of cooperative and the state of its incorporation, state law may restrict who can be admitted as a member. For example, some states preclude a for-profit corporation from becoming a member of a cooperative. The Web site findlaw.com provides access to the laws of many (but not all) states, and it shows the cooperative provisions if a given state's statutes reveal the limitations that the state places on cooperatives.

Some cooperatives may permit dealings with nonmembers on a cooperative basis. These nonmember patrons may obtain the benefits of the cooperative association, including the annual payment of patronage dividends. However, they're restricted from the right to vote and inspect the books and records of the cooperative. They're restricted from other rights that belong to full members as well. Cooperatives may do business with nonmembers for a variety of reasons (they're too numerous to list here), but nonmembers never have the same rights and privileges as members.

Many cooperatives also deal with the general public as well as their own member-patron base, separately tracking the revenue from each segment of consumer so that the cooperative aspect of operation at cost can be accurately documented and accounted for. Examples of these types of cooperatives include Ace Hardware, Ocean Spray, Land O'Lakes, and other household names.

Certain types of cooperatives can lose their tax-exempt status if they do too much business with nonmembers or derive too much income from sales that aren't related to their primary purpose. For example, rural electric cooperatives will lose their tax exemption for any year in which they earn more than 15 percent of their gross income.

Just as cooperatives have stockholders and partnerships have partners, cooperatives have members. Cooperatives may be either stock or non-stock organizations.

Collaborating for Tax Benefits

When a cooperative operates at cost by distributing its annual margin, it pays no tax on those distributions. Rather, it's a transparent entity as far as the IRS is concerned. This provides a direct tax benefit to the cooperative's members. Unlike a corporation, which gets its distributed income tax twice (once at the corporate level and then again at the shareholder level), cooperatives don't pay any income tax on their distributions of margins to members. Members who receive the distributions may be taxed on the income, if they're taxable entities. If they're tax-exempt, any patronage dividend distributions they receive generally aren't taxable to them.

Distributing the dividends: Cash and equity credits

Corporations distribute dividends, sometimes in the form of additional stock, but generally in the form of cash. Cooperative distributions of margin can also be in *equity credits*. Equity credits are undistributed profits or margin, shared by cooperative members on the same basis as the distributions would be. However, in order to qualify for tax-free distributions, at least 20 percent of any margin distribution must be paid out in cash. Equity credits are sometimes referred to as *patronage capital*.

Any portion of margin that isn't paid out in cash is still includable in the income of the member entitled to the amount as an equity credit. This retained equity is used by the cooperative for capital expenditures, growth, and other business purposes. Equity credits can be converted to cash by the cooperative on a set basis, or at the general discretion of the cooperative's board of directors when the financial health of the cooperative justifies a redemption.

Many cooperatives have an equity redemption or rotation plan in place so that each member knows when to expect to receive cash for the full value of the accumulated equity certificates. State law generally allows the cooperative to choose its method of redemption.

Special requirements for special types of cooperatives

Certain types of cooperatives receive special tax treatment by the government and are subject to stricter operating standards on what they can and can't do. For example, farmers' cooperatives can't do more than 50 percent of their business with any single member. Rural electric cooperatives that distribute electricity to rural America can't make more than 15 percent of their income from sources unrelated to their primary purpose of generating or distributing electricity.

Cooperatives that don't get any special treatment generally aren't subject to these limits. However, only income generated in pursuit of the cooperative's purpose is eligible for distribution as margin. In other words, income generated from an activity that's completely unrelated to the cooperative's purpose is taxed at the normal income tax rate for corporations.

Forming a Cooperative in Five Easy Steps

Like corporations, cooperatives are creatures of state law, and the steps in forming a cooperative are very similar to forming a corporation. The following sections guide you through the process.

Step one: Check your state's statutes

The first step in forming a cooperative is to form a corporation under your state's cooperative state statutes. The law of your particular state may say that its general corporate laws will apply, or there may be a separate provision for cooperative formation. Forming a cooperative corporation usually begins with filing the articles of organization with your state's secretary of state.

Certain types of federally regulated cooperatives (such as rural electric cooperatives) may have additional or special state requirements.

Step two: File articles of incorporation

In order to file articles of incorporation, states usually require the incorporators to be listed, and more often than not the list will constitute the cooperative's first board of directors. So, you have to identify these individuals. These folks will also likely be the first members of the cooperative. If you don't have any members yet, you need to round up some people (preferably who work in the industry) that your cooperative will be serving. Then get a board of directors in place.

Step three: Adopt some bylaws

State cooperative statutes will tell you what *must* be included in your bylaws and what *may* be included. "Must-haves" vary slightly from state to state and generally include things such as the establishment of a class (or classes) of members, a reserve fund, an educational fund, and a limit on the membership interest to one vote per member (regardless of how important the member might be to the operations of the cooperative). "May-haves" generally include things such as who should be admitted as a member, whether dues are payable, what the cost of a membership certificate should be, whether a patronage equity redemption plan is feasible, what classes of membership are needed, and other such rules.

Step four: Make some rules and policies

You need to establish rules and policies for member dues, admission, withdrawal, expulsion, meeting protocols, and other details that may not be addressed or completely clarified in the bylaws. And you need to acquire members (if you don't already have them). In most cases, a cooperative is formed out of the need of a group of similarly situated people or businesses, and so a membership base is usually readily identifiable.

Step five: Issue member shares and certificates

As the grand finale in the formation of your cooperative, you want to issue member shares or certificates. Each member is issued only one share at a nominal cost as evidence of membership. To complete the formation process, hold an organizational meeting of the members to vote on preliminary matters, such as who will be the cooperative's first set of officers and directors.

Running a Cooperative: Is It Any Different Than a Corporation?

To the outsider, the operation of a cooperative is similar to the operation of a for-profit corporation. In fact, the average consumer would not be able to distinguish a cooperative organization from a for-profit corporation.

For example, from a legal perspective, cooperatives (like corporations) hold regular meetings of the board and the members, and they elect their officers and board members. From the standpoint of operations, goods are purchased and sold, the cooperative enters into contracts and can be sued, and it performs other functions just like a corporation. In fact, unless some specific legal provision exists, cooperatives and their officers, directors, and agents don't enjoy the same types of state and federal exemptions from liabilities that are bestowed on charitable nonprofits.

A major distinguishing characteristic between corporations and cooperatives is that a cooperative needs to keep meticulous records of its dealings with its members so that it can accurately distribute its margin after the close of each fiscal year. The following sections show the other major distinctions between corporations and cooperatives.

Profit distribution

Cooperatives operate at cost, returning all of their net profit (or margin) to their members at the end of each year in an amount proportionate to the amount of business each member did with the cooperative. In other words, if you don't do business with the cooperative, you don't get a share of its margin. Conversely, with a corporation that operates on a for-profit basis, dividends are paid at a set rate per share, and the amount of dividends paid to any one shareholder depends solely on the number of shares owned. And shareholders don't need to do business with a for-profit business in order to earn a share of the company's profits.

Share transfer restrictions

Unlike in a corporation, a membership share or certificate in a cooperative is generally not freely transferable. Members usually must get permission from the cooperative's board of directors in order to transfer a membership share certificate, and the board has the power to say no. When a for-profit shareholder calls it quits and decides to sell shares to cash out, he or she usually gets cash. Not so with a terminating or withdrawing cooperative member, who may need to wait years or even decades in order to redeem his or her equity credits.

The reason for this is at the root of the cooperative philosophy: cooperatives are formed for the benefit of members and to operate at cost, and the equity credits retained from distributions of margin are used for capital investment for the benefit of all members. Redemption of equity credit will generally not be made unless it is clear to the cooperative's board that the enterprise will not suffer any economic harm or otherwise be financially jeopardized by the redemption.

The Typical Operations of a Cooperative

The day-to-day operations of a cooperative don't vary much from those of corporations in similar enterprises. There's no set formula on how operations should be conducted. However, because the nature of cooperatives varies so widely, the question of whether the cooperative operates as an agent or independent enterprise is one that frequently arises.

Cooperatives that act as an agent, bargaining on behalf of their members (such as a marketing cooperative), receive products from the members, sell them on behalf of the members, and return the proceeds of the sales to those members. In contrast, a cooperative that acts as an independent enterprise may purchase products from the membership, and then sell them just as if they had been purchased from any ordinary enterprise. In the real world, a variation or combination of these approaches is generally found in each and every cooperative.

However, there are examples of cooperatives that act strictly as agents or strictly as independent enterprises. For example, a housing cooperative is generally organized to issue membership certificates along with leases between the cooperative and its members. The member gets a membership interest in a proprietary lease, which is generally not thought of by the member as an ownership in an independent enterprise. Instead, it's thought of as a landlord/tenant relationship where the cooperative has the right to evict the member if the member doesn't pay the rent. In any event, if there's a problem with housing cooperatives, everything still comes down to what the lease says.

In day-to-day operations, the relationship of a cooperative to its members depends on the industry, the function of the cooperative, and the member composition itself. The diversity of these organizations runs the gamut.

Dealing with Some Cooperative Conundrums

While the operations of cooperatives appear to be nearly identical to those of corporations, the types of issues that co-ops face are unique. Cooperatives, for instance, don't have to deal with hostile takeover attempts, minority shareholder issues, or securities fraud. But, because cooperatives involve people, people-related issues will crop up.

For example, you may come across pushy members who have agendas that are counter to the good of the group. Every so often, a cooperative may get a complaint from a member that there's some sort of unfair treatment going on. The member may want to be on the board of directors, may want to force the cooperative to redeem outstanding equity credits, or may accuse the cooperative of not distributing enough margin.

These problems can cause real headaches and be disruptive to cooperative management. In order to resolve these issues, the cooperative generally tries to appease the unhappy member by working within its powers to give exemplary service or special attention to the squeaky wheel. Unfortunately that doesn't always work, and the member can sue the cooperative.

One common situation is where an electric cooperative serves a local business, and the owner of the business dies, holding a large amount of equity credits. The widow of the business owner approaches the cooperative and says "Hey, my spouse is now dead, and I have no use for these equity credits. Please cash me out." But depending on the financial health of the cooperative and whether a set redemption cycle is in place, the cooperative's board of directors generally holds the sole discretion to decide whether to cash out the widow or make her wait.

When the widow is told to wait and she sues the cooperative, the court will first look to the cooperative's governing documents and state law to see if the widow wins. If the cooperative's bylaws or state laws don't require redemption on death, the poor widow is out of luck if the cooperative board tells her to wait. This woman is out of luck because the court system doesn't want to get involved in the decisions that boards make. This *business judgment rule* protects the decision of the board. The court system will not second-guess decisions made by the board of directors, who sit in the best position to make such judgment calls.

In order to avoid such headaches, your cooperative is well-advised to adopt policies and procedures to address issues that have a tendency to reoccur on a regular basis. That way, an officer or board member of a cooperative can point to the policy and hopefully quell any opposition to an unpopular position or decision.

Some famous cooperatives

You may not realize it, but many cooperatives are household names. For example, you probably shop at some of these cooperatives, or maybe you have one of their products in your home. Here are just a few examples:

✔ **Ace Hardware:** Ace Hardware is a marketing cooperative that was founded in Chicago in 1924. It's currently the largest global retailer-owned cooperative with more than 4,800 stores located in 50 states and 70 countries. Its trade name ranks among the most widely recognized in America. The members of this type of cooperative are the hardware stores themselves, who purchase goods and services from the cooperative.

✔ **Ocean Spray:** Ocean Spray is an agricultural cooperative that was formed in 1930 by three cranberry growers who wanted to expand the market for cranberries. One of its members was an attorney and cranberry grower named Marcus L. Urann. In 1930, Urann invented a cranberry sauce with a long shelf life along with cranberry juice drinks. Ocean Spray was also one of the first U.S. producers to use paper bottles, which are now a mainstay in every grocery store juice aisle.

✔ **Land O'Lakes:** Land O'Lakes, Inc. has been around since 1921. It was first known as the Minnesota Cooperative Creameries Association. In 1924, set for market expansion, it decided it needed a trademark and brand name for its butter. Land O'Lakes, a tribute to Minnesota's sparkling lakes, was chosen. The popularity of the name took off, and in 1926 the cooperative changed its corporate name to Land O'Lakes Creameries, Inc., and later to Land O'Lakes, Inc.

Land O'Lakes is currently one of America's premiere farmer-owned cooperatives and offers farmers, local cooperatives, and customers across the country a large line of agricultural supplies as well as art production and business services.

Part V
Legal Landmines

The 5th Wave   By Rich Tennant

"Death and taxes are for certain,
Mr. Dooley, however, they're not
mutually exclusive."

In this part . . .

If your nonprofit organization is ready to voluntarily comply with Sarbanes-Oxley-like provisions, you've come to the right place. We devote an entire chapter in this part to guiding you to compliance. Also, this part looks at the common mistakes that nonprofits make, and explains how to help your organization avoid losing its tax-exempt status. And because just about everyone is afraid of the Internal Revenue Service, we give you some tips that will help soften the blow of being audited and smooth out any communication gaps.

Chapter 13

Existing in a World of Sarbanes-Oxley

In This Chapter

▶ Getting familiar with the key provisions of SOX

▶ Applying SOX standards to nonprofits

▶ Migrating sensibly toward full SOX compliance

▶ Taking the SOX quiz

*T*he Sarbanes-Oxley Act (SOX) was signed by President George W. Bush (with a huge wave of bipartisan support) in 2002 following two of the biggest corporate downfalls in history. Enron, the nation's largest energy company, and Worldcom, the largest telecommunications company, both filed bankruptcy mere weeks after receiving strong endorsements from stock analysts and clean bills of health from their chummy auditors. Shareholders across the nation screamed fraud, and because of this downfall, thousands of retirees lost their pensions. Since its passage, SOX has changed the way both for-profit and nonprofit businesses conduct themselves.

Although SOX doesn't apply specifically to nonprofits, nonprofit organizations of all sizes are striving to comply with its standards (or are at least becoming aware of them). This is because nonprofits must be prepared to demonstrate a commitment to good governance and so-called "internal control" over their financial reporting practices. Nonprofits, as a rule, depend on public good will and their squeaky-clean reputations to attract funds. So, needless to say, despite the organization's most altruistic motives, a financial scandal can permanently undermine its ability to attract contributions. Even before SOX came along, SOX-related words, such as "accountability," "ethics," "transparency," "duty," "full-disclosure," and "social responsibility" were part of the vernacular of nonprofit governance.

A Quick and Clean Overview of Sarbanes-Oxley

The rationale for passing SOX was to ensure the integrity of the financial statements on which the American public relies. Amazingly enough, each provision in the Act tracks to an event or abuse that occurred at a single for-profit company: Enron (see the sidebar "What went wrong at Enron" for details). The implications of SOX are staggering, and it will be years before they're fully understood. In fact, SOX has been used to justify countless data management and internal "security" projects having little or nothing to do with financial statements, but the law was not passed to deal with these unrelated issues.

For private companies, SOX goes where the federal government has never gone before. Although federal regulation of the sale of securities to protect the public is nothing new, SOX goes beyond simply prohibiting deceptive conduct and misrepresentations — it actually tells corporations how they must run their businesses. For nonprofits, which aren't technically subject to the mandates of SOX, the law has become the gold standard for good governance.

SOX defines specific duties for employees and board members and dictates the structure of boards of directors. It even tells corporations subject to it how they have to conduct their day-to-day operations.

What went wrong at Enron

Nonprofit organizations need to understand the events at Enron (which was the largest bankruptcy in history at the time) in order to understand what Congress was trying to address regarding private corporations. Understanding why SOX was passed can allow your organization to determine which concerns can be relevant to its financial reporting.

In the case of Enron, a handful of executives had paid themselves millions in bonuses and had profitably sold their own stock. Employees were prohibited from selling their Enron stock as its value plummeted because of a routine blackout period. During congressional investigations, it came to light that billions of dollars in losses had been kept off the books by hiding them in flimsy partnerships for which the chief financial officer (CFO) received huge commissions for forming. Amazingly, the board of directors had approved both the partnership transactions and the commissions to CFO Andrew Fastow (who later had to return the money and got five years in prison).

Major credit reporting agencies failed to identify the events leading up to the collapse of Enron. Moody's Investors Service, Standard & Poor's Corporation, and Fitch Rating Services all gave Enron good credit ratings a mere two and a half months prior to Enron filing for Chapter 11 bankruptcy.

The following omens that foreshadowed Enron's implosion are also present today in many non-profit organizations:

✓ **Successive resignations of key management:** On August 14, 2001, Enron CEO Jeff Skilling resigned after being in the position only six months. On October 16, 2001, coinciding with a huge restatement of third-quarter earnings, Enron announced that its CFO, Andrew Fastow, would also be replaced. SOX now requires corporations to report changes in management within four days after they occur.

Many nonprofits have equally tumultuous turnover. For this reason, Senator Charles Grassley demanded an investigation into the abrupt departure of the Red Cross CEO earlier this year (as discussed in Chapter 3).

✓ **Inaccurate and unreliable financial statements:** On October 16, 2001, Enron announced third-quarter earnings that reflected an unexpected $544,000 earnings change and a $1.2-million change in *stockholders' equity* (the value of the stockholders' interest in the company). On November 8, 2001, Enron further announced that it needed to restate its financial statements for the first and second quarters of 2001 and for the four years prior, 1997 through 2000. The grand total of overstated income was $586 million. This disaster was attributed largely to the fact that the financial statements were audited by accounting firms that were downright chummy with the management that they were supposed to be auditing.

Many nonprofits aren't required to have audited financial statements, and no rules

regulate the independence of their auditors when they do.

✓ **Off-balance-sheet transactions to hide losses:** A big factor in Enron's eventual collapse was the use of so-called *special purpose entities,* which were separate companies set up to hide Enron losses. This arrangement ensured that the losses didn't see the light of day on Enron's books. Instead, the losses showed up on the statements of the special purpose entities.

Nonprofits are vulnerable to similar type of manipulation because organizations often have multiple separately balanced funds for different programs. Improperly allocating program funds caused the Red Cross to earn a rebuke from Senator Grassley after funds earmarked for 911 were shifted to other programs.

✓ **Lack of clear document destruction policies:** On January 10, 2002, Enron's audit firm, Arthur Andersen admitted to Congress that it had destroyed or shredded an undisclosed number of documents related to Enron's use of special purpose entities to hide losses and related matters. At the time, no one within Andersen questioned or took steps to stop the shredding.

Nonprofits often rely on volunteer administrative staff or staff members who are paid less than the going rate. Without document retention policies to guide these volunteers and staff members, valuable information can inadvertently be lost or easily obscured.

Four squeaky-clean SOX objectives

In the months subsequent to the Enron collapse, no less than two dozen SOX-related bills were proposed in Congress. And President Bush announced his own ten-point plan. The following objectives emerged from the extensive testimony, press conferences, and thick packets of proposed legislation and protracted hearings that ensued:

- ✔ **Make management accountable.** Several provisions of SOX seek to ensure that management, accountants, and attorneys are held directly accountable for information that makes it onto a company's financial statements on their watches.

- ✔ **Enhance disclosure.** SOX's provisions address the fact that several key events and relatively shocking transactions having to do with corporate scandal escaped scrutiny simply because they weren't required to be disclosed to the public.

- ✔ **Conduct regular reviews.** SOX requires the SEC to look at companies more often and more closely. This new requirement is a reaction to the SEC's declining to review Enron's records for several years preceding its bankruptcy filing and consequential loss to investors.

- ✔ **Make accountants accountable.** SOX seeks to purge the accounting industry of the conflicts of interest, financial self-dealing, and plain old poor judgment that placed the investing public at risk when relying on "certified" financial statements.

The major provisions of SOX

In for-profit and nonprofit organizations alike, financial reporting problems can trigger serious and tragic consequences for investors. For this reason, SOX focuses on how for-profit companies arrive at the financial information they report to shareholders. Similarly, nonprofit stakeholders (donors, funding sources, and program recipients) need to know that the financial information that's reported on a nonprofit Form 990 is accurate. (IRS Form 990 is a combined tax return and financial statement for nonprofit organizations. You can read more about this form in Chapter 7.) Sox also sets standards for management, directors, attorneys, and auditors accountable for the end product. This section explains the most important provisions of SOX.

Clamping down on auditors

An audit isn't necessarily an adversarial process, but it's supposed to be an objective one. An *audit* is a process of verifying information and identifying information that isn't consistent with Generally Accepted Accounting Standards, or GAAS. One purpose of an audit is so that accountants can *certify* financial statements that are prepared in accordance with Generally Accepted Accounting Standards (GAAP); certification assures anyone who reviews them that the statements are GAAP-compliant.

To remove any potential for funny business, SOX addresses the important issue of auditors becoming too chummy with the clients that they're auditing.

Accounting firms, like any service company, have a financial incentive to cater to clients who pay their fees. For example, a tense audit could strain the client relationship and result in the accounting firm getting fired. This potential for conflict of interest is exacerbated if the accounting firm provides other lucrative services to the client besides the audit.

Accordingly, SOX Section 201 limits the scope of services that can be performed by auditors (see Chapter 5 for coverage of prohibited services). SOX provides that it's unlawful for a registered public accounting firm to provide any nonaudit service to an issuer contemporaneously with the audit, including:

✔ Bookkeeping or other services related to the accounting records or financial statements of the audit client

✔ Financial information systems design and implementation

✔ Appraisal or valuation services, fairness opinions, or contribution-in-kind reports

✔ Actuarial services

✔ Internal audit outsourcing services

✔ Management or human resources functions

✔ Broker, dealer, investment advisor, or investment banking services

✔ Legal and expert services unrelated to the audit

✔ Any service that the board determines, by regulation, is impermissible

SOX does allow accounting firms to perform services that aren't included in the above list. For example, accountants traditionally perform tax return preparation services.

Rotating auditors

SOX presumes that an auditor's long-time familiarity with a company compromises the quality of an audit rather than making the process more efficient each year. SOX also presumes that auditors lose their objectivity when they develop a close and comfortable relationship with the client. Accordingly, SOX Section 203 provides that the lead and concurring audit partners must rotate off of the audit every five years.

Creating committees inside companies

SOX creates a new class of worker bees within public companies. Section 301 requires that public companies who are listed with the national securities exchanges and associations (called *issuers*) form *audit committees.* These audit committees are responsible for working with the independent auditors and getting them the information they need. They're also responsible for establishing procedures on related issues, such as record retention and hearing complaints.

Each member of the audit committee must be a member of the board of directors of the issuer and must be independent.

Audit committee members can receive compensation for serving on the committee. Accountants and attorneys are prime prospects for board membership.

The audit committee of an issuer is "directly responsible" for the appointment, compensation, and oversight of the work of any registered public accounting firm hired by the company to audit its financial statements. It's also the audit committee's job to establish procedures for the "receipt, retention, and treatment of complaints" received by the issuer regarding accounting, internal controls, and auditing concerns.

SOX requires that companies pay the cost of the audit committees and give them the authority to hire independent counsel or other advisors to carry out committee functions.

Making management accountable

CEOs and CFOs are likely to be much more proactive in making sure their companies' financial statements are accurate now that they have to personally vouch for the statements and risk doing time if they're not accurate.

SOX Section 302 provides that CEOs and CFOs must personally certify the "appropriateness of the financial statements and disclosures contained in the periodic report, and that those financial statements and disclosures fairly present, in all material respects, the operations and financial condition of the issuer." A violation of this section must be knowing and intentional to give rise to liability.

In addition, Section 302 requires that the CEO and CFO disclose all significant deficiencies and material weaknesses in controls over financial reporting to both the independent accountants and the audit committee. This prevents management from taking a passive attitude toward serious weaknesses.

SOX also suggests — but doesn't require — that a corporation's federal income tax return be signed by the CFO of the corporation in order to emphasize its accuracy.

SOX Section 303 now specifically provides that it's unlawful for any officer or director of an issuer to take any action to fraudulently influence, coerce, manipulate, or mislead any auditor engaged in the performance of an audit for the purpose of rendering the financial statements materially misleading. (How could anyone ever think this type of thing was *lawful?*)

Taking back bogus bonuses

CEOs and CFOs may be required to give back their bonuses if financial statements have to be restated (changed) after an audit due to "material noncompliance" with financial reporting requirements because of fraudulent activity. SOX Section 304 provides that CEOs and CFOs must "reimburse the issuer for any bonus or other incentive-based or equity-based compensation received" during the 12 months following the issuance or filing of the noncompliant document and "any profits realized from the sale of securities of the issuer" during that period.

Ratcheting up reporting

Federal securities law is based on the premise that investors in a public company have a right to know the facts and circumstances that would reasonably and fairly influence their decisions to invest in the company.

SOX attempts to ensure that investors are fairly well-informed by adding the following provisions to existing law:

- ✔ **Reflection of accounting adjustments:** SOX Section 401(a) requires that companies' financial reports "reflect all material correcting adjustments . . . that have been identified by a registered accounting firm."

- ✔ **Disclosure of off-balance-sheet transactions:** SOX requires that a company's annual and quarterly financial reports disclose all material (significant) off-balance-sheet transactions and other relationships with unconsolidated entities that may have a material current or future effect on the company's financial condition.

- ✔ **Real-time reporting of key events:** Companies need to disclose information on material (significant) changes in their financial conditions or operations on a rapid and current basis on Form 8-K reports (see Chapter 3).

Purging company conflicts of interest

Under SOX, auditors can't accept jobs with their clients, until they have taken off a complete audit cycle. This makes sense because an auditor might otherwise hesitate to alienate a prospective employer.

Under SOX Section 206, it's unlawful for CEOs, controllers, CFOs, chief accounting officers, and persons in equivalent positions to have been employed by the company's audit firm during the one-year period preceding the audit. It's also unlawful under SOX Section 402(a) for a company to lend money to any director or executive officer. Under Section 403, directors, officers, and 10-percent owners must report designated transactions by the end of the second business day following the transaction, so that the public can follow what the "insiders" are doing.

Exercising internal control

The dreaded SOX Section 404 requires that companies include in their annual reports (Form 10-K) an *internal control report* that states:

- ✔ Management's responsibility for establishing and maintaining an adequate internal control structure and procedures for financial reporting.

- ✔ Management's assessment of the effectiveness of the internal control structure and procedures of the issuer for financial reporting. The assessment must include disclosure of any identified *material weakness* in the company's internal control over financial reporting existing at the company's fiscal year-end. (*Material* is an accounting term that means "significant." The accounting standards for what is deemed a material error depend on the type of information that's being considered.)

- ✔ Management's framework to evaluate the effectiveness of their controls.

- ✔ That the company's auditor has attested to the adequacy of management's assessment and the company's internal control over financial reporting.

Stopping the shredders

Under SOX Section 802(a), it's a felony to "knowingly" destroy or create documents to "impede, obstruct or influence" any existing or contemplated federal investigation. This is a SOX section that impacts the criminal provisions of the law and thus impacts *all* organizations, not just public companies.

Auditors are required to maintain "all audit or review work papers" for seven years from the date their report is issued.

Providing whistle-blower protection

Whistle-blowers are employees who report information about corporate fraud or mismanagement. Under SOX, employees of issuers and accounting firms are provided *whistle-blower protection.* These protections prohibit employers from taking certain actions against employees who disclose information to, among others, parties in a judicial proceeding involving a fraud claim. Whistle-blowers are also granted a remedy of special damages and attorney's fees. (For more on whistle-blowers, check out the section "Protecting whistle-blowers" later in this chapter.)

Applying SOX to the Nonprofit Arena

Nonprofits know that even a hint of scandal can send donors and other funding sources scurrying. Consider what happened at the Red Cross when the well-intentioned organization used some funds for victims of the September 11, 2001, terrorist attacks for other worthy purposes. This violation of the donor's trust and confidence and accounting protocols landed the venerable Red Cross on the front page of every newspaper in the nation. It also led to a chain of events that ultimately caused its director to resign in order to restore donor confidence. Similarly, prospective donors of the United Way all across the nation had the privilege of reading about a scandal at a local chapter involving large-scale misappropriations of donor funds.

Although only two provisions of SOX directly apply to nonprofits, its passage has rocked the nonprofit community with discussions about nonprofit account-ability and about whether nonprofits should adhere to certain provisions of the Act either on a voluntary or mandatory basis. In fact, Republican Senator Chuck Grassley of Iowa recently called for similar scrutiny of nonprofits.

The Senate Finance Committee has issued at least one draft paper calling for stronger nonprofit governance, and it has publicly debated several different proposals. Efforts to extend provisions of SOX to nonprofits met with con-cern, however, because of the additional costs it would impose on smaller nonprofits.

Many scandal-skittish states have proposed or passed regulations that extend provisions of SOX (or SOX-like provisions) to nonprofit organizations. For instance, the California Nonprofit Integrity Act of 2004 requires charities with gross revenues of $2 million or more to have an audit committee.

Specific SOX provisions for nonprofits

Although most provisions of SOX apply only to public companies, two provisions are also mandatory for nonprofits. These provisions prohibit the following:

- ✔ Retaliation against whistle-blowers who inform the appropriate people of any misconduct that happens within the company
- ✔ The destruction, alteration, or concealment of certain documents, or the impediment of investigations

Beyond these requirements, many nonprofits are voluntarily considering adopting the practices set forth in the rest of SOX as good business practice. In other words, it's unlikely that a nonprofit of any size would knowingly risk being sued without having certain safeguards in place. Many SOX-sensitive attorneys and accountants working for nonprofits recommend that every nonprofit adopt most, if not all, of the following SOX-type standards:

- ✔ **Audit committees:** Your nonprofit should create an audit committee, and it should separate the function of that committee from the finance committee. As in the private sector, your nonprofit's audit committee needs to be composed of board members who aren't compensated for serving on the committee and who don't have a financial interest or other conflict of interest with any company or person doing business with your nonprofit. (Audit committees are discussed in more detail in Chapter 10.)

✔ **Outside consultants for your audit committee:** SOX allows audit committees to hire outside consultants, and it requires the audit committee's company to pay for the consulting services. Because most nonprofit organizations have volunteer board members who may or may not be trained in business and accounting principles, it's especially important that independent, outside consultants or other advisors be available to work with the audit committee.

✔ **Procedures for adopting the auditor's report:** The nonprofit audit committee needs to meet with the outside audit firm and then recommend to the full board of directors whether the audit report should be approved or modified. The full board then formally accepts or rejects the committee's report.

✔ **Auditor independence:** SOX contains a number of requirements to ensure the independence of outside auditors. For example, SOX requires that audit firms rotate the lead partner every five years.

✔ **Bans on prohibited services:** SOX prohibits the audit firm from providing certain nonaudit services. If a nonprofit is required to have audited financial statements, it's well-advised to follow this requirement on a voluntary basis. Prohibited services include bookkeeping, financial information systems, and other services (see Chapter 5 for a more complete list).

Consistent with the standards in SOX, a nonprofit's audit committee may, however, preapprove certain types of nonaudit services outside of these categories, such as tax preparation. Additionally, auditors may be allowed to prepare Form 990 or 990-PF (for private foundations) if such services are preapproved. (These forms are discussed in more detail in Chapter 7.)

✔ **CEO/CFO certification:** Like their counterparts in the private sector, nonprofits should consider having CEOs and CFOs certify both the appropriateness of financial statements and the officers' fair presentations of the financial conditions and operations of their companies.

What most nonprofits are actually doing

In 2005, several years after the passage of SOX, the prestigious Urban Institute conducted an extensive survey (called the *National Survey of Nonprofit Governance*) to determine what nonprofits across the nation are doing with respect to many of the issues relevant to Sarbanes-Oxley. This section explores the findings of this important survey.

Forming audit committees

SOX requires for-profit, publicly traded corporations to form independent *audit committees,* which are made up of board members. (The audit committee is responsible for appointing, compensating, and overseeing the auditors, and for acting as an interface between management and the audit firm. The audit committee report, whether it has at least one financial expert, can't have employees or other individuals who are paid by the organization for professional services as members. (Check out Chapter 7 for more on audit committees.)

The Urban Institute survey found that many nonprofits in the United States (41 percent) have audit committees, and those who don't appear to be considering forming them. The survey found that most organizations (54 percent) had formed their committees after or in direct response to the passage of SOX in 2002.

The survey also asked smaller organizations that don't currently have audit committees how difficult it would be for them to form one. The majority (51 percent) of these nonprofits said that it would be either somewhat or very difficult for them to comply with a law requiring them to establish such a committee.

Of the 19 percent that said it would be very difficult to form a committee, the study found that most of them were smaller organizations. This group included mostly nonprofits with expenses of under $100,000.

Finding altruistic financial experts

SOX requires public companies to disclose whether they have at least one *financial expert* on their audit committees. A financial expert is generally someone adept at reading financial information, such as a CPA, CEO, or financial professional. Because many for-profit organizations have their own recruitment issues, it isn't surprising that 25 percent of the organizations surveyed said it would be very difficult to recruit a financial expert to serve on their audit committees. (This isn't really a surprise considering that many nonprofits don't pay board members to serve, whether they're experts or not.) Thirty-five percent of smaller organizations surveyed found the expert search very difficult.

Trying to keep their auditors independent

The reason that SOX places so much emphasis on making auditors independent from the firms that they audit is to ensure that they're objective. SOX also requires organizations to rotate their audit firms and/or lead partners every five years. Additionally, audit firms are generally prohibited from providing the organizations with other non-audit services.

The Urban Institute survey found that among those nonprofits that that did have an audit, the great majority also had the same audit firm prepare their IRS Form 990. But far fewer (20 percent) had used the same firm for other services.

More than half of the nonprofits surveyed had used the same audit firm for five years or more, and 58 percent had also used the same lead partner.

Most of the organizations (62 percent) that didn't have an independent audit said that it would be somewhat or very difficult to comply with a law requiring them to have one. Most of these organizations were the smallest organizations.

Unlike publicly traded companies, most nonprofits aren't required to have an audit — but most of them do it anyway. Sixty-seven percent of the nonprofits in the Urban Institute survey reported that they had received an audit within the previous two years. Of the larger nonprofits (those with expenses of over $500,000), more than 91 percent reported having an audit within the previous two years.

The Urban Institute survey found that many of the smaller nonprofits that didn't have their financial statements compiled or reviewed by an outside certified professional accountant opted to have them compiled or reviewed by outside accounting firms, which is a less costly option.

Getting management to sign the 990s

Under SOX, the chief executive and financial officers are responsible for certifying that the organization's financial statements were prepared using certain procedures that ensure their accuracy. SOX includes penalties for those who knowingly and intentionally violate this provision. Although this provision isn't mandatory for nonprofits, scandal-sensitive organizations should consider voluntarily complying.

According to the Urban Institute survey, the majority of nonprofits required their CEOs to sign their organization's Form 990s. However, the percentage was considerably lower (29 percent) among the very smallest nonprofits.

Reporting on internal control

SOX requires public companies to make disclosures regarding certain aspects of their finances and the internal control they exercise to make sure that the information on their financial statements is accurate.

Companies must also promptly disclose material (significant) changes in their operations and finances. Among nonprofits that conducted audits, most (76 percent) reported that they make changes publicly available.

Avoiding conflicts of interest

The Sarbanes-Oxley Act generally prohibits publicly traded companies from making loans to their directors or executives. Similarly, the Urban Institute survey found that it's rare for nonprofits to make loans to board members.

Fifty percent of nonprofits in the Urban Institute study had a conflict of interest policy for board members. Of the largest organizations, 95 percent reported having a policy, but only 23 percent of the smallest organizations reported having one.

Adopting a code of ethics

SOX requires companies to disclose whether they have adopted a code of ethics for officers (and if they haven't, they must explain why). Companies also have to report whether they've amended or waived any of the provisions of their codes of ethics.

Protecting whistle-blowers

The whistle-blower provision of SOX is one of two provisions of the Act that applies to *all* organizations, including nonprofits (see the following section to find out the other SOX provision that applies to nonprofits). SOX makes it a federal crime for any entity to retaliate against employees who report information about fraud or suspected financial misconduct within the organization.

The Urban Institute study found that among nonprofits with at least one employee, 67 percent had a formal process for staff to report complaints without fear of retaliation.

Stopping the shredders

Another provision of SOX that applies to *all* organizations (including nonprofits) makes it a federal crime to alter or destroy documents in order to prevent their use in an official proceeding (see the previous section "Protecting whistle-blowers" to find out the other SOX provision that applies to nonprofits). SOX doesn't specifically require organizations to have a written document-retention policy, but most organizations implement such policies as a precaution and to demonstrate a commitment to complying with SOX.

Determining the impact of required SOX provisions on nonprofits

What would be the potential impact of extending Sarbanes-Oxley provisions to nonprofit organizations? The Urban Institute study indicates that the smallest nonprofits would be impacted the most heavily (see the previous section "What most nonprofits are actually doing" for details on this study). According to the study, most smaller organizations didn't have one or more of the recommended SOX-like structures in place, and many reported that it would be very difficult to comply.

So, in the end, adopting mandatory SOX-like standards could mean that forming, staffing, and running small nonprofit organizations would be much more difficult.

Implementing Standards Logically: A Balanced Approach

Most nonprofit organizations have the perpetual problem of too few dollars chasing too many worthy causes. This means that, especially for smaller organizations, if they spend more money to voluntarily comply with SOX, they'll have less money to carry out their programs and missions.

Nonprofits aren't under a specific deadline to comply with SOX standards like the for-profit corporations are. In fact, for-profit corporations reported making many costly mistakes as a result of rushing to comply with deadlines. These mistakes resulted in bureaucratic structures, unnecessary projects, and redundant costs.

So, unlike their for-profit counterparts, nonprofits can (and should) strive to carefully and efficiently revamp governance structures and migrate steadily and effectively toward full compliance. In other words, don't rush it.

Specifically, nonprofits should:

- ✔ **Understand what SOX does and doesn't require.** Many for-profit companies wasted millions of dollars on useless data security programs, redundant testing, and misguided training programs, only to realize that these initiatives were extraneous to the actual legal requirements of SOX.

- ✔ **Focus on the rationale of SOX for each provision that's not mandatory.** In other words, SOX is concerned with the integrity of financial reporting, not whether data is processed efficiently or with unrelated internal procedures.

- ✔ **Adopt a logical timeline for compliance.** Don't rush to artificial deadlines. Instead, set priorities and demonstrate a pattern of continuing sustainable compliance.

- ✔ **Balance program goals with the goals of complying with SOX.** Risks within the organization should be objectively assessed by the board, and when risks are low in specific areas, your nonprofit may not need to divert program costs for immediate compliance projects.

How SOX-Savvy Is Your Nonprofit?

The Sarbanes-Oxley Act (SOX) is becoming a model for nonprofit governance. SOX provides nonprofit organizations with a template that they can use voluntarily for their own organizations so they don't have to develop structures from scratch as they grapple with governance issues.

Adopting SOX standards can ratchet up credibility with institutional and corporate donors because SOX structures and procedures are easily recognizable by decision-makers and stakeholders in the private sector. This familiarity inspires trust. However, the costs and timing of voluntary compliance must be carefully balanced against other program funding considerations.

Implementing SOX in the nonprofit arena is different than in the private sector. Nonprofits may need to adopt SOX standards incrementally, taking into account the limited resources of their organizations and the diverse nature of their boards and missions.

This brief quiz tests your knowledge about key provisions of SOX, as they may practically apply to nonprofit organizations, and it offers tips as to how your organization can get started in setting realistic compliance goals:

1. **True or False: Nonprofits should strive to comply with SOX on a timeline that corresponds roughly to the deadlines imposed on the private sector.**

   Answer: False

   SOX compliance for nonprofits is currently voluntary; nonprofits don't have to operate at a frenetic pace to implement reforms under an arbitrary deadline as is the case in the private sector. Rather, they can and should implement initiatives at a practical pace, over a time period that makes fiscal sense for their particular organizations.

   For most nonprofits, SOX compliance is an ongoing process, divided into identifiable projects and goals consistent with the staffing, training, and other available resources of the organization. Nonprofits should migrate sensibly toward the SOX model rather than viewing voluntary compliance as an all-or-nothing proposition.

2. **True or False: SOX restricts who can sit on the board of directors, increases directors' liability, and makes it more difficult to find and keep good board members.**

   Answer: False

SOX establishes only two standards as to who should sit on a board of directors. A majority of board members must be independent and the board must have at least one financial expert who's familiar with financial statements and accounting principles to serve on its audit committee. Generally, board members meet the independence requirement if they aren't receiving compensation from the organization other than for serving in their capacity as board members.

There's no evidence that SOX increases liability for the board of directors. To the contrary, it may have the opposite effect by placing greater responsibility for internal control on management.

The formation of board committees, such as the audit committee mandated by SOX, may also have the effect of limiting the liability of individual board members. Committee structures may limit responsibility for decisions to the board members directly involved in making them, rather than attributing actions to all board members regardless of whether they were involved or participated.

3. **True or False: SOX doesn't require a board to establish any committees other than an audit committee.**

   Answer: True.

   SOX doesn't require a board of directors to establish any committee other than an audit committee. However, stock exchanges, such as the NYSE or NASDAQ do require companies that list their stocks with them to have special *nominating committees* for nominating directors and *governance committees* for determining corporate governance policies. Other private sector companies have also voluntarily chosen to form *compensation committees* to determine executive compensation and *disclosure committees* to regulate public disclosures.

   Nonprofits should establish and adopt committee structures to reflect their unique missions in the community. For example, if a nonprofit isn't required to have its financial statements audited, it may decide to establish an *accounting policy committee* instead of an audit committee.

   Committee structures can be used to define responsibility and allocate work fairly and appropriately among board members with varying skills. In most organizations, it simply isn't possible to have all board members involved in every project.

4. **True or False: Under SOX, chief financial officers (CFOs) and chief executive officers (CEOs) must certify that they have personally tested all internal controls, and they're responsible for any fraud or error that occurs within the organization.**

   Answer: False

SOX requires CEOs and CFOs to personally certify that certain standards were met with respect to financial statements that their companies file with the SEC; it doesn't make them personally liable for fraud, mismanagement, or error within the organization.

Specifically, CEOs and CFOs must certify that

- They're responsible for internal control.

- The controls are designed to ensure that material financial information is made known.

- The internal controls conform to Generally Accepted Accounting Principles, or GAAP.

- They've evaluated the effectiveness of internal control and their conclusions as to its effectiveness.

- They've indicated any changes in internal control during the reporting period that could affect the financial statements.

The CEO and CFO must believe that all of the above certifications are true, and that they've performed the required evaluations. However, recent litigation indicates that management isn't responsible for acts committed by others within the organization to subvert internal controls without management's knowledge.

5. **True or False: A nonprofit organization may need to hire more than one accounting firm to perform services for it in order to comply with SOX.**

   Answer: True.

   SOX prohibits an accounting firm that performs an audit from providing other accounting or consulting services. The reason for this is that it's unethical for audit firms to help generate the financial information that's being audited.

   SOX strictly prohibits independent auditors from performing management, human resource, or investment advisor functions. Independent auditors are also prohibited from performing bookkeeping services or helping design financial information systems. They aren't allowed to provide appraisal or actuarial services either. The audit firm can, however, provide tax advice to the organization or help prepare the IRS Form 990 with prior board approval.

6. **Identify which of the following are benefits of applying appropriate SOX internal control standards to nonprofits:**

   a. Financial institutions and lenders may rely on the organization's internal control and governance systems in streamlining their own process.

b. Insurance companies may offer lower premiums.

c. It may be easier to attract qualified board members who are wary of serving on boards of organizations that lack adequate controls.

d. Internal controls inspire the confidence of donors and decision-makers in the private sector.

e. The organization may be more attractive as a candidate to participate in joint ventures and fundraising opportunities where public trust and adequate internal control are selection criteria.

f. All of the above

Answer: f. All of the above.

It's a reality that nearly all nonprofits must compete for program dollars and federal grants in some fashion. Transparency in governance and internal control inspires confidence among corporate and government donors, placing the organization at a competitive advantage. This increased transparency also enables organizations to compete more effectively for lower interest rates and insurance premiums.

7. **True or False: Cash-strapped organizations can't begin to implement SOX standards without taking needed resources away from current programs.**

Answer: False.

Organizations that don't feel they can achieve total compliance within a single fiscal year or reporting period should establish a plan to implement SOX governance structures and internal control procedures more gradually. Organizations should strive to show continuing progress and effort in this area, and to consider SOX standards in developing future policies.

Chapter 14

Some Sticky Accounting Issues That All Nonprofits Face

In This Chapter

▶ Determining when tax-exempt organizations make taxable income

▶ Identifying the true value of donations

▶ Doling out deductions and making sure donors don't overvalue contributions

▶ Understanding the requirements of the Pension Protection Act

There's no getting around the fact that nonprofit organizations need to be managed as businesses. For example, like for-profit businesses, nonprofits have to report income, and they have to file tax returns. And just as corporations and other businesses engage in tax planning, nonprofits must make certain decisions based on tax considerations. A nonprofit organization, for instance, may decide whether to engage in a particular activity based on whether income from those activities is deemed exempt or nonexempt.

This chapter looks at two areas of accounting that are unique to nonprofits: unrelated business income, and charitable contributions and allowable deductions. I also explain how you can recognize when your organization is engaging in taxable transactions and activities, and how to plan accordingly.

"Tax Exempt" Doesn't Mean "Tax Free"

Many times, with many different people, the term *nonprofit* conjures up images of an organization that pays no taxes whatsoever. For instance, these people think "If an organization is a nonprofit, it must not make a profit, right?" Well, not always. The fact that an organization is tax exempt doesn't necessarily mean that it has no tax liability. Some of a nonprofit organization's income will be subject to tax, and some of it may be exempt, depending on how the income is legally characterized.

So, how do you know which funds your nonprofit must pay taxes on and which are exempt? It's not easy, but the IRS tries to make it simpler by using two major distinctions to identify which income is subject to tax and which you can keep tax free. Here are the two distinctions:

- ✔ **Earned versus unearned income:** The IRS makes a distinction between money people donate to an organization, and income that an organization earns by selling its products and services.

- ✔ **Related versus unrelated business income:** After a distinction is made between earned and unearned income, the IRS makes a further distinction between income that's earned from activities and products related to the organization's tax-exempt purpose, and profit-making activities that bear no relationship to the organization's purpose for being.

Confused? Who wouldn't be? But, never fear. The following sections explain the reasons for these complicated tax distinctions, and tell you what they mean in practical terms for your organization.

Distinguishing between earned and unearned income

As far as an IRS agent is concerned, nonprofit income comes in two flavors: *unearned* and *earned*.

Unearned income is usually exempt from taxes, whereas earned income is taxed just like it would be for a for-profit organization involved in a business venture.

Unearned income is received from donations, grants, and other sources to support the organization in its operation and mission. Usually, the donors of unearned income expect nothing in return for their grants or donations, other than having the nonprofit apply the donated funds to its charitable mission.

In contrast, earned income is the income an organization gets for products and services sold to the public by the nonprofit organization. When an organization receives this type of income, the person or entity from which the income is received expects to receive something of value in return. An example of earned income might be a fee for a summer camp for underprivileged kids. Or, another example might be the selling of adaptive devices to disabled individuals (for organizations who benefit the groups being serviced).

Understanding unrelated business income

When a nonprofit organization derives income from a trade or business that's "regularly carried on" and isn't "substantially related" to the performance by the nonprofit to its exempt purpose or function, that income may likely be classified by the Internal Revenue Service (IRS) as *unrelated business income*. (Check out the section "Testing for unrelated income" for an explanation on how the IRS determines what's considered unrelated business income.)

Nonprofits that have $1,000 or more in unrelated business taxable income must file IRS Form 990-T and pay taxes on this type of income. This form is discussed in more detail in Chapter 7.

You may be asking yourself the question "Why can't the government just leave these nice nonprofit organizations alone?" The simple answer is this: When nonprofits start competing with for-profit organizations, people get a sour view that the exempt organization may not be acting to fulfill its mission or accomplish its tax-exempt purpose, but might instead be using its exemption to shelter income that would otherwise be taxable.

It isn't fair then, from a fiscal policy standpoint, to give nonprofits a free tax ride on their unrelated business income so they can compete with the for-profit businesses. The nonexempt vendor would suffer unfair competition — and that's if it could stay in business at all.

For example, consider this commercially unfair example: Suppose your local fast-food vendor is charging sales tax and selling food with enough of a margin to cover its own 34-percent income taxes. Now imagine what would happen if a local church put up a tax-exempt fast-food stand offering the same menu at a 34-percent discount reflecting its lower (nontaxable) operating costs. Doesn't sound too fair, does it? This is one reason that the IRS takes a hard look at the relationship of a nonprofit organization's income relative to its tax-exempt purpose.

Testing for unrelated income

The IRS doesn't have specific rules to deal with every bake sale, charity auction, and fundraiser that nonprofits can concoct. Instead, IRS regulations specify three general tests. Income is considered unrelated to an organization's purpose if it meets *all* of the following:

> ✔ **It's trade- or business-related:** To pass this test, income must come from a trade or business performed by the nonprofit or from selling goods and services similar to those sold by for-profit entities.

✔ **It's regularly carried on:** The business activity that generates the income must be "regularly carried on." In plain English, this means that the activity has a frequency and continuity comparable to commercial activities of for-profit organizations.

For example, if a hospital operates a sandwich stand for one week per year at a county fair, that activity wouldn't be considered "regularly carried on." However, if that same hospital operated a year-round sandwich stand on the corner of the busiest intersection in town, this would be considered a business activity that was regularly carried on.

✔ **It has no substantial relationship to the exempt purpose:** Generally speaking, an activity has no substantial relationship to furthering the exempt purpose of a nonprofit organization if it's unrelated to the organization's mission. (You can find out more about missions in Chapter 4.)

So, if the hospital from the example in the previous bullet can't show how selling sandwiches at its year-round sandwich stand furthers its exempt purpose, it's likely to meet this third test as well.

As the three tests above indicate, a trade or business is related to an organization's exempt purpose only when it has a significant relationship to achieving the exempt purpose of the organization. This also means that if an activity is conducted on a scale larger than is reasonably necessary to perform an exempt purpose, you may come across some tax consequences. So, in other words, if the activity doesn't contribute solely to the accomplishment of the exempt purpose, the part of the activity that's unnecessary would be considered unrelated trade or business.

For example, income generated from a theatre in a museum that shows educational films while the museum is open to the public wouldn't be considered unrelated business income. However, if the museum shows commercially released films and operates the theatre as a motion picture theatre that's open to the public when the museum is closed, that activity would be considered unrelated trade or business.

Making exceptions

With every rule comes plenty of exceptions — and the IRS follows suit with its unrelated income laws. It excludes, for instance, certain trade or business activities from the definition of unrelated trade or business that may otherwise fall into this trap. For example, a trade or business in which substantially all of the work is performed without compensation by a volunteer workforce isn't considered an unrelated trade or business.

Checking out IRS Publication 598 for more examples of unrelated income

Determining unrelated business income isn't always easy or intuitive. That's why the Internal Revenue Service (IRS) offers a special publication, Publication 598, titled *Tax on Unrelated Business Income of Exempt Organizations,* which gives various examples of unrelated business income.

One example of unrelated business income provided by the IRS focuses on museum greeting card sales. In this example, an art museum that exhibits modern art also sells greeting cards that display printed reproductions of selected works from other art collections. Each card is imprinted with the name of the artist, the title or subject matter of the work, the date or period of its creation (if known), and the museum's name. The cards contain appropriate greetings and are personalized on request.

The organization sells the cards in the shop that it operates within the museum and sells them at quantity discounts to retail stores. It also sells the cards by mail order through a catalog that's advertised in magazines and other publications throughout the year. As a result, a large number of cards are sold at a significant profit.

The museum is exempt as an educational organization on the basis of its ownership, maintenance, and exhibition for public viewing of works of art. Accordingly, the IRS takes the position that the sale of greeting cards with printed reproductions of art works contributes to the museum's exempt educational purposes by enhancing public awareness, interest, and appreciation of art. The IRS believes that the cards may encourage more people to visit the museum itself to share in educational programs. The fact that the cards are promoted and sold in a commercial manner at a profit and in competition with commercial greeting card publishers doesn't alter the fact that the activity is related to the museum's exempt purpose. Therefore, according to this IRS-provided example, these sales activities are *not* unrelated income.

Also, certain income is excluded when tallying up what constitutes unrelated business income. For example, under the law, royalties, rents, gains, and losses from the sale of property, dividends, interest, and investment income are all excluded from the income that counts toward unrelated business taxable income.

Other activities that are specifically excluded from the definition of unrelated trade or business include business activities that are carried out for the convenience of members. This exclusion encompasses any trade or business carried on by an organization primarily for the convenience of its members, students, patients, officers, or employees. An example of this type of exclusion is a school cafeteria. Another exemption would be the selling of donated merchandise, which means that any trade or business that sells merchandise received as a contribution or gift would also be excluded. Thrift shop operations of exempt organizations, such as Goodwill Stores, would be exempt under this exclusion.

The controversy over the NCAA's tax-exempt status and unrelated business income

In November 2006, Fox News reported that Myles Brand, the president of the National Collegiate Athletic Association (NCAA), wrote a 25-page letter to Congress defending the organization's tax-exempt status. He argued that the organization's primary mission is education.

The NCAA often comes under attack because of the enormous amount of revenue it generates and the exorbitant salaries it pays coaches. In 1998, 82 percent of the organization's $220-million budget came from television revenues. And the coach salaries are called into question because of pay to coaches like Mike Kryzewski, who's coach of the men's basketball program at Duke. He has a lifetime contract with Duke that pays a salary of $800,000 per year, but when other benefits and allowances are added in, his earnings average about $1.5 million. It's reported that he also earns another $1.5 million from his endorsements for Nike. While Kryzewski is one of the higher paid coaches, others also have no problem raking in the cash. Taxpayers periodically question why the NCAA continues to keep its tax-exempt status, and

why the federal government subsidizes college athletics when it seems that the money helps pay for ever-increasing coaching salaries, some of which reach seven-figures.

In his letter to Congress, Brand argued that pay for coaches is on par with other highly recruited faculty members and said that the NCAA shouldn't be punished merely because television networks will pay millions (or even billions) of dollars to televise games. Brand wrote "If the educational purpose of college basketball could be preserved only by denying the right to telecast the events, students, university faculty and staff, alumni, the institutions of higher education themselves, and even the American taxpayer would ultimately lose."

So, given the popularity of college athletics, it's unlikely that the NCAA will lose its tax-exempt status, and the issue of whether the income it generates is actually unrelated business income will continue to be a sacred cow that Congress will begrudgingly ignore.

Reporting unrelated business income

How does the IRS know about your organization's unrelated business income? The answer is that it requires your organization to self-report. In other words, the IRS expects that you'll follow the honor system. If you fail to report, or if you underreport your income, you may face penalties for negligence, substantial understatement of tax, and fraud. (The IRS can find out about your negligence because it conducts audits of nonprofit organizations as discussed in Chapter 15.)

Nonprofits must report unrelated business income on IRS Form 990-T, which is titled *Exempt Organization Business Income Tax Return*. All exempt organizations that have *gross income* (gross receipts minus the cost of goods sold) from an unrelated trade or business of $1,000 or more must file this form. (This requirement is discussed in more detail in Chapter 14.)

Calculating the tax due for unrelated business income

The tax rate for unrelated business income varies depending on the type of entity that's reporting it. The IRS provides a separate method for taxing the unrelated business income of trusts, and a separate method for taxing the unrelated business income of nonprofit corporations. Generally, both methods use a graduated rate system that caps at a certain income level, after which a flat rate of tax applies. Both methods are also *progressive,* meaning that as the amount of income increases, so does the rate of tax — until, of course, the top tax rate is reached. The top rate is then used as a flat rate of tax on all income over the amount needed to reach the top rate.

With the exception of certain retirement accounts and educational accounts, you must file Form 990-T by the 15th day of the 5th month after the end of the tax year for your organization. An automatic six-month extension of time is available for corporations, and a three-month automatic extension is available for trusts. Form 990-T is filed with the Internal Revenue Service Center in Ogden, Utah. IRS Form 990-T and detailed instructions for completing the form are available at `www.irs.gov/charities/index.html` under the "Forms and publications" link.

Valuing Donations Realistically

Even if your nonprofit avoids competing with for-profit businesses, it may still have some explaining to do to the IRS regarding your unearned income. (See the section "Distinguishing between earned and unearned income" for a quick review of what unearned income is.) Even though unearned income is generally exempt from taxation, this type of income has its own set of issues when it comes to valuing contributions from donors.

In theory, a donor is responsible for placing a value on non-cash contributions (a building, a piece of land, or a rare work of art). But, a nonprofit organization also has to estimate the value, because a nonprofit that accepts donations with inflated values assigned to them risks losing its exempt status. Your organization also needs to know how much the donated property is worth so that it can reflect the value accurately in its own financial statements and know the true value of its asset portfolio. Why? Because overvalued assets can cost your organization its credibility.

Here's an example: In 2003, the Wyobraska Wildlife Museum in Gering, Nebraska, was a small facility far from any large population area. This museum held more than 800 big game trophies and exotic animals, which were simply tossed into an old railroad car and three other storage facilities (they obviously were worth a lot if they got that kind of treatment!). The museum reported that its collection was valued at over $4.2 million. This value had been assigned because it was the value that the donors placed on the taxidermy carcasses it donated — and the museum blindly accepted the donor values.

After an April 14, 2005, article in the *Washington Post* titled "Big Game Hunting Brings Big Tax Breaks" exposed the practice of wealthy hunters taking inflated tax deductions from the donation of their trophy kills to pseudomuseums, the IRS cracked down. Now taxidermy deductions are limited to the cost of preparing, stuffing, or mounting the animal. Deductions for travel and costs relating to the hunting and killing of the animal are no longer allowed.

The implications of incorrectly valuing your organization's donations can be damaging, so in this section, I explain how you can avoid problems.

Figuring out if your donors are reporting realistic values

Figuring out how much a non-cash donation is worth can be a complex process for even the most adept nonprofit organization.

The general rule is that received property is valued at its *fair market value* as of the date of the contribution. Fair market value is the price for which that property would sell between a willing buyer and a willing seller, with neither being required to act and both having reasonable knowledge of the relevant facts.

Determining the value of donated property would be simple if a fixed formula could be used. Unfortunately, it isn't that easy. There's no single formula that always applies in determining a property's value. Because formulas don't lend themselves to valuing property (at least as far as the IRS is concerned), donors are advised to use other more objective methods, including the cost or selling price of the item, the sales of comparable properties, the replacement costs, and the opinion of experts.

Using cost or selling price to establish value

If the donor bought the property recently, taking a look at the purchase price can be a good starting point. In fact, the purchase price of the property may be the best indicator of fair market value if the buyer and seller weren't compelled to enter into a transaction and the market didn't change between the date of the purchase and the valuation.

The cost of the property, or its actual selling price, may be relevant if the following factors are met:

- The purchase or sale occurred close to the time that the valuation date is made.
- The purchase and sale is at an arm's length offer.
- The buyer and seller both know all the relevant facts.

An *arm's length offer* refers to an offer from a willing buyer to a willing seller where neither party is required to purchase. For example, items obtained at a liquidation or fire sale aren't considered to be at arm's length, because the seller may not be so willing to unload property at the price it's being sold for, but generally in that situation, the seller has no choice in the matter.

Also, if the seller places restrictions or limitations on the property being sold, that value of the property will be affected. For example, if a parcel of land is sold but the seller retains an easement to cross over the land to access another parcel of land, the buyer wouldn't be able to build anything that might obstruct the path to the other piece of land. In this case, the value of the land would be affected.

A factor that might affect the cost or selling price would be unusual market conditions. These are conditions that may depress the usual prices or make them skyrocket. Even though the sales price of property at an arm's length transaction in an open market is generally the best indicator of fair market value, sales that occur in a market that's artificially supported or stimulated may not offer a true representation of value. That's why comparable sales data needs to be taken from sales at an arm's length transaction in an open market in order to be valid.

If cost or selling price is going to be used for valuing a deduction, ask the following questions:

- Do the terms of the sale limit what can be done with the property?
- Was the arm's length offer to buy the property close to the valuation date?
- Was the purchase or sale of the property reasonably close to the date of contribution?

Comparing sales of similar property

If your organization is going to compare sales of similar property to ensure that your donors are reporting realistic values, the trustworthiness of valuation (from the IRS' standpoint) depends on the degree of similarity between the properties you're comparing.

The two properties must be similar in terms of:

- ✔ **The timing of the sale:** Both sales must have taken place in the relevant time period.

- ✔ **The circumstances of the sale:** The price paid in both sales must be related solely to the value that the buyer and seller feel the property is worth, and not to other factors, such as family relationship.

- ✔ **The conditions of the market in which the sale was made:** Temporary fluctuations in the market can be caused by all sorts of events. So, the two properties being compared should both have been sold during times when market conditions were relatively stable.

This type of valuation method is particularly suited for real estate, but it can also be applied to other types of sales as well. The most important aspect of this form of valuation is the degree of similarity of between the comparable property and the donated property, which must be close enough so that the selling price would be considered relevant by reasonably well-informed buyers and sellers.

Consider the following example offered by the IRS: You give a rare, old book to your former college. The book is a third edition and is in poor condition because of a missing back cover. You discover that there was a sale for $300, near the valuation date, of the first edition of the book that was in good condition. Although the contents are the same, the books are not at all similar because of the different editions and their physical condition. So, little consideration would be given to the selling price of the $300 property by knowledgeable buyers or sellers.

So, if your organization decides to use the comparable sales data method, be sure to consider the following questions:

- ✔ How similar is the comparable property to the donated property? Was the sale at arm's length?

- ✔ What was the condition of the market at the time of the sale?

- ✔ How close is the date of the sale to the valuation date?

Considering replacement cost as a basis for value

Another way of valuing property may be to use its replacement cost. Under this method, the cost of buying, building, or manufacturing property that's similar to the donated item might be considered when establishing its fair market value.

The use of replacement cost as a valuation method has serious limitations, because often the cost to replace a donated item on the valuation date bears no relationship to its fair market value. Also, if the supply of the donated item is more or less than the actual demand for it, the replacement cost becomes less important.

When determining the replacement cost of donated property, first find the estimated replacement cost of the item as if it's new, and then subtract depreciation, wear and tear, and obsolescence. The result is the fair market value. But, remember that you need to be able to show the relationship between the depreciated property and the fair market value, as well as how the estimated replacement cost of the item as if new was determined.

If the donor intends to use replacement cost as a valuation method, ask the following questions:

- ✔ What would it cost to replace the property that's being donated?
- ✔ What's the relationship between the fair market value and the replacement cost?
- ✔ Is the demand for the donated property more or less than the supply of it?

Playing it safe with an appraisal expert opinion

Want to take the easy way out and simply have someone tell you how much a donation is worth? Get an appraisal! If your organization decides to go this route, you need to find an expert. But remember that you have to be picky when choosing an expert. For example, if your Uncle Louie gives you an ashtray hat and says "It's one of a kind and worth a hundred thousand dollars," you can bet that his "expertise" definitely won't cut it. However, if a certified appraiser who deals in (and collects) rare ashtray hats gives you an opinion that this particular hat is extremely rare and would fetch at least $5 on the open market, that's probably a more reliable source and of more use in establishing the value of your cherished item.

It would be nice if this was a foolproof way of establishing value, but it isn't. So, whatever you do, don't consider this method an insurance policy against the IRS second-guessing the value a donor has assigned to a piece of property.

When a nonprofit should get a qualified appraisal

A *qualified appraisal* is one that's made not earlier than 60 days prior to the date of the appraised party's contribution, that doesn't involve an appraisal fee based on a percentage of the appraised value of the property, that includes certain information required by the IRS (like the property's description, its physical condition, the qualification of the appraisal, and other relevant information), and that's prepared and signed by a qualified appraiser.

Appraisals are generally required if the deduction being claimed for donated property is more than $5,000 and needs to be reported using IRS Form 8283, which is filed with the donor's individual income tax return. (You can take a look at IRS Form 8283 in Appendix A.) So, for example, if you give a number of rare books to different charities and the total amount for your planned deduction exceeds $5,000, you need to obtain a qualified appraisal. Unfortunately, the cost of obtaining the appraisal isn't allowable as part of the charitable deduction. However, appraisal fees may qualify for a miscellaneous deduction subject to the 2-percent limit as an itemized deduction on the donor's individual income tax return.

Appraisals aren't required for certain types of property, including the following:

- ✔ Nonpublicly traded stock of $10,000 or less
- ✔ A vehicle (for example, a car, boat, or airplane) donated after December 31, 2004, if the deduction is limited to the gross proceeds from the vehicle's sale
- ✔ Qualified intellectual property (for example, a patent) donated after June 3, 2004
- ✔ Certain publicly traded securities (for example, stocks and bonds) that are listed on an exchange
- ✔ Any donation, made after June 3, 2004, of stock in trade, inventory, or property held primarily for sale to customers in the ordinary course of business
- ✔ A donation made by a corporation before June 4, 2004

If you claim a deduction of more than $500,000 for property donated after June 3, 2004, you must attach a qualified appraisal to your return — unless the deduction was for a contribution of cash, inventory, publicly traded stock, or intellectual property.

An appraiser's opinion is only as good as the facts on which it's based. Without good facts, it's simply a guess. And just because an appraiser is "certified" by being a member of a professional appraiser's organization doesn't automatically establish his or her level of competency, or vice versa. In any event, it's important to remember that an appraiser's opinion isn't binding on the IRS.

Predicting the unpredictable

Plenty of problems can arise when valuing property for charitable donation purposes, and your organization may find itself in the middle of a controversy.

But, by knowing the common errors that can happen, you can better prepare yourself. Here are the two most common mistakes:

✓ **Relying too heavily on past events that may not fairly reflect the future earnings and fair market value of an item.** For example, suppose a donor contributes the rights of a successful patent to your organization. Prior to the donation, the patent went through many sales stages. For example, when the invention was first introduced to the marketplace, the patent initially generated high revenues. This was followed by a prolonged stable period of sales, and then a gradually declining period of sales leveled off to a steady sales history at the time of the donation. If an appraiser were to give too much weight to the high sales period in this example, the valuation would lack integrity. In this instance, more weight should likely be given to the current sales figures in determining value.

✓ **Placing a value on property in anticipation of future events that have yet to occur.** As far as the IRS is concerned, you can only base the value of an item on events that have already occurred, or those that could be reasonably expected at the time of the gift (for example, the maturity date of a savings bond).

Dealing with Donations, Deductions, and Donors Who Overvalue Their Items

People donate all kinds of things to charitable organizations. The value of this stuff may or may not be readily apparent. For example, if your donors write a check for a cash contribution each week to your church, the value of the donation is obviously straightforward. But, if your donors contribute a truckload of clothes, some unique artwork, or a stamp collection, the fair market value issue becomes a bit trickier — both for the donors and for your organization. But, this section can help you stay on the right track.

From the perspective of the donor, the deduction from giving the gift, grant, or donation may or may not be a significant consideration. For example, tax-exempt organizations that make gifts or grants to other tax-exempt organizations aren't concerned about receiving a deduction. On the other hand, individuals are routinely interested in whether a deduction is available — and if so, they want to know how much that deduction or contribution will be worth to them when it comes time to filing their tax returns.

Handing out deductions

Because the availability of a deduction may be a primary motivator for many of your donors, make sure your organization becomes familiar with the rules for doling out the deductions. Here are the basic rules according to category of donation:

- ✔ **Household goods:** The items in this group, which includes furniture, appliances, and linens, are generally worth much less than the price paid for them when they were new. This type of property may have little or no market value because of its worn condition. Or, it may have an increased value if it's an antique, in which case an appraisal will likely be required.

- ✔ **Used clothing and other personal items:** As with household goods, these personal items are usually worth much less than their original selling price, and the value of such items is generally set by the value that a purchaser may pay at a thrift store or consignment shop. If the clothing is something of an intrinsically higher value, such as a fur coat or an expensive gown, the donor may have to file the special IRS Form 8283 with his or her return to report the value and how he or she arrived at that value (see the sidebar "When a nonprofit should get a qualified appraisal" for more on this form).

- ✔ **Gems and jewelry:** These items almost always require an appraisal because of the unique and specialized nature of the items. Typically an appraisal would describe the type of gem, its condition, style, cut, and setting, and whether it's currently in fashion. Sentimental or personal value doesn't come into play here, but if the jewelry was owned by a famous person, such as Elvis or Marilyn Monroe, its value may increase.

- ✔ **Paintings, antiques, and art:** All I can say here is call your appraiser. If the art is valued at $20,000 or more, a complete copy of the signed appraisal must be attached to the donor's return, along with a photo of the donated property. If the art donated is valued at $50,000 or more, the donor can request a *statement of value* from the IRS for the item being claimed. A statement of value can be requested by sending in a copy of the qualified appraisal, a completed IRS Form 8283, and a user fee (the fee the IRS charges to review your materials) of $2,500 plus $250 for each item in excess of three.

- ✔ **Collections:** Common types of collections that may be donated include books, manuscripts, stamps, coins, autographs, sports memorabilia, guns, photos, records, and natural history items. Because of the varied nature of these items, the method of determining fair market value is likewise broad. Estimates of value through collector's publications or dealer price lists are useful, but an old-fashioned appraisal may also be used.

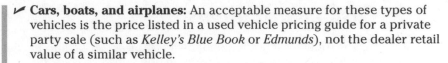

✔ **Cars, boats, and airplanes:** An acceptable measure for these types of vehicles is the price listed in a used vehicle pricing guide for a private party sale (such as *Kelley's Blue Book* or *Edmunds*), not the dealer retail value of a similar vehicle.

The deduction for donating a car, boat, or plane is generally limited to the gross proceeds of its sale by the receiving organization. If the value of the vehicle donated is more than $500, a *contemporaneous* written acknowledgement from the donee organization (that is the receiving organization) is required. An acknowledgment is considered contemporaneous if it is furnished within 30 days after the date of the sale or the contribution.

Just because an item is worth its weight in gold to your donor doesn't mean the IRS will see things the same way. If the donor overstates the value of an item on his or her tax return, penalties may apply. If your organization routinely allows donors to overstate valuations, it can lose its exempt status.

Penalizing donors who overvalue

Your organization may not be doing donors any favors by letting them overvalue their deductions. For instance, overzealous donors who deduct too much face a penalty of 20 percent of the taxes they should have paid. This hefty penalty applies if the value of the property that the donor claims on the return is 200 percent or more of the correct amount, *and* they underpaid their tax by more than $5,000 because of that overstatement.

Are your donors too rich to worry about a paltry 20-percent penalty? Have them try the IRS's 40-percent penalty on for size. This penalty applies where the value of the claimed deduction is more than 400 percent of the correct amount, and the donor underpaid his or her tax by more than $5,000 because of the overstatement.

The Requirements of the Pension Protection Act

President George W. Bush signed the Pension Protection Act (PPA) into law on August 17, 2006. Not only does the PPA protect pensions, it also creates a number of rules that apply to nonprofit organizations as well as to donors who make gifts and contributions to tax-exempt organizations.

This section gives a quick rundown of how these new rules may affect donors and the charities to which they generously contribute.

Cash contributions

For the well-meaning churchgoer who throws a $5 bill into the collection plate every Sunday and takes a deduction for those contributions on his or her tax return, prior law allowed the taxpayer to use their own written records, such as a log or diary of the contributions where the amount was less than $250.

The PPA has changed things dramatically. Under this new act, no matter how small the amount, no deduction is allowed for contributions made after August 17, 2006, unless the donor maintains a bank record (such as a cancelled check) or obtains a written communication from the donee organization showing the name of the charity and the date and amount of the contribution.

Clothing and household items

For contributions made after August 17, 2006, the PPA doesn't allow a deduction for a charitable contribution of clothing or household items unless they're in good used condition or better. Also, unless a qualified appraisal is attached to the taxpayer's return, no deduction is allowed for a single article of clothing or a household item that's valued at more than $500.

Appreciated personal property

Let's say that a donor is finally willing to part with that old painting hanging in his garage; the one that he bought at a rummage sale for $25 and that's now worth $25,000. The art-loving donor may deduct the fair market value of the $25,000 painting if he contributes it to an art museum that will display it. If, on the other hand, the donor contributes the painting to a museum who sells it within three years of the contribution, the deduction is limited to the painting's tax basis: $25.

Fractional interests

A *fractional interest* is one where a donor gives away the right to possess or use an object for a given period of time. For example, consider the donor who owns a valuable art collection, which is located at her summer home. When during the winter months she flees the cold and gives the local museum the right to display her art collection she's giving them a fractional interest in it.

This type of contribution was previously allowed, but under the PPA, they're no longer allowed unless both of the following conditions are met:

✔ Immediately before the contribution, all of the interests in the property are owned either by the donor or by the donor and the donee organization.

✔ The donor must contribute the remaining interest in the property to the same donee organization within 10 years of the initial donation or, if earlier, before the donor's death.

This is one of the PPA's most controversial and criticized provisions, because it significantly curtails the desirability of making fractional gifts of art work to museums.

Facade easements

A *facade easement* is an easement by a property owner who, for a price, agrees not to alter or change the outward appearance of his or her historic home. Facade easements can be contributed, and a charitable deduction can be taken for the contribution. The PPA limits the facade easement deduction to easements that:

✔ Preserve the building's *entire* exterior

✔ Prohibit any exterior change inconsistent with the structure's historic character

✔ Are substantiated by a qualified appraisal

Also, the PPA states that any deduction in excess of $10,000 must be accompanied by a $500 user fee to the IRS.

Chapter 15

Communicating Comfortably with the IRS

· ·

In This Chapter

▶ Becoming familiar with the Tax Exempt/Government Entities Division

▶ Responding to soft contacts

▶ Requesting information with a determination letter

▶ Knowing the best ways to survive an IRS audit

· ·

As the nation's taxing authority, the Internal Revenue Service (IRS) is both revered and feared by taxpayers of all types, including nonprofit organizations. Because nonprofits, like everyone else, are required to pay tax on some or all of their income, the need to communicate with the IRS arises occasionally for some organizations and constantly for others.

As you can imagine, most people are as comfortable receiving a letter from the IRS as they are sitting in a dentist's chair with a screaming drill headed for their mouths. Nonprofit organizations are no different than private citizens in this regard.

When questions about tax forms and returns arise, you or someone from your organization will need to answer them, which often involves meeting with IRS agents and answering IRS notices. This chapter can help you prepare for those fun meetings.

The Tax Exempt and Government Entities Division of the IRS

To say that the IRS is a complicated entity would be an understatement. I could write several books on what it does and how it works (and I still probably wouldn't be able to cover it all). Suffice it to say that the IRS collects taxes from five primary areas, including organizations that fall within the following groups:

- Small business/self-employed

- Wage and investment

- Large and mid-size businesses

- Criminal investigation

- Tax-exempt and government entities

Nonprofit organizations are generally concerned with, and will interact most prominently with, the Tax Exempt and Government Entities Division (TE/GE Division), so that's what the remainder of this chapter will cover. The TE/GE Division sprang to life in 1999 as part of the overhaul of the IRS. Although the TE/GE Division interacts mostly with nonprofits, it also deals with tax-qualified retirement plans (such as 401(k)s, profit sharing, and pension plans) as well as government entities. Even though nonprofits generally don't pay much in the way of income tax, they do pay more than $220 billion in employment taxes and income tax withholding. In fact, the TE/GE Division estimates that this customer base controls over $8.2 trillion in assets!

In a nutshell, the TE/GE Division helps organizations understand and comply with tax law, and it protects the public by applying the tax law. In doing its job, the Division addresses the following basic needs of nonprofit organizations:

- **Education:** The TE/GE Division provides education to nonprofits by advising them about what areas of the tax law might affect them.

- **Communication:** The TE/GE Division communicates with these nonprofits, supplying a real, live person to talk to and interface with at the IRS in connection with their nonprofit issues and questions.

- **Issuance of rulings:** The Division's rulings generally deal with specific areas that are applicable to tax-exempt organizations that are either unclear in the industry or that require special attention at the request of a specific customer.

- **Entrance into agreements:** The TE/GE Division has the authority to enter into agreements with customers who may have either fallen out of compliance or need to work out some sort of problem with the IRS. When entering these agreements, the organizations agree to comply with certain requirements in order to avoid further action by the IRS.

- **Examination of returns:** The TE/GE performs an examination function, much like the other branches of the IRS. The Division looks for *noncompliance,* which can be caused by anything from not filing a Form 990 to not reporting an honorarium received by an officer of a nonprofit as income (check out Chapter 7 for more on filing the dreaded Form 990).

- **Taxpayer assistance:** The TE/GE Division provides customer account services. These services help taxpayers file returns more efficiently, accurately, and timely. The TE/GE also provides answers to questions that the customer base may have and supplies information on any issues that may arise.

Understanding why your organization is taxed

In 1862, President Abraham Lincoln and Congress needed a way to finance the Civil War, and so they created the position of Commissioner of Internal Revenue to head up the nation's tax collection agency. It was a great way to pay for war expenses (and apparently still is). Income tax was repealed 10 years later, but Congress revived it in 1894. One year later, the Supreme Court ruled it unconstitutional (those were the good old days).

Fast-forward on the timeline to 1913, when Wyoming ratified the 16th Amendment, which gave Congress the authority to enact a tax on income. Later that same year, the very first individual income tax form (1040) came on the scene, and Congress decided to enact a 1 percent personal income tax on anyone with income above $3,000. The tax increased to 6 percent if a person's income was more than $500,000.

Five years later during World War I, the highest tax bracket rose to 77 percent, which was used to pay for war expenses. After World War I, the income tax dropped sharply, all the way down to 24 percent in 1929, and then rose again during the Great Depression. Then came World War II. To make sure that taxes would be collected, Congress passed a payroll withholding requirement, which is when quarterly tax payments came into being.

The taxing agency was revamped in the 1950s, and the official name, "Internal Revenue Service," was also adopted. Finally, in 1998, the IRS Restructuring and Reform Act again modernized the IRS, with a view toward a private sector model and customer service.

Soft Contacts: Friendly Notes from the IRS

The TE/GE Division believes in reaching out to the public in non-intimidating ways (to the extent that's possible for an arm of the IRS). These friendly communiqués are referred to as *soft contacts*. In case you're unfamiliar with soft contacts, the following sections tell you how to identify and handle them.

Knowing a soft contact when you see one

The most common type of soft contact is a letter from the IRS to a nonprofit organization asking for information about a certain function of the organization's activities. Some functions that the IRS may be curious about include questions about fundraising activities and the organization's accounting practices.

In 2004, the IRS contacted more than 1,800 public charities and private foundations through the mail to request compensation practice information. About 1,200 of these initial contacts were what are commonly referred to as *compliance checks.*

A compliance check is an IRS review to determine whether an organization is following proper recordkeeping and reporting procedures. However, remember that a compliance check isn't an audit. Instead, it's a friendly review that's designed to alert an organization to potential errors.

Responding to a soft contact

If you're the lucky recipient of a soft contact or a compliance check letter, chances are the contact was triggered by some part of your IRS Form 990 being incorrectly answered or omitted entirely. (The most frequently omitted information generally refers to loans, deferred compensation, and fringe benefits of nonprofit organizations.)

When you receive this type of contact from the IRS, you should respond as fully and accurately as possible to the questions that it asks and within the time frame that the letter specifies. These types of letters are sent for a reason. In other words, they aren't meant to be left unopened in the back of your file cabinet! Seriously, the IRS is likely seeking information that can help your organization run more efficiently and help the industry overall. And, as with most organizations, if you don't respond, you may receive further correspondence of a less congenial nature.

Contacting TE/GE Customer Account Services

Nonprofit officers and directors, as well as their accountants, may have questions about the best way to report information on annual IRS Form 990 (discussed in Chapter 7). They may even have choices to make as to how to treat certain income and expense items on the form. Sometimes organizations are even confronted with issues that affect their ongoing tax-exempt status. If you find yourself in one or more of these predicaments, you should consider contacting TE/GE Customer Account Services. One of the goals of the TE/GE Division is to help educate its customer base. It provides an easy way to interface with a live person to answer technical and procedural questions concerning nonprofit organizations and charities.

The easiest way to contact TE/GE Customer Account Services is to simply call (877) 829-5500, which is a toll-free number. (I told you they were friendly!) If you express yourself better in writing, your issue is extremely complicated, or for some other reason you prefer to communicate in writing, you can contact TE/GE Customer Account Services at:

Internal Revenue Service
Exempt Organizations Determinations
P.O. Box 2508
Cincinnati, OH 45201

You can contact your local IRS office, but the Cincinnati, Ohio, facility of the IRS is generally designated as the "go to" location for handling customer base questions.

Contacts with the TE/GE Customer Account Services can be done on an anonymous basis, so if you're concerned that revealing your identity may lead to some sort of audit, you can put your mind at ease.

Prior to calling or writing, you should note that the IRS doesn't provide legal advice, and it can't tell you what direction is best for your organization. If you need more directional advice, contact your lawyer.

If your question is one that's so unique, novel, or without precedent, you may be required to request a determination letter on the issue (check out the section "Sending a Determination Letter" later in this chapter for details).

Deciding when to get a lawyer

Your organization may need to call upon a tax lawyer to help with procedural issues, answer highly technical questions, and otherwise tell you whether you're moving in the right direction. And if your lawyer can't help you directly, he or she may be able to tell you who can.

Sending a Determination Letter

A *determination letter request* is a letter in which you ask the IRS to give your organization some advice on a matter before it actually becomes controversial, or before your organization falls into noncompliance. For example, an organization may want to know if a particular fundraising program will be subject to income tax. That same organization may also have questions about the forms that it's required to file for the fundraiser.

Even though you can prepare a determination letter request on your own, nonprofit organizations generally enlist the aid of an attorney or accountant to dot all the i's and cross all the t's.

The determination letter request is usually a lengthy letter for your organization and attorneys to prepare. It entails some cost, and it requires you to set forth a specific set of facts (not hypothetical) that the IRS can directly address.

In response to your request for a determination, you'll likely receive a *private letter ruling,* which gives you specific advice that's applicable only to the questions you asked about in your determination letter request.

According to IRS regulations, some exempt organizations *must* request a private letter ruling for certain issues, including advance approval of scholarship programs, voluntary termination of a private foundation, and certain changes in accounting methods and periods.

Surviving an IRS Audit

Imagine getting a phone call or letter from the IRS informing you that your nonprofit organization has been selected for an audit. During this jarring initial contact, the IRS usually tells you what year it's going to examine your organization, and what information its staff plans to review. The worst aspect of an audit, however, is that the process is inconvenient and time-consuming. It's also pretty intimidating. But, chances are your nonprofit's return was selected for a reason. The most common audit triggers come from information that's reported (or not reported) on the annual Form 990. This section is here to help.

Looking at things from the auditor's perspective

When the IRS initiates an audit of your nonprofit, it usually tells you upfront the issues that it will be looking at on your return. So, it's a good idea to look at the items with which the IRS is concerned. Go over these issues with others in your organization, and make sure that the people who will be communicating with the IRS understand the issues that will be discussed. You should also try to figure out why the IRS is taking the position that it is.

Identifying any errors

In preparation for the audit, get a copy of your organization's Form 990 for the year in question, exactly as it was filed (with all attachments). Focusing on the entries that are of concern to the IRS, check all the calculations for accuracy. Also, review any documentation supporting these entries.

If you do find an error, there's little chance that it can be corrected once an audit is underway. However, this isn't the end of the world! IRS auditors will work with you to help resolve the errors. If it ultimately turns out that there's no discernable error on your nonprofit's return, you'll know you're in good shape.

When reviewing your nonprofit's Form 990, you might also look for items that weren't identified as part of the audit, but that you may be questioned about after the audit is underway. Examples of such items for nonprofits include information on expenses (especially with regard to salaries, compensation, and employee benefits) and printing and publications. So that you aren't caught off guard, it's important to be prepared to answer questions on all out-of-the-ordinary entries.

Studying filings from other tax years

After reviewing the return for the year in question, take a look at the return for the preceding year (and subsequent year, if available). You need to perform this check because when selecting a nonprofit return for audit, the IRS may very well look at the returns filed for the years before and after the year in question to see if the items of interest have been reported consistently. If the items in question appear to be unusual or outside the normal range for its category or the dollar level of your nonprofit (and the reporting is consistent), an audit of the years prior and subsequent to the return being audited may follow, especially if the return for the year in question is found to be in error.

Getting your ducks and digits in a row

Many audits simply question a few line items, which may be easily substantiated by providing the records relating to the entry on the return. In some cases, if the audit is narrowly focused, a face-to-face meeting with the auditor may not be necessary, and support for the items in question can be provided by mail or facsimile. However, if the records are voluminous and/or could be better explained in person, it may be best to present them to the auditor in person. Either way, your records need to be in some kind of order.

If your records are already organized, great. If not, you (or your accountant) need to put them together in short order, and in a logical manner. All records may be pertinent, so having them organized and readily available is important.

If records aren't available for some reason, be prepared to explain why (for example, lost due to relocation or floods). "My dog ate it" isn't a good excuse. Some acceptable excuses, however, might include

- ✔ Transition of employees
- ✔ Data loss due to theft or damage
- ✔ Pressing matters within the organization

If you need some tips on organizing your records, take a look at the following sections.

Keep copies of everything

It's important to keep original copies of all records that are within your control. So, if you need to provide records to substantiate an item, make a copy and keep the original. It's also a good idea to keep a list of all documentation that you provided to the auditor, as well as the date provided, for your non-profit's records.

Communicate promptly

Surprisingly, some nonprofits that receive letters from the IRS don't respond. To put it mildly, this is a poor strategy. When the IRS writes you, it isn't sending you a holiday greeting or a credit card application. In other words, this isn't junk mail, and you're best advised to open any correspondence immediately to find out why the IRS deems it necessary to communicate with your organization.

Appoint a point person

If a letter from the IRS requests anything more than a simple explanation of an item and requires you to contact the Service, do so at your earliest convenience. For these purposes, your nonprofit organization should have a *point person* who always communicates with the IRS so that the organization can speak with one voice. This point person should be the nonprofit organization's controller, chief financial officer, accountant, or attorney. For smaller organizations that don't have those positions, it's best to appoint the treasurer, president, or some other high-ranking officer.

After your organization's representative is appointed, his or her first conversation with the IRS auditor should be to get all the relevant information that's available, such as what items are under review (if you aren't already aware of that), when and where they want to meet, what records are requested, and the name of all the relevant parties at the IRS.

During the initial conversation, it's also a good idea for the point person to casually ask for the name and phone number of the group manager. The point person may find it difficult to get this important information in later stages of contact because auditors are incredibly busy folks who are often in the field. Also, it may be necessary to contact someone else within the audit group at one time or another, and getting the name of the group manager in charge of the audit upfront is less likely to upset the auditor than if requested later on, especially if things aren't going well or personalities differ.

Stay one step ahead

As you begin communicating with the IRS, you'll quickly get a better sense of what it's interested in reviewing. At this point, then, you should stay a step ahead by considering whether the item being reviewed might lead the auditor to look at other items on the return that aren't currently in question. For example, if the auditor is interested in reviewing compensation, review your nonprofit organization's policies and procedures on expense reimbursement, travel, receipt of gifts, and other compensatory items.

If you're trying to stay one step ahead, it's also important to gather all substantiation necessary to support information reported on the particular entry in question. That way you can begin to decide the best way to explain the line item entry to the auditor. If you're missing records, be able to explain why. And finally, make a list of any questions that you may have for the auditor, and if you're meeting in person, prepare your documentation for presentation.

Meeting face to face

If a face-to-face meeting with an IRS auditor is required, it will likely take place on the premises of your nonprofit organization. This helps the auditor get a feel for the operations of the organization, meet the staff, scope out the physical layout of the enterprise, and basically understand the nature of the operations. If this on-site meeting isn't practical, or if your nonprofit's schedule or the auditor's schedule can't accommodate the meeting, your organization then needs to send its representative to the office of the auditor for the meeting.

Your representative, or point person, needs to be completely prepared for the meeting with the auditor (see the section "Appoint a point person" earlier in this chapter for details on a point person's duties). Here are some preparation tips for a face-to-face meeting:

- ✔ The point person should have all necessary documentation, paperwork, records, and other substantiation prepared and ready to give to the auditor as the meeting progresses.

- ✔ The point person should respectfully and politely guide the meeting through the various issues presented, and should answer any questions fully and fairly.

> ✔ If any necessary answers or documents can't be readily produced at the meeting, the point person should gather and forward those items to the auditor within a reasonable time frame that's agreed on by the IRS.
>
> ✔ If any negotiable issues arise, they should be worked out and agreed to during the course of the audit. You should also agree on the time frame for responding.

Following up with the auditor

After the meeting, I highly suggest that you follow up with the auditor in writing to confirm any results of the audit that were discussed orally. This follow-up establishes a record of understanding for later reference, and allows the auditor to note any disagreements.

Ending on a good note

Hopefully your audit will go smoothly, painlessly, and quickly. If an agreement is required or an error is found, the auditor will generally work with your organization to help resolve the issues raised and see that future compliance isn't a problem. If you have any questions, don't hesitate to contact the exempt organization's section of the TE/GE Division. (Refer to the section "Contacting TE/GE Customer Account Services" earlier in this chapter for contact info.) These IRS workers really can be very helpful!

Part VI
The Part of Tens

The 5th Wave   By Rich Tennant

"I've had a lot of experience running nonprofit organizations. My last three positions were managing Internet companies."

In this part . . .

This part offers checklists on some of the most important nonprofit topics, including what to ask when
becoming a board member, what activities lead an organization to lose its tax-exempt status, and how you can use
the media to your advantage. We also provide a list of
online resources that can help your organization with its
day-to-day business.

Chapter 16

More Than Ten Web Sites Every Nonprofit Should Visit

In This Chapter

▶ Finding useful info on Guidestar, USA.gov, and the Internet Nonprofit Center

▶ Surfing other helpful sites

*N*ot knowing what you don't know is worse than knowing what you don't know. If you're in the latter camp, the Web sites in this chapter can help educate you and help you understand that there's a lot more that you don't know. There's something for everyone on at least one of the sites I discuss here — give them a try and find your favorite.

Guidestar

For guidance on nonprofit information, visit GuideStar's Web site at www.guidestar.org. GuideStar is said to be the leading source of information on U.S. nonprofits. GuideStar provides a searchable database of more than 1.5 million IRS-recognized nonprofit organizations. This is the go-to site for a look at the tax information of your favorite nonprofit. The site offers three levels of accessibility: GuideStar Premium, GuideStar Select, and GuideStar Basic. Each of the three versions has a demo that interested Web surfers can view and test-drive to discover the capabilities of the selected tier. Here's a rundown of the three options:

✔ **GuideStar Premium:** This high-end option is the best option for the dedicated philanthropist or professional user. It offers maximum search fields for precision searching, at-a-glance information in search results, and more ways than the other options to sort the organizations found in searches. It provides the most comprehensive financial and other data available. The current subscription rate is $100 a month or $1,000 a year.

✔ **GuideStar Select:** This version of GuideStar targets professionals and enthusiasts by providing flexible searches, at-a-glance information, and sortable results. This mid-tier option allows narrowing of searches by city and state. The subscription rate for this service is currently $30 a month or $300 a year.

✔ **GuideStar Basic:** So, maybe you've got no money and no job, but you're still somewhat of an enthusiast in the nonprofit world. You're in luck because GuideStar hasn't forgotten you! This basic, no frills version of GuideStar provides a free simple search vehicle for enthusiastic users who just want to verify a nonprofit's legitimacy or view a nonprofit's recent Form 990s. This free service is offered by GuideStar due to the generosity of a number of foundations. However, users can't use the site without entering their login information.

Whether you're an enthusiast or just a snoop, GuideStar has the straight scoop on your favorite nonprofit.

The Internet Nonprofit Center

Who would have thought that you could find a nonprofit center on the Internet? The Internet Nonprofit Center, that's who! Located at www. nonprofits.org, this site is a subset of a larger, multicultural Web site called Idealist.org, which is available in 11 languages. This organization, found at www.idealist.org, promotes altruistic motives under links such as Imagine, Connect, Find, Post, Reach Out, and Donate.

Launched by a project called Action Without Borders in the early 1990s and edited by Putnam Barber, the Internet Nonprofit Center's Web site compiles frequently asked questions (and answers, of course) from e-communications on nonprofits.

Upon arrival at www.nonprofits.org, Internet Nonprofit Center visitors immediately find the main Nonprofit FAQ (frequently asked questions) pane, which lists five link categories: organization, management, regulation, resources, and development. Each link takes the surfer to a range of resources — at least 20 sublinks under each of the five main categories — that in turn lead downstream to topical discussions, blogs, and further resource and informational links.

On the right-hand side of the main pane, you can find more links, which lead you to the frequently asked questions. And if you're looking for a volunteer opportunity or internship (or a number of other nonprofit items), check out the Find box, where you can search the database.

The Internet Nonprofit Center Web site has remarkable a depth and breadth of information and guidance for anyone interested in any aspect of the nonprofit sector. Try it — you'll like it.

USA.gov

To find out what type of information the U.S. government offers, visit www.USA.gov (or you can jump straight to the nonprofit tab by going to www.usa.gov/business/business_gateway.shtml). This Web site is the U.S. Government's office Web portal to more information than you could read in a lifetime. It bills itself as a network of links to federal government information and services of interest to the public (and especially to nonprofit organizations), and it lives up to that claim.

While all of the other tabs on this site are helpful and chock-full of information, the For Businesses and Nonprofits tab is the most applicable to the subject matter of this book, and is the real reason we're even discussing this site.

You can find some great info under the For Business and Nonprofits tab. For example, consider the following, which you can find by clicking on the Nonprofit Organizations link:

- ✔ If you're looking for a grant, information on a grant, how to write a grant, how to make grants, or how grants are granted, check out the heading Grants, Loans, and Other Assistance. Under this heading are links to state and local funding directories, faith-based and community initiatives, surplus government property for governments and nonprofits, writing grant proposals, and much more.

- ✔ Under the Management and Operations heading, you can find links to information regarding charitable activities, such as state forms and information, and nonprofit standard mail eligibility. The links under this heading can help you get useful tips on managing and operating your organization, no matter what size it may be.

- ✔ Under the Tax Information heading, you can find links to tons of tax information, including federal tax information for charities and nonprofits and a tax guide for churches and religious organizations. These links take you directly to information put out by the IRS in simple language to help you understand tax issues and deal with them before they become tax problems.

USA.gov is *the* place to go for quick-find info on government resources at both the federal and state levels — it's a must-visit, if for no other reason than to say you've been there (done that, saw the movie, and bought the T-shirt).

CompassPoint

To navigate the many paths of information available for nonprofits, visit www.compasspoint.org. CompassPoint.org is a nonprofit service that offers consulting, training, and research to nonprofits by providing management tools, resources, and strategies. CompassPoint works with community-based nonprofit organizations to assist with staffing, governance, financial and business planning, and technology.

Of particular interest on this site are the bookstore, which offers a host of selections on nonprofit topics, and the resource directory. The resource directory is helpful for funders.

Also check out the Nonprofit Genie (FAQs) at www.compasspoint.org/askgenie/index.php. It's an excellent source of information on nonprofit management with topics such as how to start-up a nonprofit organization and technology planning for nonprofits.

NASCOnet.org

The National Association of State Charity Officials (NASCO), whose Web site can be found at www.nasconet.org, is an association of state offices that oversees charitable organizations in the United States. The requirements and procedures for forming charitable organizations differ from state to state. So, NASCOnet.org provides state-specific info for nonprofits and links to the U.S. Charity Offices for information relevant to the state in which your organization operates.

In addition, you may also find interesting the federal government information in the IRS section of this Web site. You'll find links to information on obtaining and maintaining federal tax-exempt status.

Other Worthwhile Sites

If the preceding list of Web sites hasn't given you a case of information overload, you'll find the following roster of additional sites for nonprofits helpful. They can provide you with even more info in just about any area of interest that you may have.

- ✓ **The NCNA** (www.ncna.org): This association is a network of 41 state and regional associations with a collective membership of more than 20,000 community nonprofits.

- ✓ **Opportunity Knocks** (www.opportunitynocs.org): This is a resource for finding employment opportunities in the nonprofit sector. Job seekers can search a database of available nonprofit jobs online.

- ✓ **Community Career Center** (www.nonprofitjobs.org): This Web site helps connect nonprofit employers and prospective management members. It provides a job board and résumé posting service, in addition to member services.

- ✓ **Nonprofit guides** (www.npguides.org): At this Web site, you can find nationally recognized nonprofit guides, free sample grants, and grant-writing tools that help nonprofit organizations.

- ✓ **BoardSource** (www.boardsource.org): This site helps strengthen the effectiveness of nonprofits by providing publications, management tools, and consulting for nonprofit executives.

- ✓ **Internet Resources for Nonprofits** (www.uticapubliclibrary.org/non-profit/directory.html): At this site, you'll find more than 1,100 Web links, online directories, and useful sources of free information for and about nonprofit organizations and community leadership.

- ✓ **Nonprofit @ Adobe** (blogs.adobe.com/nonprofit): The Nonprofit @ Adobe blog is a resource for anyone in the nonprofit technology world.

- ✓ **OMB Watch for nonprofit issues** (www.ombwatch.org/npadv): At this site, you find news and articles relating to relations between the United States government and the nonprofit sector.

- ✓ **Nonprofit Academic Centers Council** (www.naccouncil.org): The Nonprofit Academic Centers Council is a membership organization dedicated to the advancement and networking of centers that focus on the study of nonprofit organizations, philanthropy, and volunteerism. This site provides a wealth of reference sources and information on fellowship programs.

Chapter 17

Ten Questions to Ask Before Agreeing to Join a Nonprofit Board

In This Chapter

▶ Getting the appropriate info before joining a board

▶ Understanding your obligations as a board member

▶ Looking at the legal liabilities of serving on a board

Some boards seem to lead their organizations very effectively, moving smoothly through strategic agendas that include holding management accountable to the mission of the organization. Other boards become bogged down with bickering or paralyzed by apathy, inertia, and inexperience — while the staff seems to run the place.

So, before you commit to helping fulfill a company's mission by joining its board, it's important to get a realistic (as opposed to idealistic) view of the organization. To help you do just that, this chapter shows you how to assess the legal and financial shape of the organization *before* you commit.

Who's on the Current Board and How Did They Get There?

You can tell a lot about how much a board will accomplish by looking at who's sitting on it. Ask, as diplomatically as possible about the skills and experience of the people on the board. Knowing this information will clue you in as to the areas in which the board is particularly strong or weak. For example, if no one on the board has an accounting background or any experience reading financial statements, you may want to ask how the board exercises any financial oversight responsibilities it may have.

Most board members of nonprofit organizations are recruited by existing board members or someone in the organization, such as a CEO or executive director. You also may be asked to join a board because you have expressed a commitment to the organization in the past by volunteering or giving money. Or, you may even be asked to join because you seem to have the skills to get things done.

In any event, because most board positions pay either nothing or very little, many board members decide to sign on because of personal commitment or as a community networking opportunity.

Board members may be selected or appointed in a variety of ways. How they are appointed can affect the credentials and perspective of the board members. For example:

- ✔ **Nepotism is a factor for foundations:** In a public charity, new board members are often nominated by sitting board members. In larger public charities, the organization may have a nominating committee who submits names to the board. If you're on the board of a private foundation, board members may be appointed because they contributed money to establish the foundation or are related to someone who did.

  Private foundations, as discussed in Chapter 11, often allow donors to control the funds that they make available for philanthropic purposes, and this greatly influences who's selected to serve on a board.

- ✔ **What the organization's bylaws say:** The *bylaws* of an organization state how the board members are selected. For example, the bylaws may state that the directors are elected by the organization's membership or are selected by a vote of the existing directors for a term of years. (See Chapter 4 for more on creating bylaws for your nonprofit.)

- ✔ **Restrictions imposed as to whether board members must be independent:** Some organizations have provisions in their bylaws that require a majority of their directors to be *independent,* which means that they can't be employed by or have certain types of financial relationships with the nonprofit organization. (Check out Chapter 8 for more on independence provisions.) This type of provision is becoming more prevalent in nonprofit bylaws after the advent of the Sarbanes-Oxley Act, which is discussed in Chapter 13.

How Long Are the Director's Terms?

Be sure to check out the term of years for which directors are appointed on the board because you may be making anywhere from a two- to five-year commitment. Commitments can be broken, and priorities can change, but resignation can be sticky. And resignation is something that other board members can talk you out of by reminding you of the terms.

On the other hand, if the term is extremely short (such as one to two years), and you're planning on proposing a relatively controversial agenda after you're on the board, you may want to ask yourself whether you'll have the time to push it through before they push you off.

In any event, information about the term limits of board members is usually spelled out in the organization's bylaws.

How Many Board Members Does It Take to Get Anything Done?

As an individual board member, you'll basically be powerless. You're only one vote on a board that must act as a group. The bylaws will specify how many members your board has (usually between six and twelve). The bylaws will also specify how many board members must be present to conduct business and to put a matter up for a vote. This number is called a *quorem*.

Before you agree to sit on a nonprofit board, be sure you understand how many members are required for a quorum, and whether meetings must take place in person or whether they can occur by phone in order to convene a quorum.

What Committees Does the Board Control?

One way that you can have a more powerful voice on a board is by being appointed to a *committee*. A committee is a subgroup of board members (which can be as small as one person) that's authorized by the board to gather information or act on an issue. Examples of typical committees include the following:

- **Audit committees:** These types of committees work with the nonprofit organization's auditors or accountants and make sure that the financial reports that are generated are based on accurate information supplied by the organization. (Flip to Chapter 10 for more on audit committees.)

- **Programming committees:** These committees are often formed to carry out specific programs (such as a yoga class or a Bible study group) or to look at the feasibility of undertaking new ones.

✔ **Fundraising committees:** Because no nonprofit could exist without donors and a source of funds, many organizations have committees that convene to explore fundraising opportunities, and report to the board.

✔ **Community relations and outreach committees:** Community relations and outreach are closely related to fundraising, but they also may involve creating a community awareness of the nonprofit.

Boards can delegate acting power to committees. So, if you're joining a nonprofit and a particular program is of importance to you, ask before joining the board (for instance while they're in the process of recruiting you to work for free) if there's an opportunity to be appointed to a committee that handles the project in which you're interested.

Can 1 See the Books and Records of the Organization?

Many states have laws that require members of nonprofit organizations to make books and records available for inspection by members. Additionally, forms filed with the Internal Revenue Service (IRS) must be made available. At a minimum, you have a right to see the organization's Form 990-PF. The 990-PF is a gold mine of information because it usually contains a copy of the organization's bylaws and articles of incorporation.

If the organization is too small to be required to file a 990-PF, and it has any source of funds whatsoever, it should have some sort of accounting records. These accounting records may be something as simple as a check register. If the organization balks in providing you this information before you agree to sit on the board, consider yourself warned because a red flag has been waved.

Many boards also keep minutes of their meetings. You can tell a lot about what goes on during meetings from the minutes, such as what topics on the agenda may have provoked detailed discussion. The minutes also reflect how organized the board is in meeting its goals.

What's the Organization's Financial Situation?

One of the first things you want to look for is what money is coming into the organization, and then you need to know where it's going. If this information isn't clear to you from looking at the 990-PF or other available records, ask.

Some other good questions to start investigating are in the following list:

- ✔ **Overall budget:** How large is the organization's budget? The answer will tell you how much money the board is actually responsible for administering.

- ✔ **Allocation of funds:** What percentage of program revenues goes directly to programs as opposed to administrative expenses and overhead? Generally speaking, the higher the percentage, the more effective the organization.

- ✔ **Salaries and expenses:** Are the organization's salaries and expenses reasonable? This generally depends on the organization in relation to other similar organizations. (See Chapter 6 for more on compensating officers and directors.)

Is the Organization Current on Its Payroll Taxes?

One of the most important obligations of a nonprofit organization is to pay its employees, along with any payroll taxes and other obligations. It's important to remember that a nonprofit's tax-exempt status relates only to certain revenues earned by the organization, not to the salaries and wages (see Chapter 5 for more on gaining tax-exempt status).

No federal income tax withholding is required in the cases of ministers and members of religious orders. Their wages for religious duties aren't subject to mandatory withholding. But, any compensation not related to religious duties is subject to federal income tax withholding. Their compensation is also subject to self-employment tax, which is a responsibility of the individual, not of the church employer. In addition to federal requirements, state and local jurisdictions may have their own requirements for withholding amounts from employees' wages.

In the event that a nonprofit organization fails to pay its taxes, the IRS can impose substantial penalties on the organization. In theory, the board members can be sued for allowing these penalties to pile up. If the organization also fails to maintain its status as a nonprofit under state and federal law, board members and directors can be held personally liable (because no active corporate entity is in place to shield them), particularly if the board has approved the use of the funds that were required to be withheld for other purposes.

What tax-exempt organizations must withhold

Your nonprofit organization is responsible for paying Social Security and Medicare taxes for all employees earning $100 or more a year, except ministers and members of religious orders. (The exemption from Social Security and Medicare taxes applies to services performed by duly ordained members of a church in the exercise of their ministry.)

The good news is that if your organization is tax-exempt as provided under Section 501(c)(3) of the Internal Revenue Code (as discussed in Chapter 5), it may be exempt from federal unemployment taxes. For example, organizations exempt from federal unemployment taxes generally include nonprofits that

✔ Are organized and operated exclusively for religious, charitable, scientific, public safety, literary, or educational purposes.

✔ Are operated for the prevention of cruelty to children or animals.

✔ Are operated on a nonprofit basis.

✔ Have devoted no substantial part of their activities to lobbying or political activities.

IRS Publication 15-A (*Employer's Supplemental Tax Guide, Supplement to Circular E*) explains the federal unemployment tax withholding requirements and who is exempt from them and is available at www.IRS.gov/publications.

What Are the Responsibilities of the Directors?

Before you accept any position — paid or unpaid — it's a good idea to know what your responsibilities entail. Some boards are advisory only, which means that they have little say or responsibility in the day-to-day management of the organization. In fact, many boards leave day-to-day management to the CEO, executive director, or other paid staff person, and this person always reports back to the board. However, other boards are held to a high degree of responsibility.

A common problem with respect to volunteer nonprofit boards is that the paid staff members may be held to vague standards of accountability because volunteer board members may not view themselves as having the same role as the directors when it comes to making sure that the mission of the organization is met. You may also find that when you join a board, you take on some new financial responsibilities. For example, you may be required to make a minimum contribution to the organization, or you may have to help make up shortfalls in the organization's revenues at the end of the year.

In most nonprofit organizations, however, board members' duties consist of at least some of the following:

- **Determining the organization's ongoing mission and purpose:** This is one of the key, universal roles of any board member.

- **Selecting the executive director:** Most boards (other than purely advisory ones) have some role in hiring, firing, evaluating, and supervising the executive directors.

- **Overseeing organizational planning:** This duty usually involves communicating with the executive director to ensure that the resources and staff of the organization are used effectively to accomplish its mission.

- **Raising funds and enhancing the public image of the organization:** Board members are often actively involved in soliciting funds for the organization and raising its visibility on the public radar.

- **Serving as a "court of appeal":** If staff and stakeholders believe that an organization isn't meeting its mission, it's imperative that they're able to go to the board of directors with the issue.

When, Where, and How Often Does the Board Meet?

This may seem like a trivial question relative to other issues, but it can be a key determining factor for recruiting board members, because as a practical matter, in many organizations, it's difficult to get a board to change its meeting place or time. This can be critical in getting certain types of individuals to serve.

For example, a board that meets midday at a suburban venue may find itself hard-pressed to recruit directors that work downtown. On the other hand, the meeting time and place may be ideal for a board comprised of stay-at-home parents or retirees. It's increasingly common for organizations to allow meetings to take place by phone conference, but it's far from the norm.

Most boards that play active management roles in their organizations meet at least monthly, and may convene additional meetings if emergencies arise.

Is the Board Being Sued or Has It Ever Been Sued?

Litigation may be inevitable in some sound organizations, particularly in those that deal with controversial causes, but pending lawsuits are something you definitely want to ask about and understand before you commit to a leadership role. Understanding pending lawsuits is important because, personal liability issues aside, litigation is always distracting. It's a sign of conflict and it's a diversion of organizational resources that could be used for the organization's mission.

Most state laws shield directors of nonprofit organizations who are acting within the scope of their authority from direct personal liability. Nevertheless, a lawsuit is never a good thing. However, it becomes a problem when the board is found to have exceeded its authority or to have taken actions that have nothing to do with its mission.

For example, if a nonprofit board that deals with domestic abuse issues decides it would be a great idea to publish the names of individuals the board thinks are *potentially* abusive in a local newspaper, there's a chance that the board will be deemed to have acted outside the scope of its authority. If held personally liable, the board members would have to defend the action on their own or determine if their own professional liability insurance covered the claim.

Chapter 18

Ten Ways to Lose Tax-Exempt Status

In This Chapter

▶ Activities that nonprofits should avoid

▶ Laws that nonprofits must comply with

*T*housands of organizations in the United States each year apply for and receive tax-exempt recognition from the Internal Revenue Service (IRS). Despite meeting the initial requirements, many of them later find themselves in the throes of high-profile IRS investigations, which subject them to just about the worst kind of publicity a nonprofit can get.

To keep you on track, this chapter warns you of ten actions that can quickly put your organization in jeopardy of being excommunicated by the IRS and ostracized by donors and other critical funding sources.

Engage in Plenty of Nonexempt Activities

Performing *nonexempt activities* (those activities that make a profit for your nonprofit organization) is a surefire way to lose your tax-exempt status. A tax-exemption is analogous to a government subsidy for a worthy activity. Nonprofit organizations are considered tax exempt because Congress has chosen to support what they do, and it has told the IRS to give them a free ride on the tax train.

But that free ride only lasts as long as the organizations are performing exempt deeds — not the ones that compete with their private business counterparts (what an unfair advantage that would be!).

Some examples of nonprofit activities that the IRS may frown upon include the following:

- ✔ Selling products and services that clearly compete with the private sector

- ✔ Conducting activities unrelated to the nonprofit mission

- ✔ Engaging in business activities that allow benefit board members to benefit or profit in a manner that's a clear conflict of interest

A nonprofit organization must spell out its activities in its governing documents. These documents are called *articles of incorporation,* or some other name, depending on what state you're in. The articles must make clear that the organization's activities are pretty much limited to the exempt purposes. The articles can't authorize the organization to engage in substantial non-exempt or profit-making activities.

For more information concerning types of charitable organizations and their activities, download Publication 557 from the IRS Web site (www.irs.gov/publications) or contact your local IRS office.

Get Involved in Prohibited Political Activities

Regardless of how sympathetic a particular pundit may be to the organization's mission, nonprofit organizations can't use their funds to support political candidates.

Congress approved this ban on political campaign activity by charities and churches in 1954. In 1987, Congress amended the language to clarify that the prohibition also applies to statements in opposition of candidates.

Even though nonprofits can't endorse political candidates, they *can* endorse issues. Many nonprofits routinely lobby for issues in the political arena. Nonprofits champion a variety of causes, and such advocacy may be their primary mission. Here are a few examples:

- ✔ People for the Ethical Treatment of Animals (PETA) is an organization whose primary mission is the advocacy of animal rights.

- ✔ The American Cancer Society is a nonprofit that's visible in many states and localities with respect to anti-smoking legislation.

How political activity can affect your nonprofit status: A real-life example

In September 2006, the Internal Revenue Service (IRS) announced that it had revoked the nonprofit 501(c)(3) status of Youth Ministries, Inc., which did business as Operation Rescue West (ORW). The IRS generally doesn't publish its reasons for exempt status in detail, but the media speculated that the organization pushed the limits of its exemption by placing a large advertisement that solicited tax-deductible donations to help "defeat [John Kerry] in November and enable President Bush to appoint a pro-life Supreme Court Justice to finally overturn *Roe v. Wade.*"

The fate of ORW is a stark reminder that while nonprofit organizations are free to educate members and the public, they must do so within the limits of charitable laws. Organizations that want to directly participate in the election process must renounce their charitable status.

The IRS published Fact Sheet 2006-17, which outlines how churches and all 501(c)(3) organizations can stay within the law regarding the ban on political activity. You can access this document on the IRS Web site at www.irs. gov/newsroom/article/0,,id=154712,00.html.

Become a Partnership

Under 501(c)(3), a nonprofit organization must be some type of corporation fund, association, or foundation. Partnerships aren't on the IRS's list of acceptable legal entities. The legal types of nonprofit organizations are discussed in more detail in Chapter 5. A *charitable trust* is a fund or foundation and will qualify, but sole proprietorships and partnerships don't qualify and need not apply!

Divert Some of Your Organization's Earnings to Private Individuals

Dole out money to private individuals within a nonprofit and you'll lose your tax-exempt status — pronto. In a nonprofit, no individual is supposed to have his or her pockets lined with the organization's money. Also, a legit nonprofit organization can't be operated for the benefit of private interests, such as the people who created it, the creator's family, or any sort of for-profit business endeavor.

This type of private benefit may be present in less obvious ways than direct deposits to an officer's bank account; it may be found to occur where there are unjustifiable incidents of extravagant vacations, excessive compensation, an insider's purchase of the nonprofit's assets for less than fair market value, or other creative ways to milk the organization.

Farm Out Control of Your Operations

Tax-exempt organizations must manage their own affairs or have them managed by other nonprofits. They can't hire for-profit entities to manage their operations or carry out their tax-exempt operations.

In a 2003 court battle (*St. David's Health Care System v. United States*), an organization lost its tax-exempt status when it entered into a partnership joint venture with a for-profit healthcare system. In this case, the court held that in such situations the nonprofit partner must have the "capacity to ensure that the partnership's operations further charitable purposes." The court reasoned that a "nonprofit should lose its tax exempt status if it cedes control."

Fail to Limit Your Commercial Activities

Nonprofits aren't allowed to compete with private businesses on a tax-free basis because doing so would give them a grossly unfair competitive advantage.

If your nonprofit engages in a business venture that's unrelated to its purpose (like operating a pizza parlor when its mission is to help fund medical research projects), the profits from that venture are taxable. However, if the organization as a whole has too much taxable income, it may lose its tax-exempt status altogether. For this reason, successful nonprofit groups, such as the National Geographic Society, have had to spin off business projects that became too profitable.

Require Donations in Exchange for Your Organization's Services

In 2006, the IRS revoked the tax-exempt status of many nonprofit, down-payment assistance organizations that were operating under the guise of charitable organizations but were *requiring* applicants to make a "donation."

Often these mandatory donations were really fees for commercial services. For example, certain down payment assistance and credit counseling programs have lost their tax-exempt status in recent years by channeling funds to mortgage companies, brokers, and other private parties.

Skip Filing IRS Form 990 for Three Years in a Row

On August 17, 2006, President Bush signed into law the Pension Protection Act of 2006. Under the new law, a nonprofit's tax-exempt status is automatically revoked if the organization fails to file a Form 990 for three years in a row (flip to Chapter 7 for more details on Form 990s). After they have their status revoked, these organizations have to reapply for exempt status (which is no easy job) or show reasonable cause for failure to file the return.

Worse yet, under this law, the IRS publishes a list of the organizations that have had their tax-exempt status revoked. The IRS even notifies the state charity officials of the organization's change in status, free of charge, so the state can take appropriate action.

The law doesn't say as much, but because the IRS publishes a notice that a charity's exemption is revoked, it's pretty much assumed that a donor who makes a gift to a charity that's on the public shaming list isn't entitled to a charitable deduction. And of course, as you probably can imagine, causing a donor to lose out on tax deductions is a fabulous way to tarnish your reputation.

Support Terrorist Activities

Terrorism isn't an exempt activity. You won't find it listed under Section 501(c) of the Internal Revenue Code.

But seriously, all joking aside, multinational organizations or organizations who aid in charitable causes overseas are facing strict scrutiny in this area. In this day and age, companies that make contributions are responsible for understanding counter-terrorism regulations, and making sure that their well-intentioned dollars don't benefit terrorists or terrorist organizations.

Executive Order 13224, straight from the President, freezes the assets of individuals and organizations that support terrorism, knowingly or otherwise. Corporations can run into trouble if they have a program of matching employee donations and inadvertently let some slip through to terrorist organizations.

Pay Your Executives Exorbitant Salaries

The IRS has issued a number of guidelines as to when executive compensation is deemed excessive and when an organization has run afoul of its charitable mission as a result. Nonprofits are required to report salaries on their tax returns, and services like GuideStar post tax returns of nonprofits on the Internet so the public can assess this information as well. (Check out Chapter 6 for more info on compensating your officers and directors.)

IRS policies also address freebie fringe benefits, such as paid vacations, spousal travel, and golf outings. And don't forget that the IRS also frowns on transactions that create a conflict of interest. For example, personal loans to directors or executives, as discussed in Chapter 6, are no-nos.

Chapter 19

Ten Tips for Dealing with the Media

In This Chapter

▶ Handling the media effectively

▶ Using the media to your advantage

▶ Presenting your nonprofit through the media

*M*ost nonprofit organizations need to use the media or have its spotlight cast on them at some point during their existence. It may be an ongoing relationship or only a quick 15 minutes of fame. Regardless of the nature and extent to which your organization wants or gets media attention, there are certain tips that can help improve the experience and give you an edge in maximizing the opportunity to offer your story to the world. While many of the tips in this chapter may apply to any type of organization, those organizations involved in fundraising or consciousness-raising activities should find these tips particularly thought-provoking and hopefully useful as well.

Acquaint Yourself with Your Local Media

Before you assess how to deal with the media, you need to fundamentally understand what media outlets may be listening to (or looking at) your organization. Review the likely radio stations, television channels, and local and regional newspapers. Get to know the reporters and television personalities, and determine what their reporting styles may be. This study of the media is crucial when evaluating who to talk to about your story, and how to spin it. By carefully choosing who to approach about a particular matter, you can maximize the opportunity to expose your announcement or news story to the right audience at the right time.

Create Your Message

If you have important news that needs to be covered, it has to be interesting. And developing the right message to make your pitch to the media is the key to success. Make your message short and sweet to get the media person's attention, and have backup information on hand with all the correct facts in order. By doing so, you give yourself a good chance at getting the right person to listen to your story and report it with the message *you* craft — rather than having the wrong message sent to your intended audience.

Be Prepared When Being Interviewed

Imagine that you've successfully created interest in your story, and a reporter asks you for an interview. One of the first things you need to find out is what interest the interviewer has in the story. Once you know this fact, you can formulate the message in a way that helps them with their mission. Create a loose script that includes bullet points you want to cover, making sure that the most important points are first. If the interview is conducted over the phone (as are most newspaper and radio interviews), feel free to grab prepared materials and read your sound bite directly from them.

In any event, make sure that your message is delivered — and don't be timid about repeating your most important point or points. Repetition emphasizes the importance of these points and highlights your areas of concern to the reporter.

Keep Control of the Story

If you have a message that causes a stir, or if something causes the media to focus on your organization, keep control of the story. In other words, make sure that you're ready with the right answers to the questions that you know reporters will ask. The most media-savvy people within an organization know how to steer an answer. In answering a tough question, these smooth-talkers can address the primary issue succinctly, and then move on to a topic that's part of the story but hasn't yet been covered. It's a sure-fire, time-tested method that you can hear whenever you listen to a politician being interviewed, a lawyer publicly commenting on a big case, or a government official talking about some issue within his or her department.

Don't Avoid the Press

The rules on dealing with the media don't change when you're in a crisis situation. One of the worst public relations moves an organization can make is to attempt to avoid the media. We've all seen on television a person cornered by a mob of reporters while making a mad dash to an awaiting car, only to lean briefly into a sea of microphones and say "No comment" before being whisked away. What inevitably follows this disastrous clip is the local media reporter summarizing the story that the person refused to comment on, and (if the reporter is doing his or her job correctly) making the story as interesting as possible. Unfortunately, this good reporting job usually means commenting on suspected scandal, insinuating criminal activity or embezzlement, or speculating on whatever other facts may relate to the story and catch the public's interest.

If the media approaches you and you aren't ready to comment, don't avoid them. Instead, tell them you want to address all of their concerns directly, and then you can schedule a press conference or other meeting to do just that. This tactic gives your organization the time to decide how to create the message, control the story, and consult with a media specialist, if necessary, to make sure that the opportunity to comment is maximized and becomes a positive for the organization.

Hire Professional PR Help When Necessary

Depending on the size of your organization's operating budget, its mission, and its specific situation, you may consider hiring a public relations (PR) professional. Good PR firms have people who are well-connected and wired into the network of media people. They know each other by first name and have instant access at the appropriate times. These PR professionals can help you form your message and can coach you on how to deliver it. They prepare the press releases, the campaign slogans, the handout materials, or any other media-related functions you need. If you can afford these professionals, we highly suggest that you invest in them. They function and assist as effectively in fundraising campaigns as they do in organizational emergencies. Sometimes, even for smaller organizations, it's well worth the money to get a professional involved.

Remember That Nothing Is Ever "Off the Record"

We've all seen those outtakes where an unsuspecting person thought that the camera was no longer rolling and proceeded to make some stupid remark that was completely contrary to what he or she was just saying, framing him or her, at best, as some sort of non-credible source or, at worst, some sort of hypocritical buffoon. If these folks had control over the camera or microphone, they'd never be put into compromising situations. So too, it is with the press.

When you say "This is off the record" or someone tells you during an interview that something they say is off the record, it really isn't. Nothing is ever off the record. In fact, that's when the reporters sharpen their pencils and pay the most attention. They're just hoping that your guard will be down and you'll let something slip. If you need to comment on anything off the record, keep control of the story and answer the question in a manner that leads the story where you want it to go.

Gather the Forces When Appropriate

Whether you want to get the word out about a fundraising event or about your organization's position on a controversial issue, a highly effective method of disseminating that information is through your staff and volunteers. Find out which people in these groups are willing to speak and tour the circuit of public forums to get the message out. Not only does this get the word out on the street, but it also raises the visibility of your organization within the community and lets others know more about your mission and philosophy.

One note of caution: Speakers are representatives of the organization, and their audiences will form opinions of the speakers and associate your organization with that opinion. So, make your speaker selections carefully! Tell them that they are the message.

Know the Difference between News and Advertising

This tip seems intuitive, but on slow news days you can always see old news stories that are simply being rehashed. Some of these stories come close to being thinly veiled advertisements for how well a company is doing or for promoting its line of products. We aren't saying that these stories aren't newsworthy, but there's definitely a time and a place for everything — and the time to break a news story is when it's fresh, not months or years old. For example, if you plan to hire a new CEO for your organization, that's news on or before the date it actually happens, but it becomes advertising to run the story months afterward.

Even a newbie reporter can see through ploys, so save your credibility and know what's newsworthy and what's not.

Surf the 'Net

You can pick up a lot of great public relations tips and strategies simply by surfing the Web sites of organizations that have the resources to hire the biggest and best public relations firms.

Whether you're a sophisticated national public charity or a community-based club, your organization probably has a Web site. You can bet most other nonprofits have them too, and they probably use them as major public relations tools. Many also post their press releases on their Web sites. You can take a look at what other organizations similar to yours are doing regarding Web designs, blogging, and media blitzing.

Part VII
Appendixes

"They call it 'stealing', I call it 'safeguarding our nonprofit status.'"

In this part . . .

*I*f you're looking for some useful reference materials, you're in luck — this part contains such documents. For example, we provide sample nonprofit bylaws and a sample audit committee report. We also include a directory of contact information for state and regulatory authorities and select articles from the Model Nonprofit Corporation Act of 1987.

Appendix A

Sample Nonprofit Bylaws

BYLAWS OF _____

ARTICLE I – NAME, PURPOSE

Section 1: The name of the organization shall be
_____.

Section 2: The _____ is organized exclusively for
charitable, scientific, and educational purposes, more specifically to
_____.

ARTICLE II – MEMBERSHIP

Section 1: Membership shall consist only of the members of the Board of
Directors, which shall be _____ in number and shall elect a Chair by simple
majority.

ARTICLE III – ANNUAL MEETING

Section 1: Annual Meeting. The date of the regular annual meeting shall be
set by the Board of Directors who shall also set the time and place.

Section 2: Special Meetings. Special meetings may be called by the Chair.

Section 3: Notice. Notice of each meeting shall be given to each voting
member, by mail, not less than ten days before the meeting.

ARTICLE IV – BOARD OF DIRECTORS

Section 1: Board Role, Size, Compensation. The Board is responsible for overall policy and direction of the Council, and delegates responsibility for day-to-
day operations to the Council Director and committees. The Board shall have
up to _____ and not fewer than _____ members. The Board receives no compensation other than reasonable expenses.

Section 2: Meetings. The Board shall meet at least _____, at an
agreed upon time and place.

Section 3: Board Elections. Election of new directors or election of current directors to a second term will occur as the first item of business at the annual meeting of the corporation. Directors will be elected by a majority vote of the current directors.

Section 4: Terms. All Board members shall serve _____ year terms, but are eligible for re-election.

Section 5: Quorum. A quorum must be attended by at least _____ percent of the Board members before business can be transacted or motions made or passed.

Section 6: Notice. An official Board meeting requires that each Board member have written notice two weeks in advance.

Section 7: Officers and Duties. There shall be four officers of the Board consisting of a Chair, Vice-Chair, Secretary, and Treasurer. Their duties are as follows:

The Chair shall convene regularly scheduled Board meetings and shall preside or arrange for other members of the executive committee to preside at each meeting in the following order: Vice-Chair, Secretary, and Treasurer.

The Vice-Chair will chair committees on special subjects as designated by the Board.

The Secretary shall be responsible for keeping records of Board actions, including overseeing the taking of minutes at all Board meetings, sending out meeting announcements, distributing copies of minutes and the agenda to each Board member, and assuring that corporate records are maintained.

The Treasurer shall make a report at each Board meeting. The Treasurer shall chair the finance committee, assist in the preparation of the budget, help develop fundraising plans, and make financial information available to Board members and the public.

Section 8: Vacancies. When a vacancy on the Board exists, nominations for new members may be received from present Board members by the Secretary two weeks in advance of a Board meeting. These nominations shall be sent out to Board members with the regular Board meeting announcement, to be voted upon at the next Board meeting. These vacancies will be filled only to the end of the particular Board member's term.

Section 9: Resignation, Termination, and Absences. Resignation from the Board must be in writing and received by the Secretary. A Board member shall be dropped for excess absences from the Board if s/he has three unexcused absences from Board meetings in a year. A Board member may be removed for other reasons by a three-fourths vote of the remaining directors.

Section 10: Special Meetings. Special meetings of the Board shall be called upon the request of the Chair or one-third of the Board. Notices of special meetings shall be sent out by the Secretary to each Board member postmarked two weeks in advance.

ARTICLE V – COMMITTEES

Section 1: The Board may create committees as needed, such as audit, fundraising, nominating, membership, etc. The Board Chair appoints all committee chairs.

Section 2: Executive Committee. The four officers serve as the members of the Executive Committee. Except for the power to amend the Articles of Incorporation and Bylaws, the Executive Committee shall have all of the powers and authority of the Board of Directors in the intervals between meetings of the Board of Directors, subject to the direction and control of the Board of Directors.

Section 3: Audit Committee. The Chair of the Board of Directors shall serve on the Audit Committee, which shall also include three other Board members. The Audit Committee is responsible for developing and reviewing fiscal procedures and an annual budget. The Board must approve the budget, and all expenditures must be within the budget. Any major change in the budget must be approved by the Board. Annual reports are required to be submitted to the Board, showing income, expenditures and pending income, and any unusual audit adjustments.

Section 4: The financial records of the organization are public information and shall be made available to the membership, Board members, and the public.

ARTICLE VI – AMENDMENTS

Section 1: These Bylaws may be amended when necessary by a two-thirds majority of the Board of Directors. Proposed amendments must be submitted to the Secretary to be sent out with regular Board announcements.

These Bylaws were approved at a meeting of the Board of Directors of

_____ on

_____, 20_____.

Appendix B

Sample Audit Committee Report

• •

*T*he Audit Committee (the "Committee") of the **XYZ Company** Board of Directors (the "Board") consists of (number _____) of independent Directors pursuant to the requirements of the New York Stock Exchange, NASDAQ, and the Securities and Exchange Commission.

The Committee has a written charter that is publicly available for review at (Web site _____).

The Board has determined that the following Directors are financial experts as defined by the rules of the Securities and Exchange Commission:

(name _____)

(name _____)

(Web site _____)

The following Committee members serve on other public company audit committees as indicated below:

(name _____) (Board _____)

(name _____) (Board _____)

(Web site _____) (Board _____)

The Committee has determined that the simultaneous service on these public company audit committees does not impair the ability of the Directors.

The Committee had _____ meetings during 20_____. Of these meetings, _____ included sessions of the Committee with the independent auditors, _____ included sessions with the internal auditor, and _____ included sessions with management.

The Company also had _____ conference calls with _____ related to the Company's earnings and financial statements.

Responsibility for the financial statements of XYZ Company is delegated as follows:

✔ Board of Directors: The Committee oversees the Company's financial reporting process on behalf of the Board of Directors.

✔ Management: Management has primary responsibility for the financial statements of XYZ Company and the reporting process.

✔ Independent audit firm: The independent audit firm of _____ is responsible for expressing an opinion on the conformity of the Company's consolidated audited financial statements with Generally Accepted Accounting Principles.

The Committee has reviewed and discussed with management and the independent auditors the audited financial statements of XYZ Company and all matters pertinent to the preparation of the financial statements.

The Committee has pre-approved the following with respect to the services of the independent auditors:

✔ All audit services

✔ Permitted non-audit services

✔ The related fees for such services provided by the independent auditors

The Committee's charter allows delegation of the following authority, which has been assigned to subcommittees: [describe authority]

The Committee recommended to the Board of Directors, and the Board approved, that the audited financial statements be included in the Company's Annual Report on Form 10-K for the year ended December 31, 20_____, for filing with the Securities and Exchange Commission.

Audit Committee Signatures:

_____

_____

_____

_____

Appendix C

State Regulatory Authorities for Nonprofits

• •

Alabama
Office of the Attorney General
11 South Union St., 3rd Floor
Montgomery, AL 36130
Phone: (334) 242-7335
Web site: www.ago.state.al.us/consumer_charities.cfm

Alaska
Office of the Attorney General
1031 W. 4th Ave., Suite 200
Anchorage, AK 99501
Phone: (907) 465-2133
Web site: www.law.state.ak.us/department/civil/consumer/
cpindex.html

Arizona
Office of the Secretary of State
1700 W. Washington St.
Phoenix, AZ 85007
Phone: (602) 542-4285
Web site: www.azsos.gov/business_services/Charities.htm

Office of the Attorney General
1275 W. Washington St.
Phoenix, AZ 85007
Phone: (602) 542-5025
Web site: www.attorneygeneral.state.az.us

Arkansas
Office of the Attorney General
323 Center St., Suite 200
Little Rock, AR 72201-2610
Phone: (501) 682-2007
Web site: www.ag.state.ar.us/index_high.htm

California
Office of the Attorney General
1300 I St., Suite 1130
Sacramento, CA 95814
Phone: (916) 445-2021
Web site: `caag.state.ca.us/charities/statutes.htm`

Colorado
Office of the Secretary of State
Licensing Division
1700 Broadway #300
Denver, CO 80290
Phone: (303) 860-6934
Information Center Web site: `www.sos.state.co.us`
Licensing Center Web site: `www.sos.state.co.us/pubs/bingo_raffles/main.htm`

Department of Law
1525 Sherman St., 5th Floor
Denver, CO, 80203
Phone: (303) 866-5189

Connecticut
Office of the Attorney General
Public Charities Unit
55 Elm St.
Hartford, CT 06106
Phone: (860) 808-5318
Web site: `www.cslib.org/attygenl/mainlinks/tabindex8.htm`

Delaware
Department of Justice
Securities Division
820 N. French St.
Wilmington, DE 19801
Phone: (302) 577-8600
Web site: `www.state.de.us/attgen/main_page/links.htm`

District of Columbia
Department of Consumer and Regulatory Affairs
941 N. Capitol St. NE, 7th Floor
Washington, DC 20002
Phone: (202) 442-4400
Web site: `dcra.dc.gov/dcra/site/default.asp`

Florida
Department of Agriculture and Consumer Services
Consumer Affairs
2005 Apalachee Parkway
Terry Rhodes Building
Tallahassee, FL 32399-6500
Phone: (850) 488-2221
Web site: doacs.state.fl.us/onestop/cs/solicit.html

Georgia
Office of the Secretary of State
Securities and Business Regulation Division
2 Martin Luther King Jr. Dr. SE, Suite 802, West Tower
Atlanta, GA 30334
Phone: (404) 656-3920
Web site: www.sos.state.ga.us/securities/
charities_paid_solicitors.htm

Georgia Bureau of Investigation
Investigative Division, Bingo Unit
P.O. Box 370808
Decatur, GA 30037-0808
Phone: (404) 244-2600
Web site: www.ganet.org/gbi/idbingo.html

Hawaii
Department of the Attorney General
425 Queen St.
Honolulu, HI 96813-5045
Phone: (808) 586-1500
Web site: www.hawaii.gov/ag/charities

Idaho
Office of the Attorney General
Consumer Protection Unit
700 W. Jefferson St.
P.O. Box 83720
Boise, ID 83720
Phone: (208) 334-2424
Web site: www2.state.id.us/ag/consumer/index.htm

Illinois
Office of the Attorney General
Charitable Trust Bureau
100 W. Randolph St., 3rd Floor
Chicago, IL 60601
Phone: (312) 814-2595
Web site: www.ag.state.il.us/charities/index.html

Indiana
Office of the Attorney General
Consumer Protection Division
302 W. Washington St., 5th Floor
Indianapolis, IN 46204
Phone: (317) 232-6330
Web site: www.state.in.us/attorneygeneral

Iowa
Department of Justice
Consumer Protection Division
1305 E. Walnut St.
Des Moines, IA 50319
Phone: (515) 281-5926
Web site: www.state.ia.us/government/ag/consumer.html

Kansas
Office of the Secretary of State
Memorial Hall, 1st Floor
120 SW 10th Ave.
Topeka, KS 66612
Phone: (785) 296-4564
Web site: www.kssos.org/main.html

Office of the Attorney General
Consumer Protection Division
120 SW 10th St., 2nd Floor
Topeka, KS 66612
Phone: (785) 296-2215
Web site: www.kansas.gov/ksag/divisions/consumer/main.htm

Kentucky
Office of the Attorney General
Consumer Protection Division
The Capitol, Suite 118
700 Capitol Ave.
Frankfort, KY 40601
Phone: (502) 696-5389
Web site: ag.ky.gov/default.htm

Louisiana
Office of the Attorney General
Consumer Protection Division
P.O. Box 94005
Baton Rouge, LA 70804-9095
Phone: (225) 326-6465
Web site: www.ag.state.la.us

Maine
Office of Licensing and Registration
Department of Professional and Financial Regulation
35 State House Station
Augusta, ME 04333
Phone: (207) 624-8603
Web site: www.state.me.us/pfr/olr/categories/cat10.htm

Office of the Attorney General
Consumer Protection Division
6 State House Station
Augusta, ME 04333-0006
Phone: (207) 626-8800
Web site: www.maine.gov/ag/clenotice.htm

Maryland
Office of the Secretary of State
Charitable Organizations Division
State House
Annapolis, MD 21401
Phone: (410) 974-5534
Web site: www.sos.state.md.us/charity/charityhome.htm

Massachusetts
Office of the Attorney General
Division of Public Charities
One Ashburton Place, Room 1813
Boston, MA 02108
Phone: (617) 727-2200
Web site: http://www.ago.state.ma.us/

Michigan
Office of the Attorney General
Charitable Trust Section
G. Mennen Williams Building, 7th Floor
525 W. Ottawa St.
P.O. Box 30212
Lansing, MI 48909
Phone: (517) 373-1152
Web site: www.michigan.gov/ag/

Minnesota
Office of the Attorney General
Charities Division
1400 Bremer Tower
445 Minnesota St.
St. Paul, MN 55101-2130
Phone: (651) 296-3353
Phone: (651) 296-6172 for registration/forms
Web site: www.ag.state.mn.us/charities

Mississippi
Office of the Secretary of State
Regulation and Enforcement Unit
P.O. Box 136
Jackson, MS 39205-0136
Phone: (601) 359-2663
Web site: www.sos.state.ms.us/regenf/charities/charities.asp

Office of the Attorney General
Consumer Protection Division
P.O. Box 22947
Jackson, MS 39225-2947
Phone: (601) 359-4230
Web site: www.ago.state.ms.us./divisions/consumer

Missouri
Office of the Attorney General
Consumer Protection Division, Charities Unit
200 W. High St.
P.O. Box 899
Jefferson City, MO 65102
Phone: (573) 751-3321
Web site: www.ago.mo.gov/consumer-programs.htm

Montana
Office of the Attorney General
Consumer Protection Office
1219 8th Ave.
P.O. Box 200151
Helena, MT 59620-0151
Phone: (406) 444-4500
Web site: www.doj.mt.gov/consumer

Nebraska
Office of the Attorney General
Consumer Protection Division
2115 State Capitol
Lincoln, NE 68509
Phone: (402) 471-2682
Web site: www.ago.state.ne.us

Nevada
Office of the Attorney General
Bureau of Consumer Protection
100 N. Carson St.
Carson City, NV 89710-4717
Phone: (775) 684-1100
Web site: ag.state.nv.us

New Hampshire
Department of Justice
Division of Charitable Trusts
33 Capitol St.
Concord, NH 03301-6397
Phone: (603) 271-3658
Web site: www.doj.nh.gov/charitable

New Jersey
Department of Law and Public Safety
Office of Consumer Protection
124 Halsey St.
Newark, NJ 07102
Phone: (973) 504-6200
Web site: www.state.nj.us/lps/ca/ocp.htm

New Mexico
Office of the Attorney General
Registry of Charitable Organizations
111 Lomas Blvd. NW, Suite 300
Albuquerque, NM 87102
Phone: (505) 222-9046
Web site: www.ago.state.nm.us/divs/cons/charities/
charities.htm

New York
Office of the Attorney General
The Charities Bureau
120 Broadway
New York, NY 10271
Phone: (212) 416-8000
Web site: www.oag.state.ny.us/charities/charities.html

North Carolina
Department of the Secretary of State
Charitable Solicitation Licensing Section
P.O. Box 29622
Raleigh, NC 27626-0622
Phone: (919) 807-2214
Web site: www.secretary.state.nc.us/csl/
licensing.asp?dtm=497685185185185

Department of Justice
Consumer Protection Division
9001 Mail Service Center
Raleigh, NC 27699-9001
Phone: (919) 716-6400
Web site: www.ncdoj.com/consumerprotection/cp_about.jsp

North Dakota
Office of the Secretary of State
Administrative and Licensing Division
600 E. Boulevard Ave., Dept. 108
Bismarck, ND 58505-0500
Phone: (701) 328-3665
Web site: www.nd.gov/sos/nonprofit

Office of the Attorney General
Consumer Protection and Antitrust Division
4025 State St.
P.O. Box 1054
Bismarck, ND 58502-1054
Phone: (701) 328-3404
Web site: www.ag.state.nd.us

Ohio
Office of the Attorney General
Charitable Law Section
150 E. Gay St., 23rd Floor
Columbus, OH 43215-3130
Phone: (614) 466-3180
Web site: www.ag.state.oh.us/business/char_organizations.asp

Oklahoma
Office of the Secretary of State
Charitable Organizations
2300 N. Lincoln Blvd., Suite 101
Oklahoma City, OK 73105-4897
Phone: (405) 521-3912
Web site: www.sos.state.ok.us

Office of the Attorney General
Consumer Protection Division
4545 N. Lincoln Blvd., Suite 260
Oklahoma City, OK 73105-3498
Phone: (405) 521-3921
Web site: www.oag.state.ok.us/oagweb.nsf/consumer!openpage

Oregon
Department of Justice
Charitable Activities Section
1515 SW 5th Ave, Suite 410
Portland, OR 97201-5451
Phone: (971) 673-1880
Web site: www.doj.state.or.us/charigroup/index.shtml

Pennsylvania
Department of State
Bureau of Charitable Organizations
207 North Office Building
Harrisburg, PA 17120
Phone: (717) 783-1720
Web site: www.dos.state.pa.us/char/site/default.asp

Office of the Attorney General
Charitable Trusts and Organizations Section
14th Floor, Strawberry Square
Harrisburg, PA 17120
Phone: (717) 783-2853
Web site: www.attorneygeneral.gov/consumers.aspx?id=227

Rhode Island
Department of Business Regulation
Charitable Organizations
233 Richmond St., Suite 232
Providence, RI 02903-4232
Phone: (401) 222-3048
Web site: www.dbr.state.ri.us/char_orgs.html

Department of the Attorney General
Charitable Trusts Unit of the Civil Division
150 S. Main St.
Providence, RI 02903
Phone: (401) 274-4400
Web site: www.riag.state.ri.us/civil/charitable.php

South Carolina
Office of the Secretary of State
Public Charities Division
P.O. Box 11350
Columbia, SC 29211
Phone: (803) 734-1790
Web site: www.scsos.com

Office of the Attorney General
Charitable Trust Division
P.O. Box 11549
Columbia, SC 29211
Phone: (803) 734-3970
Web site: www.scattorneygeneral.org

South Dakota
Office of the Attorney General
Consumer Protection Division
1302 E. Hwy. 14, Suite 3
Pierre, SD 57501-8503
Phone: (605) 773-4400
Web site: www.state.sd.us/attorney/office/divisions/consumer

Tennessee
Office of the Secretary of State
Division of Charitable Solicitations
312 Eight Ave. North
8th Floor, Snodgrass Tower
Nashville, TN 37243
Phone: (615) 741-2555
Web site: www.state.tn.us/sos/charity.htm

Office of the Attorney General
Consumer Advocate and Protection Division
P.O. Box 20207
Nashville, TN 37202-0207
Phone: (615) 741-1671
Web site: www.attorneygeneral.state.tn.us

Texas
Office of the Attorney General
Consumer Protection
P.O. Box 12548
Austin, TX 78711-2548
Phone: (512) 463-2100
Web site: www.oag.state.tx.us/consumer/charitabletrusts.shtml
www.sos.state.tx.us/corp/nonprofit_org.shtml

Utah
Department of Commerce
Division of Consumer Protection
P.O. Box 146704
Salt Lake City, UT 84114
Phone: (801) 530-6601
Web site: www.dcp.utah.gov

Office of the Attorney General
Consumer Assistance/Commercial Enforcement Division
P.O. Box 142320
Salt Lake City, UT 84114
Phone: (801) 538-9600
Web site: attygen.state.ut.us/consumerassistance.html

Vermont
Office of the Attorney General
Consumer Protection
109 State St.
Montpelier, VT 05609-1001
Phone: (802) 828-3171
Web site: www.atg.state.vt.us/display.php?smod=10

Virginia
Department of Agriculture and Consumer Services
Office of Consumer Affairs
P.O. Box 1163
Richmond, VA 23218
Phone: (804) 786-2042
Web site: www.vdacs.virginia.gov/allforms.html

Office of the Attorney General
Anti-Trust & Consumer Litigation Section
900 East Main St., 2nd Floor
Richmond, VA 23219
Phone: (804) 786-2071
Web site: www.oag.state.va.us

Washington
Office of the Secretary of State
Charitable Solicitations and Trusts
P.O. Box 40234
Olympia, WA 98504-0234
Phone: (360) 753-0863
Web site: www.secstate.wa.gov/charities

Office of the Attorney General
Consumer Protection Division
900 4th Ave., Suite 2000
Seattle, WA 98164-1012
Phone: (206) 464-6684
Web site: www.atg.wa.gov

West Virginia
Office of the Secretary of State
State Capitol Bldg. 1, Suite 157-K
1900 Kanawha Blvd. East
Charleston, WV 25305-0770
Phone: (304) 558-6000
Web site: www.wvsos.com/charity/main.htm

Office of the Attorney General
Consumer Protection Division
P.O. Box 1789
Charleston, WV 25326
Phone: (304) 558-8986
Web site: www.wvago.us

Wisconsin
Department of Regulation and Licensing
P.O. Box 8935
Madison, WI 53708-8935
Phone: (608) 266-2112
Web site: drl.wi.gov/boards/rco/index.htm

Department of Justice
Office of the Attorney General
P.O. Box 7857
Madison, WI 53707-7857
Phone: (608) 266-1221
Web site: www.doj.state.wi.us/dls/crimlitt.asp

Wyoming
Office of the Attorney General
Consumer Protection Unit
123 State Capitol
Cheyenne, WY 82002
Phone: (307) 777-7874
Web site: attorneygeneral.state.wy.us/consumer.htm

Appendix D

Selections from the Revised Model Nonprofit Corporation Act (1987)

Chapter 2: Organization

Section 2.01. Incorporators.

One or more persons may act as the incorporator or incorporators of a corporation by delivering articles of incorporation to the secretary of state for filing.

Section 2.02. Articles of Incorporation.

(a) The articles of incorporation must set forth:

(1) a corporate name for the corporation that satisfies the requirements of section 4.01;

(2) one of the following statements:

(i) This corporation is a public benefit corporation.

(ii) This corporation is a mutual benefit corporation.

(iii) This corporation is a religious corporation;

(3) the street address of the corporation's initial registered office and the name of its initial registered agent at that office;

(4) the name and address of each incorporator;

(5) whether or not the corporation will have members; and

(6) provisions not inconsistent with law regarding the distribution of assets on dissolution.

(b) The articles of incorporation may set forth:

(1) the purpose or purposes for which the corporation is organized, which may be, either alone or in combination with other purposes, the transaction of any lawful activity;

(2) the names and addresses of the individuals who are to serve as the initial directors;

(3) provisions not inconsistent with law regarding:

(i) managing and regulating the affairs of the corporation;

(ii) defining, limiting, and regulating the powers of the corporation, its board of directors, and members (or any class of members); and

(iii) the characteristics, qualifications, rights, limitations and obligations attaching to each or any class of members.

(4) any provision that under this Act is required or permitted to be set forth in the bylaws.

(c) Each incorporator and director named in the articles must sign the articles.

(d) The articles of incorporation need not set forth any of the corporate powers enumerated in this Act.

Section 2.03. Incorporation.

(a) Unless a delayed effective date is specified, the corporate existence begins when the articles of incorporation are filed.

(b) The secretary of state's filing of the articles of incorporation is conclusive proof that the incorporators satisfied all conditions precedent to incorporation except in a proceeding by the state to cancel or revoke the incorporation or involuntarily dissolve the corporation.

Section 2.04. Liability for Preincorporation Transactions.

All persons purporting to act as or on behalf of a corporation, knowing there was no incorporation under this Act, are jointly and severally liable for all liabilities created while so acting.

Section 2.05. Organization of Corporation.

(a) After incorporation:

(1) if initial directors are named in the articles of incorporation, the initial directors shall hold an organizational meeting, at the call of a majority of the

directors, to complete the organization of the corporation by appointing officers, adopting bylaws, and carrying on any other business brought before the meeting;

(2) if initial directors are not named in the articles, the incorporator or incorporators shall hold an organizational meeting at the call of a majority of the incorporators:

(i) to elect directors and complete the organization of the corporation; or

(ii) to elect a board of directors who shall complete the organization of the corporation.

(b) Action required or permitted by this Act to be taken by incorporators at an organizational meeting may be taken without a meeting if the action taken is evidenced by one or more written consents describing the action taken and signed by each incorporator.

(c) An organizational meeting may be held in or out of this state in accordance with section 8.21.

Section 2.06. Bylaws.

(a) The incorporators or board of directors of a corporation shall adopt bylaws for the corporation.

(b) The bylaws may contain any provision for regulating and managing the affairs of the corporation that is not inconsistent with law or the articles of incorporation.

Chapter 7: Members' Meetings and Voting

Subchapter A: Meetings and Action Without Meetings

Section 7.01. Annual and Regular Meetings.

(a) A corporation with members shall hold a membership meeting annually at a time stated in or fixed in accordance with the bylaws.

(b) A corporation with members may hold regular membership meetings at the times stated in or fixed in accordance with the bylaws.

(c) Annual and regular membership meetings may be held in or out of this state at the place stated in or fixed in accordance with the bylaws. If no place is stated in or fixed in accordance with the bylaws, annual and regular meetings shall be held at the corporation's principal office.

(d) At the annual meeting:

(1) The president and chief financial officer shall report on the activities and financial condition of the corporation; and

(2) The members shall consider and act upon such other matters as may be raised consistent with the notice requirements of sections 7.05 and 7.23(b).

(e) At regular meetings the members shall consider and act upon such matters as may be raised consistent with the notice requirements of sections 7.05 and 7.23(b).

(f) The failure to hold an annual or regular meeting at a time stated in or fixed in accordance with a corporation's bylaws does not affect the validity of any corporate action.

Chapter 8: Directors and Officers

Subchapter A: Board of Directors

Section 8.01. Requirement for and Duties of Board.

(a) Each corporation must have a board of directors.

(b) Except as provided in this Act or subsection (c), all corporate powers shall be exercised by or under the authority of, and the affairs of the corporation managed under the direction of, its board.

(c) The articles may authorize a person or persons to exercise some or all of the powers which would otherwise be exercised by a board. To the extent so authorized any such person or persons shall have the duties and responsibilities of the directors, and the directors shall be relieved to that extent from such duties and responsibilities.

Section 8.02. Qualifications of Directors.

All directors must be individuals. The articles or bylaws may prescribe other qualifications for directors.

Section 8.03. Number of Directors.

(a) A board of directors must consist of three or more individuals, with the number specified in or fixed in accordance with the articles or bylaws.

(b) The number of directors may be increased or decreased (but to no fewer than three) from time to time by amendment to or in the manner prescribed in the articles or bylaws.

Section 8.04. Election, Designation and Appointment of Directors.

(a) If the corporation has members, all the directors (except the initial directors) shall be elected at the first annual meeting of members, and at each annual meeting thereafter, unless the articles or bylaws provide some other time or method of election, or provide that some of the directors are appointed by some other person or designated.

(b) If the corporation does not have members, all the directors (except the initial directors) shall be elected, appointed or designated as provided in the articles or bylaws. If no method of designation or appointment is set forth in the articles or bylaws, the directors (other than the initial directors) shall be elected by the board.

Section 8.05. Terms of Directors Generally.

(a) The articles or bylaws must specify the terms of directors. Except for designated or appointed directors, the terms of directors may not exceed five years. In the absence of any term specified in the articles or bylaws, the term of each director shall be one year. Directors may be elected for successive terms.

(b) A decrease in the number of directors or term of office does not shorten an incumbent director's term.

(c) Except as provided in the articles or bylaws:

(1) the term of a director filling a vacancy in the office of a director elected by members expires at the next election of directors by members; and

(2) the term of a director filling any other vacancy expires at the end of the unexpired term that such director is filling.

(d) Despite the expiration of a director's term, the director continues to serve until the director's successor is elected, designated or appointed and qualifies, or until there is a decrease in the number of directors.

Subchapter C: Standards of Conduct

Section 8.30. General Standards for Directors.

(a) A director shall discharge his or her duties as a director, including his or her duties as a member of a committee:

(1) in good faith;

(2) with the care an ordinarily prudent person in a like position would exercise under similar circumstances; and

(3) in a manner the director reasonably believes to be in the best interests of the corporation.

(b) In discharging his or her duties, a director is entitled to rely on information, opinions, reports, or statements, including financial statements and other financial data, if prepared or presented by:

(1) one or more officers or employees of the corporation whom the director reasonably believes to be reliable and competent in the matters presented;

(2) legal counsel, public accountants or other persons as to matters the director reasonably believes are within the person's professional or expert competence;

(3) a committee of the board of which the director is not a member, as to matters within its jurisdiction, if the director reasonably believes the committee merits confidence; or

(4) in the case of religious corporations, religious authorities and ministers, priests, rabbis or other persons whose position or duties in the religious organization the director believes justify reliance and confidence and whom the director believes to be reliable and competent in the matters presented.

(c) A director is not acting in good faith if the director has knowledge concerning the matter in question that makes reliance otherwise permitted by subsection (b) unwarranted.

(d) A director is not liable to the corporation, any member, or any other person for any action taken or not taken as a director, if the director acted in compliance with this section.

(e) A director shall not be deemed to be a trustee with respect to the corporation or with respect to any property held or administered by the corporation, including without limit, property that may be subject to restrictions imposed by the donor or transferor of such property.

Section 8.31. Director Conflict of Interest.

(a) A conflict of interest transaction is a transaction with the corporation in which a director of the corporation has a direct or indirect interest. A conflict of interest transaction is not voidable or the basis for imposing liability on the director if the transaction was fair at the time it was entered into or is approved as provided in subsections (b) or (c).

(b) A transaction in which a director of a public benefit or religious corporation has a conflict of interest may be approved:

(1) in advance by the vote of the board of directors or a committee of the board if:

(i) the material facts of the transaction and the director's interest are disclosed or known to the board or committee of the board; and

(ii) the directors approving the transaction in good faith reasonably believe that the transaction is fair to the corporation; or

(2) before or after it is consummated by obtaining approval of the:

(i) attorney general; or

(ii) [describe or name] court in an action in which the attorney general is joined as a party; or

(c) A transaction in which a director of a mutual benefit corporation has a conflict of interest may be approved if;

(1) the material facts of the transaction and the director's interest were disclosed or known to the board of directors or a committee of the board and the board or committee of the board authorized, approved, or ratified the transaction; or

(2) the material facts of the transaction and the director's interest were disclosed or known to the members and they authorized, approved, or ratified the transaction.

(d) For purposes of this section, a director of the corporation has an indirect interest in a transaction if (1) another entity in which the director has a material interest or in which the director is a general partner is a party to the transaction or (2) another entity of which the director is a director, officer, or trustee is a party to the transaction.

(e) For purposes of subsections (b) and (c) a conflict of interest transaction is authorized, approved, or ratified, if it receives the affirmative vote of a majority of the directors on the board or on the committee, who have no direct or indirect interest in the transaction, but a transaction may not be authorized, approved, or ratified under this section by a single director. If a majority of the directors on the board who have no direct or indirect interest in the transaction vote to authorize, approve, or ratify the transaction, a quorum is present for the purpose of taking action under this section. The presence of, or a vote cast by, a director with a direct or indirect interest in the transaction does not affect the validity of any action taken under subsections (b)(1) or (c)(1) if the transaction is otherwise approved as provided in subsection (b) or (c).

(f) For purposes of subsection (c)(2), a conflict of interest transaction is authorized, approved, or ratified by the members if it receives a majority of the votes entitled to be counted under this subsection. Votes cast by or voted under the control of a director who has a direct or indirect interest in the transaction, and votes cast by or voted under the control of an entity described in subsection (d)(1), may not be counted in a vote of members to determine whether to authorize, approve, or ratify a conflict of interest transaction under subsection (c)(2). The vote of these members, however, is counted in determining whether the transaction is approved under other sections of this Act. A majority of the voting power, whether or not present, that are entitled to be counted in a vote on the transaction under this subsection constitutes a quorum for the purpose of taking action under this section.

(g) The articles, bylaws, or a resolution of the board may impose additional requirements on conflict of interest transactions.

Section 8.32. Loans to or Guaranties for Directors and Officers.

(a) A corporation may not lend money to or guaranty the obligation of a director or officer of the corporation.

(b) The fact that a loan or guaranty is made in violation of this section does not affect the borrower's liability on the loan.

Section 8.33. Liability for Unlawful Distributions.

(a) Unless a director complies with the applicable standards of conduct described in section 8.30, a director who votes for or assents to a distribution made in violation of this Act is personally liable to the corporation for the amount of the distribution that exceeds what could have been distributed without violating this Act.

(b) A director held liable for an unlawful distribution under subsection (a) is entitled to contribution:

(1) from every other director who voted for or assented to the distribution without complying with the applicable standards of conduct described in section 8.30; and

(2) from each person who received an unlawful distribution for the amount of the distribution whether or not the person receiving the distribution knew it was made in violation of this Act.

Subchapter D: Officers

Section 8.40. Required Officers.

(a) Unless otherwise provided in the articles or bylaws, a corporation shall have a president, a secretary, a treasurer and such other officers as are appointed by the board.

(b) The bylaws or the board shall delegate to one of the officers responsibility for preparing minutes of the directors' and members' meetings and for authenticating records of the corporation.

(c) The same individual may simultaneously hold more than one office in a corporation.

Section 8.41. Duties and Authority of Officers.

Each officer has the authority and shall perform the duties set forth in the bylaws or, to the extent consistent with the bylaws, the duties and authority prescribed in a resolution of the board or by direction of an officer authorized by the board to prescribe the duties and authority of other officers.

Section 8.42. Standards of Conduct for Officers.

(a) An officer with discretionary authority shall discharge his or her duties under that authority:

(1) in good faith;

(2) with the care an ordinarily prudent person in a like position would exercise under similar circumstances; and

(3) in a manner the officer reasonably believes to be in the best interests of the corporation and its members, if any.

(b) In discharging his or her duties an officer is entitled to rely on information, opinions, reports, or statements, including financial statements and other financial data, if prepared or presented by:

(1) one or more officers or employees of the corporation who the officer reasonably believes to be reliable and competent in the matters presented;

(2) legal counsel, public accountants or other persons as to matters the officer reasonably believes are within the person's professional or expert competence; or

(3) in the case of religious corporations, religious authorities and ministers, priests, rabbis or other persons whose position or duties in the religious organization the officer believes justify reliance and confidence and who the officer believes to be reliable and competent in the matters presented.

(c) An officer is not acting in good faith if the officer has knowledge concerning the matter in question that makes reliance otherwise permitted by subsection (b) unwarranted.

(d) An officer is not liable to the corporation, any member, or other person for any action taken or not taken as an officer, if the officer acted in compliance with this section.

Section 8.43. Resignation and Removal of Officers.

(a) An officer may resign at any time by delivering notice to the corporation. A resignation is effective when the notice is effective unless the notice specifies a future effective date. If a resignation is made effective at a future date and the corporation accepts the future effective date, its board of directors may fill the pending vacancy before the effective date if the board provides that the successor does not take office until the effective date.

(b) A board may remove any officer at any time with or without cause.

Section 8.44. Contract Rights of Officers.

(a) The appointment of an officer does not itself create contract rights.

(b) An officer's removal does not affect the officer's contract rights, if any, with the corporation. An officer's resignation does not affect the corporation's contract rights, if any, with the officer.

Section 8.45. Officers' Authority To Execute Documents.

Any contract or other instrument in writing executed or entered into between a corporation and any other person is not invalidated as to the corporation by any lack of authority of the signing officers in the absence of actual knowledge on the part of the other person that the signing officers had no authority to execute the contract or other instrument if it is signed by any two officers in Category 1 below or by one officer in Category 1 below and one officer in Category 2 below.

Category 1 – The presiding officer of the board and the president.

Category 2 – A vice president, the secretary, treasurer and executive director.

Subchapter E: Indemnification

Section 8.50. Subchapter Definitions.

In this subchapter:

(1) "Corporation" includes any domestic or foreign predecessor entity of a corporation in a merger or other transaction in which the predecessor's existence ceased upon consummation of the transaction.

(2) "Director" means an individual who is or was a director of a corporation or an individual who, while a director of a corporation, is or was serving at the corporation's request as a director, officer, partner, trustee, employee, or agent of another foreign or domestic business or nonprofit corporation, partnership, joint venture, trust, employee benefit plan, or other enterprise. A director is considered to be serving an employee benefit plan at the corporation's request if the director's duties to the corporation also impose duties on, or otherwise involve services by, the director to the plan or to participants in or beneficiaries of the plan. "Director" includes, unless the context requires otherwise, the estate or personal representative of a director.

(3) "Expenses" include counsel fees.

(4) "Liability" means the obligation to pay a judgment, settlement, penalty, fine (including an excise tax assessed with respect to an employee benefit plan), or reasonable expenses actually incurred with respect to a proceeding.

(5) "Official capacity" means: (i) when used with respect to a director, the office of director in a corporation; and (ii) when used with respect to an individual other than a director, as contemplated in section 8.56, the office in a corporation held by the officer or the employment or agency relationship undertaken by the employee or agent on behalf of the corporation. "Official capacity" does not include service for any other foreign or domestic business or nonprofit corporation or any partnership, joint venture, trust, employee benefit plan, or other enterprise.

(6) "Party" includes an individual who was, is or is threatened to be made a named defendant or respondent in a proceeding.

(7) "Proceeding" means any threatened, pending, or completed action, suit or proceeding whether civil, criminal, administrative, or investigative and whether formal or informal.

Section 8.51. Authority To Indemnify.

(a) Except as provided in subsection (d), a corporation may indemnify an individual made a party to a proceeding because the individual is or was a director against liability incurred in the proceeding if the individual:

(1) conducted himself or herself in good faith; and

(2) reasonably believed:

(i) in the case of conduct in his or her official capacity with the corporation, that his or her conduct was in its best interests; and

(ii) in all other cases, that his or her conduct was at least not opposed to its best interests; and

(3) in the case of any criminal proceeding, had no reasonable cause to believe his or her conduct was unlawful.

(b) A director's conduct with respect to an employee benefit plan for a purpose the director reasonably believed to be in the interests of the participants in and beneficiaries of the plan is conduct that satisfies the requirements of subsection (a)(2)(ii).

(c) The termination of a proceeding by judgment, order, settlement, conviction, or upon a plea of nolo contendere or its equivalent is not, of itself, determinative that the director did not meet the standard of conduct described in this section.

(d) A corporation may not indemnify a director under this section:

(1) in connection with a proceeding by or in the right of the corporation in which the director was adjudged liable to the corporation; or

(2) in connection with any other proceeding charging improper personal benefit to the director, whether or not involving action in his or her official capacity, in which the director was adjudged liable on the basis that personal benefit was improperly received by the director.

(e) Indemnification permitted under this section in connection with a proceeding by or in the right of the corporation is limited to reasonable expenses incurred in connection with the proceeding.

Section 8.52. Mandatory Indemnification.

Unless limited by its articles of incorporation, a corporation shall indemnify a director who was wholly successful, on the merits or otherwise, in the defense of any proceeding to which the director was a party because he or she is or was a director of the corporation against reasonable expenses actually incurred by the director in connection with the proceeding.

Section 8.53. Advance for Expenses.

(a) A corporation may pay for or reimburse the reasonable expenses incurred by a director who is a party to a proceeding in advance of final disposition of the proceeding if:

(1) the director furnishes the corporation a written affirmation of his or her good faith belief that he or she has met the standard of conduct described in section 8.51;

(2) the director furnishes the corporation a written undertaking, executed personally or on the director's behalf, to repay the advance if it is ultimately determined that the director did not meet the standard of conduct; and

(3) a determination is made that the facts then known to those making the determination would not preclude indemnification under this subchapter.

(b) The undertaking required by subsection (a)(2) must be an unlimited general obligation of the director but need not be secured and may be accepted without reference to financial ability to make repayment.

(c) Determinations and authorizations of payments under this section shall be made in the manner specified in section 8.55.

Section 8.54. Court-Ordered Indemnification.

Unless limited by a corporation's articles of incorporation, a director of the corporation who is a party to a proceeding may apply for indemnification to the court conducting the proceeding or to another court of competent jurisdiction. On receipt of an application, the court after giving any notice the court considers necessary may order indemnification in the amount it considers proper if it determines:

(1) the director is entitled to mandatory indemnification under section 8.52, in which case the court shall also order the corporation to pay the director's reasonable expenses incurred to obtain court-ordered indemnification; or

(2) the director is fairly and reasonably entitled to indemnification in view of all the relevant circumstances, whether or not the director met the standard of conduct set forth in section 8.51(a) or was adjudged liable as described in section 8.51(d), but if the director was adjudged so liable indemnification is limited to reasonable expenses incurred.

Section 8.55. Determination and Authorization of Indemnification.

(a) A corporation may not indemnify a director under section 8.51 unless authorized in the specific case after a determination has been made that indemnification of the director is permissible in the circumstances because the director has met the standard of conduct set forth in section 8.51.

(b) The determination shall be made:

(1) by the board of directors by majority vote of a quorum consisting of directors not at the time parties to the proceeding;

(2) if a quorum cannot be obtained under subdivision (1), by majority vote of a committee duly designated by the board of directors (in which designation directors who are parties may participate), consisting solely of two or more directors not at the time parties to the proceeding;

(3) by special legal counsel:

(i) selected by the board of directors or its committee in the manner prescribed in subdivision (1) or (2); or

(ii) if a quorum of the board cannot be obtained under subdivision (1) and a committee cannot be designated under subdivision (2), selected by majority vote of the full board (in which selection directors who are parties may participate); or

(4) by the members of a mutual benefit corporation, but directors who are at the time parties to the proceeding may not vote on the determination.

(c) Authorization of indemnification and evaluation as to reasonableness of expenses shall be made in the same manner as the determination that indemnification is permissible, except that if the determination is made by special legal counsel, authorization of indemnification and evaluation as to reasonableness of expenses shall be made by those entitled under subsection (b)(3) to select counsel.

(d) A director of a public benefit corporation may not be indemnified until 20 days after the effective date of written notice to the attorney general of the proposed indemnification.

Section 8.56. Indemnification of Officers, Employees and Agents.

Unless limited by a corporation's articles of incorporation:

(1) an officer of the corporation who is not a director is entitled to mandatory indemnification under section 8.52, and is entitled to apply for court-ordered indemnification under section 8.54 in each case, to the same extent as a director;

(2) the corporation may indemnify and advance expenses under this subchapter to an officer, employee, or agent of the corporation who is not a director to the same extent as to a director; and

(3) a corporation may also indemnify and advance expenses to an officer, employee, or agent who is not a director to the extent, consistent with public

policy, that may be provided by its articles of incorporation, bylaws, general or specific action of its board of directors, or contract.

Section 8.57. Insurance.

A corporation may purchase and maintain insurance on behalf of an individual who is or was a director, officer, employee, or agent of the corporation, or who, while a director, officer, employee, or agent of the corporation, is or was serving at the request of the corporation as a director, officer, partner, trustee, employee, or agent of another foreign or domestic business or nonprofit corporation, partnership, joint venture, trust, employee benefit plan, or other enterprise, against liability asserted against or incurred by him or her in that capacity or arising from his or her status as a director, officer, employee, or agent, whether or not the corporation would have power to indemnify the person against the same liability under section 8.51 or 8.52.

Section 8.58. Application of Subchapter.

(a) A provision treating a corporation's indemnification of or advance for expenses to directors that is contained in its articles of incorporation, bylaws, a resolution of its members or board of directors, or in a contract or otherwise, is valid only if and to the extent the provision is consistent with this subchapter. If articles of incorporation limit indemnification or advance for expenses, indemnification and advance for expenses are valid only to the extent consistent with the articles.

(b) This subchapter does not limit a corporation's power to pay or reimburse expenses incurred by a director in connection with appearing as a witness in a proceeding at a time when the director has not been made a named defendant or respondent to the proceeding.

Chapter 10: Amendment of Articles of Incorporation and Bylaws

Subchapter A: Articles of Incorporation

Section 10.01. Authority To Amend.

A corporation may amend its articles of incorporation at any time to add or change a provision that is required or permitted in the articles or to delete a provision not required in the articles. Whether a provision is required or permitted in the articles is determined as of the effective date of the amendment.

Section 10.02. Amendment by Directors.

(a) Unless the articles provide otherwise, a corporation's board of directors may adopt one or more amendments to the corporation's articles without member approval:

(1) to extend the duration of the corporation if it was incorporated at a time when limited duration was required by law;

(2) to delete the names and addresses of the initial directors;

(3) to delete the name and address of the initial registered agent or registered office, if a statement of change is on file with the secretary of state;

(4) to change the corporate name by substituting the word "corporation," "incorporated," "company," "limited," or the abbreviation "corp.," "inc.," "co.," or "ltd.," for a similar word or abbreviation in the name, or by adding, deleting or changing a geographical attribution to the name; or

(5) to make any other change expressly permitted by this Act to be made by director action.

(b) If a corporation has no members, its incorporators, until directors have been chosen, and thereafter its board of directors, may adopt one or more amendments to the corporation's articles subject to any approval required pursuant to section 10.30. The corporation shall provide notice of any meeting at which an amendment is to be voted upon. The notice shall be in accordance with section 8.22(c). The notice must also state that the purpose, or one of the purposes, of the meeting is to consider a proposed amendment to the articles and contain or be accompanied by a copy or summary of the amendment or state the general nature of the amendment. The amendment must be approved by a majority of the directors in office at the time the amendment is adopted.

Section 10.03. Amendment by Directors and Members.

(a) Unless this Act, the articles, bylaws, the members (acting pursuant to subsection (b)), or the board of directors (acting pursuant to subsection (c)) require a greater vote or voting by class, an amendment to a corporation's articles to be adopted must be approved:

(1) by the board if the corporation is a public benefit or religious corporation and the amendment does not relate to the number of directors, the composition of the board, the term of office of directors, or the method or way in which directors are elected or selected;

(2) except as provided in subsection 10.02(a), by the members by two-thirds of the votes cast or a majority of the voting power, whichever is less; and

(3) in writing by any person or persons whose approval is required by a provision of the articles authorized by section 10.30.

(b) The members may condition the amendment's adoption on receipt of a higher percentage of affirmative votes or on any other basis.

(c) If the board initiates an amendment to the articles or board approval is required by subsection (a) to adopt an amendment to the articles, the board may condition the amendment's adoption on receipt of a higher percentage of affirmative votes or any other basis.

(d) If the board or the members seek to have the amendment approved by the members at a membership meeting, the corporation shall give notice to its members of the proposed membership meeting in writing in accordance with section 7.05. The notice must state that the purpose, or one of the purposes, of the meeting is to consider the proposed amendment and contain or be accompanied by a copy or summary of the amendment.

(e) If the board or the members seek to have the amendment approved by the members by written consent or written ballot, the material soliciting the approval shall contain or be accompanied by a copy or summary of the amendment.

Section 10.04. Class Voting by Members on Amendments.

(a) The members of a class in a public benefit corporation are entitled to vote as a class on a proposed amendment to the articles if the amendment would change the rights of that class as to voting in a manner different than such amendment affects another class or members of another class.

(b) The members of a class in a mutual benefit corporation are entitled to vote as a class on a proposed amendment to the articles if the amendment would:

(1) affect the rights, privileges, preferences, restrictions or conditions of that class as to voting, dissolution, redemption or transfer of memberships in a manner different than such amendment would affect another class;

(2) change the rights, privileges, preferences, restrictions or conditions of that class as to voting, dissolution, redemption or transfer by changing the rights, privileges, preferences, restrictions or conditions of another class.

(3) increase or decrease the number of memberships authorized for that class;

(4) increase the number of memberships authorized for another class;

(5) effect an exchange, reclassification or termination of the memberships of that class; or

(6) authorize a new class of memberships.

(c) The members of a class of a religious corporation are entitled to vote as a class on a proposed amendment to the articles only if a class vote is provided for in the articles or bylaws.

(d) If a class is to be divided into two or more classes as a result of an amendment to the articles of a public benefit or mutual benefit corporation, the amendment must be approved by the members of each class that would be created by the amendment.

(e) Except as provided in the articles or bylaws of a religious corporation, if a class vote is required to approve an amendment to the articles of a corporation, the amendment must be approved by the members of the class by two-thirds of the votes cast by the class or a majority of the voting power of the class, whichever is less.

(f) A class of members of a public benefit or mutual benefit corporation is entitled to the voting rights granted by this section although the articles and bylaws provide that the class may not vote on the proposed amendment.

Section 10.05. Articles of Amendment.

A corporation amending its articles shall deliver to the secretary of state articles of amendment setting forth:

(1) the name of the corporation;

(2) the text of each amendment adopted;

(3) the date of each amendment's adoption;

(4) if approval of members was not required, a statement to that effect and a statement that the amendment was approved by a sufficient vote of the board of directors or incorporators;

(5) if approval by members was required:

(i) the designation, number of memberships outstanding, number of votes entitled to be cast by each class entitled to vote separately on the amendment, and number of votes of each class indisputably voting on the amendment; and

(ii) either the total number of votes cast for and against the amendment by each class entitled to vote separately on the amendment or the total number of undisputed votes cast for the amendment by each class and a statement that the number cast for the amendment by each class was sufficient for approval by that class.

(6) if approval of the amendment by some person or persons other than the members, the board or the incorporators is required pursuant to section 10.30, a statement that the approval was obtained.

Section 10.06. Restated Articles of Incorporation.

(a) A corporation's board of directors may restate its articles of incorporation at any time with or without approval by members or any other person.

(b) The restatement may include one or more amendments to the articles. If the restatement includes an amendment requiring approval by the members or any other person, it must be adopted as provided in section 10.03.

(c) If the restatement includes an amendment requiring approval by members, the board must submit the restatement to the members for their approval.

(d) If the board seeks to have the restatement approved by the members at a membership meeting, the corporation shall notify each of its members of the proposed membership meeting in writing in accordance with section 7.05. The notice must also state that the purpose, or one of the purposes, of the meeting is to consider the proposed restatement and contain or be accompanied by a copy or summary of the restatement that identifies any amendments or other change it would make in the articles.

(e) If the board seeks to have the restatement approved by the members by written ballot or written consent, the material soliciting the approval shall contain or be accompanied by a copy or summary of the restatement that identifies any amendments or other change it would make in the articles.

(f) A restatement requiring approval by the members must be approved by the same vote as an amendment to articles under section 10.03.

(g) If the restatement includes an amendment requiring approval pursuant to section 10.30, the board must submit the restatement for such approval.

(h) A corporation restating its articles shall deliver to the secretary of state articles of restatement setting forth the name of the corporation and the text of the restated articles of incorporation together with a certificate setting forth:

(1) whether the restatement contains an amendment to the articles requiring approval by the members or any other person other than the board of directors and, if it does not, that the board of directors adopted the restatement; or

(2) if the restatement contains an amendment to the articles requiring approval by the members, the information required by section 10.05; and

(3) if the restatement contains an amendment to the articles requiring approval by a person whose approval is required pursuant to section 10.30, a statement that such approval was obtained.

(i) Duly adopted restated articles of incorporation supersede the original articles of incorporation and all amendments to them.

(j) The secretary of state may certify restated articles of incorporation, as the articles of incorporation currently in effect, without including the certificate information required by subsection (h).

Section 10.07. Amendment Pursuant to Judicial Reorganization.

(a) A corporation's articles may be amended without board approval or approval by the members or approval required pursuant to section 10.30 to carry out a plan of reorganization ordered or decreed by a court of competent jurisdiction under federal statute if the articles after amendment contain only provisions required or permitted by section 2.02.

(b) The individual or individuals designated by the court shall deliver to the secretary of state articles of amendment setting forth:

(1) the name of the corporation;

(2) the text of each amendment approved by the court;

(3) the date of the court's order or decree approving the articles of amendment;

(4) the title of the reorganization proceeding in which the order or decree was entered; and

(5) a statement that the court had jurisdiction of the proceeding under federal statute.

(c) This section does not apply after entry of a final decree in the reorganization proceeding even though the court retains jurisdiction of the proceeding for limited purposes unrelated to consummation of the reorganization plan.

Section 10.08. Effect of Amendment and Restatement.

An amendment to articles of incorporation does not affect a cause of action existing against or in favor of the corporation, a proceeding to which the corporation is a party, any requirement or limitation imposed upon the corporation or any property held by it by virtue of any trust upon which such property is held by the corporation or the existing rights of persons other than members of the corporation. An amendment changing a corporation's name does not abate a proceeding brought by or against the corporation in its former name.

Subchapter B: Bylaws

Section 10.20. Amendment by Directors.

If a corporation has no members, its incorporators, until directors have been chosen, and thereafter its board of directors, may adopt one or more amendments to the corporation's bylaws subject to any approval required pursuant to section 10.30. The corporation shall provide notice of any meeting of directors at which an amendment is to be approved. The notice shall be in accordance with section 8.22(c). The notice must also state that the purpose, or one of the purposes, of the meeting is to consider a proposed amendment to the bylaws and contain or be accompanied by a copy or summary of the amendment or state the general nature of the amendment. The amendment must be approved by a majority of the directors in office at the time the amendment is adopted.

Section 10.21. Amendment by Directors and Members.

(a) Unless this Act, the articles, bylaws, the members (acting pursuant to subsection (b)), or the board of directors (acting pursuant to subsection (c)) require a greater vote or voting by class, an amendment to a corporation's bylaws to be adopted must be approved:

(1) by the board if the corporation is a public benefit or religious corporation and the amendment does not relate to the number of directors, the composition of the board, the term of office of directors, or the method or way in which directors are elected or selected;

(2) by the members by two-thirds of the votes cast or a majority of the voting power, whichever is less; and

(3) in writing by any person or persons whose approval is required by a provision of the articles authorized by section 10.30.

(b) The members may condition the amendment's adoption on its receipt of a higher percentage of affirmative votes or on any other basis.

(c) If the board initiates an amendment to the bylaws or board approval is required by subsection (a) to adopt an amendment to the bylaws, the board may condition the amendment's adoption on receipt of a higher percentage of affirmative votes or on any other basis.

(d) If the board or the members seek to have the amendment approved by the members at a membership meeting, the corporation shall give notice to its members of the proposed membership meeting in writing in accordance with section 7.05. The notice must also state that the purpose, or one of the purposes, of the meeting is to consider the proposed amendment and contain or be accompanied by a copy or summary of the amendment.

(e) If the board or the members seek to have the amendment approved by the members by written consent or written ballot, the material soliciting the approval shall contain or be accompanied by a copy or summary of the amendment.

Section 10.22. Class Voting by Members on Amendments.

(a) The members of a class in a public benefit corporation are entitled to vote as a class on a proposed amendment to the bylaws if the amendment would change the rights of that class as to voting in a manner different than such amendment affects another class or members of another class.

(b) The members of a class in a mutual benefit corporation are entitled to vote as a class on a proposed amendment to the bylaws if the amendment would:

(1) affect the rights, privileges, preferences, restrictions or conditions of that class as to voting, dissolution, redemption or transfer of memberships in a manner different than such amendment would affect another class;

(2) change the rights, privileges, preferences, restrictions or conditions of that class as to voting, dissolution, redemption or transfer by changing the rights, privileges, preferences, restrictions or conditions of another class;

(3) increase or decrease the number of memberships authorized for that class;

(4) increase the number of memberships authorized for another class;

(5) effect an exchange, reclassification or termination of all or part of the memberships of that class; or

(6) authorize a new class of memberships.

(c) The members of a class of a religious corporation are entitled to vote as a class on a proposed amendment to the bylaws only if a class vote is provided for in the articles or bylaws.

(d) If a class is to be divided into two or more classes as a result of an amendment to the bylaws, the amendment must be approved by the members of each class that would be created by the amendment; and

(e) If a class vote is required to approve an amendment to the bylaws, the amendment must be approved by the members of the class by two-thirds of the votes cast by the class or a majority of the voting power of the class, whichever is less.

(f) A class of members is entitled to the voting rights granted by this section although the articles and bylaws provide that the class may not vote on the proposed amendment.

Subchapter C: Articles of Incorporation and Bylaws

Section 10.30. Approval by Third Persons.

The articles may require an amendment to the articles or bylaws to be approved in writing by a specified person or persons other than the board. Such an article provision may only be amended with the approval in writing of such person or persons.

Section 10.31. Amendment Terminating Members or Redeeming or Canceling Memberships. Optional section.

(a) Any amendment to the articles or bylaws of a public benefit or mutual benefit corporation that would terminate all members or any class of members or redeem or cancel all memberships or any class of memberships must meet the requirements of the Act and this section.

(b) Before adopting a resolution proposing such an amendment, the board of a mutual benefit corporation shall give notice of the general nature of the amendment to the members.

(c) After adopting a resolution proposing such an amendment, the notice to members proposing such amendment shall include one statement of up to 500 words opposing the proposed amendment if such statement is submitted by any five members or members having three percent or more of the voting power, whichever is less, not later than twenty days after the board has voted to submit such amendment to the members for their approval. In public benefit corporations the production and mailing costs shall be paid by the requesting members. In mutual benefit corporations the production and mailing costs shall be paid by the corporation.

(d) Any such amendment shall be approved by the members by two-thirds of the votes cast by each class.

(e) The provisions of section 6.21 shall not apply to any amendment meeting the requirements of the Act and this section.

Chapter 11: Merger

Section 11.01. Approval of Plan of Merger.

(a) Subject to the limitations set forth in section 11.02, one or more nonprofit corporations may merge into a business or nonprofit corporation, if the plan of merger is approved or provided in section 11.03.

(b) The plan of merger must set forth:

(1) the name of each corporation planning to merge and the name of the surviving corporation into which each plans to merge;

(2) the terms and conditions of the planned merger;

(3) the manner and basis, if any, of converting the memberships of each public benefit or religious corporation into memberships of the surviving corporation; and

(4) if the merger involves a mutual benefit corporation, the manner and basis, if any, of converting memberships of each merging corporation into memberships, obligations or securities of the surviving or any other corporation or into cash or other property in whole or part.

(c) The plan of merger may set forth:

(1) any amendments to the articles of incorporation or bylaws of the surviving corporation to be effected by the planned merger; and

(2) other provisions relating to the planned merger.

Section 11.02. Limitations on Mergers by Public Benefit or Religious Corporations.

(a) Without the prior approval of [insert name of appropriate court] in a proceeding which the attorney general has been given written notice, a public benefit or religious corporation may merge only with:

(1) a public benefit or religious corporation;

(2) a foreign corporation that would qualify under this Act as a public benefit or religious corporation;

(3) a wholly-owned foreign or domestic business or mutual benefit corporation, provided the public benefit or religious corporation is the surviving corporation and continues to be a public benefit or religious corporation after the merger; or

(4) a business or mutual benefit corporation, provided that: (i) on or prior to the effective date of the merger, assets with a value equal to the greater of the fair market value of the net tangible and intangible assets (including goodwill) of the public benefit corporation or the fair market value of the public benefit corporation if it were to be operated as a business concern are transferred or conveyed to one or more persons who would have received its assets under section 14.06(a)(5) and (6) had it dissolved; (ii) it shall return, transfer or convey any assets held by it upon condition requiring return, transfer or conveyance, which condition occurs by reason of the merger, in

accordance with such condition; and (iii) the merger is approved by a majority of directors of the public benefit or religious corporation who are not and will not become members or shareholders in or officers, employees, agents or consultants of the surviving corporation.

(b) At least 20 days before consummation of any merger of a public benefit corporation or a religious corporation pursuant to (a)(4), notice, including a copy of the proposed plan of merger, must be delivered to the attorney general.

(c) Without the prior written consent of the attorney general or of [insert name of appropriate court] in a proceeding in which the attorney general has been given notice, no member of a public benefit or religious corporation may receive or keep anything as a result of a merger other than a membership or membership in the surviving public benefit or religious corporation. The court shall approve the transaction if it is in the public interest.

Section 11.03. Action on Plan by Board, Members and Third Persons.

(a) Unless this Act, the articles, bylaws or the board of directors or members (acting pursuant to subsection (c)) require a greater vote or voting by class, a plan of merger to be adopted must be approved:

(1) by the board;

(2) by the members, if any, by two-thirds of the votes cast or a majority of the voting power, whichever is less; and

(3) in writing by any person or persons whose approval is required by a provision of the articles authorized by section 10.30 for an amendment to the articles or bylaws.

(b) If the corporation does not have members, the merger must be approved by a majority of the directors in office at the time the merger is approved. In addition the corporation shall provide notice of any directors' meeting at which such approval is to be obtained in accordance with section 8.22(c). The notice must also state that the purpose, or one of the purposes, of the meeting is to consider the proposed merger.

(c) The board may condition its submission of the proposed merger, and the members may condition their approval of the merger, on receipt of a higher percentage of affirmative votes or on any other basis.

(d) If the board seeks to have the plan approved by the members at a membership meeting, the corporation shall give notice to its members of the proposed membership meeting in accordance with section 7.05. The notice must also state that the purpose, or one of the purposes, of the meeting is to consider the plan of merger and contain or be accompanied by a copy or summary of the plan. The copy or summary of the plan for members of the surviving corporation shall include any provision that, if contained in a proposed amendment to the articles of incorporation or bylaws, would entitle members to vote on the provision. The copy or summary of the plan for members of the disappearing corporation shall include a copy or summary of the articles and bylaws that will be in effect immediately after the merger takes effect.

(e) If the board seeks to have the plan approved by the members by written consent or written ballot, the material soliciting the approval shall contain or be accompanied by a copy or summary of the plan. The copy or summary of the plan for members of the surviving corporation shall include any provision that, if contained in a proposed amendment to the articles of incorporation or bylaws, would entitle members to vote on the provision. The copy or summary of the plan for members of the disappearing corporation shall include a copy or summary of the articles and bylaws that will be in effect immediately after the merger takes effect.

(f) Voting by a class of members is required on a plan of merger if the plan contains a provision that, if contained in a proposed amendment to articles of incorporation or bylaws, would entitle the class of members to vote as a class on the proposed amendment under section 10.04 or 10.22. The plan is approved by a class of members by two-thirds of the votes cast by the class or a majority of the voting power of the class, whichever is less.

(g) After a merger is adopted, and at any time before articles of merger are filed, the planned merger may be abandoned (subject to any contractual rights) without further action by members or other persons who approved the plan in accordance with the procedure set forth in the plan of merger or, if none is set forth, in the manner determined by the board of directors.

Section 11.04. Articles of Merger.

After a plan of merger is approved by the board of directors, and if required by section 11.03, by the members and any other persons, the surviving or acquiring corporation shall deliver to the secretary of state articles of merger setting forth:

(1) the plan of merger;

(2) if approval of members was not required, a statement to that effect and a statement that the plan was approved by a sufficient vote of the board of directors;

(3) if approval by members was required:

(i) the designation, number of memberships outstanding, number of votes entitled to be cast by each class entitled to vote separately on the plan, and number of votes of each class indisputably voting on the plan; and

(ii) either the total number of votes cast for and against the plan by each class entitled to vote separately on the plan or the total number of undisputed votes cast for the plan by each class and a statement that the number cast for the plan by each class was sufficient for approval by that class;

(4) if approval of the plan by some person or persons other than the members or the board is required pursuant to section 11.03(a)(3), a statement that the approval was obtained.

Section 11.05. Effect of Merger.

When a merger takes effect:

(1) every other corporation party to the merger merges into the surviving corporation and the separate existence of every corporation except the surviving corporation ceases;

(2) the title to all real estate and other property owned by each corporation party to the merger is vested in the surviving corporation without reversion or impairment subject to any and all conditions to which the property was subject prior to the merger;

(3) the surviving corporation has all liabilities and obligations of each corporation party to the merger;

(4) a proceeding pending against any corporation party to the merger may be continued as if the merger did not occur or the surviving corporation may be substituted in the proceeding for the corporation whose existence ceased; and

(5) the articles of incorporation and bylaws of the surviving corporation are amended to the extent provided in the plan of merger.

Section 11.06. Merger with Foreign Corporation.

(a) Except as provided in section 11.02, one or more foreign business or nonprofit corporations may merge with one or more domestic nonprofit corporations if:

(1) the merger is permitted by the law of the state or country under whose law each foreign corporation is incorporated and each foreign corporation complies with that law in effecting the merger;

(2) the foreign corporation complies with section 11.04 if it is the surviving corporation of the merger; and

(3) each domestic nonprofit corporation complies with the applicable provisions of sections 11.01 through 11.03 and, if it is the surviving corporation of the merger, with section 11.04.

(b) Upon the merger taking effect, the surviving foreign business or nonprofit corporation is deemed to have irrevocably appointed the secretary of state as its agent for service of process in any proceeding brought against it.

Section 11.07. Bequests, Devises and Gifts.

Any bequest, devise, gift, grant, or promise contained in a will or other instrument of donation, subscription, or conveyance, that is made to a constituent corporation and that takes effect or remains payable after the merger, inures to the surviving corporation unless the will or other instrument otherwise specifically provides.

Chapter 12: Sale Of Assets

Section 12.01. Sale of Assets in Regular Course of Activities and Mortgage of Assets.

(a) A corporation may on the terms and conditions and for the consideration determined by the board of directors:

(1) sell, lease, exchange, or otherwise dispose of all, or substantially all, of its property in the usual and regular course of its activities; or

(2) mortgage, pledge, dedicate to the repayment of indebtedness (whether with or without recourse), or otherwise encumber any or all of its property whether or not in the usual and regular course of its activities.

(b) Unless the articles require it, approval of the members or any other person of a transaction described in subsection (a) is not required.

Section 12.02. Sale of Assets Other Than in Regular Course of Activities.

(a) A corporation may sell, lease, exchange, or otherwise dispose of all, or substantially all, of its property (with or without the goodwill) other than in the usual and regular course of its activities on the terms and conditions and for the consideration determined by the corporation's board if the proposed transaction is authorized by subsection (b).

(b) Unless this Act, the articles, bylaws, or the board of directors or members (acting pursuant to subsection (d)) require a greater vote or voting by class, the proposed transaction to be authorized must be approved:

(1) by the board;

(2) by the members by two-thirds of the votes cast or a majority of the voting power, whichever is less; and

(3) in writing by any person or persons whose approval is required by a provision of the articles authorized by section 10.30 for an amendment to the articles or bylaws.

(c) If the corporation does not have members the transaction must be approved by a vote of a majority of the directors in office at the time the transaction is approved. In addition the corporation shall provide notice of any directors' meeting at which such approval is to be obtained in accordance with section 8.22(c). The notice must also state that the purpose, or one of the purposes, of the meeting is to consider the sale, lease, exchange, or other disposition of all, or substantially all, of the property or assets of the corporation and contain or be accompanied by a copy or summary of a description of the transaction.

(d) The board may condition its submission of the proposed transaction, and the members may condition their approval of the transaction, on receipt of a higher percentage of affirmative votes or on any other basis.

(e) If the corporation seeks to have the transaction approved by the members at a membership meeting, the corporation shall give notice to its members of the proposed membership meeting in accordance with section 7.05. The notice must also state that the purpose, or one of the purposes, of the meeting is to consider the sale, lease, exchange, or other disposition of all, or substantially all, of the property or assets of the corporation and contain or be accompanied by a copy or summary of a description of the transaction.

(f) If the board needs to have the transaction approved by the members by written consent or written ballot, the material soliciting the approval shall contain or be accompanied by a copy or summary of a description of the transaction.

(g) A public benefit or religious corporation must give written notice to the attorney general twenty days before it sells, leases, exchanges, or otherwise disposes of all, or substantially all, of its property if the transaction is not in the usual and regular course of its activities unless the attorney general has given the corporation a written waiver of this subsection.

(h) After a sale, lease, exchange, or other disposition of property is authorized, the transaction may be abandoned (subject to any contractual rights), without further action by the members or any other person who approved the transaction in accordance with the procedure set forth in the resolution proposing the transaction or, if none is set forth, in the manner determined by the board of directors.

Chapter 13: Distributions

Section 13.01. Prohibited Distributions.

Except as authorized by section 13.02, a corporation shall not make any distributions.

Section 13.02. Authorized Distributions.

(a) A mutual benefit corporation may purchase its memberships if after the purchase is completed:

(1) the corporation would be able to pay its debts as they become due in the usual course of its activities; and

(2) the corporation's total assets would at least equal the sum of its total liabilities.

(b) Corporations may make distributions upon dissolution in conformity with chapter 14 of this Act.

Chapter 14: Dissolution

Subchapter A: Voluntary Dissolution

Section 14.01. Dissolution by Incorporators or Directors and Third Persons.

(a) A majority of the incorporators or directors of a corporation that has no members may, subject to any approval required by the articles or bylaws, dissolve the corporation by delivering to the secretary of state articles of dissolution.

(b) The corporation shall give notice of any meeting at which dissolution will be approved. The notice shall be in accordance with section 8.22(c). The notice must also state that the purpose, or one of the purposes, of the meeting is to consider dissolution of the corporation.

(c) The incorporators or directors in approving dissolution shall adopt a plan of dissolution indicating to whom the assets owned or held by the corporation will be distributed after all creditors have been paid.

Section 14.02. Dissolution by Directors, Members and Third Persons.

(a) Unless this Act, [fill in name of any relevant state law,] the articles, bylaws or the board of directors or members (acting pursuant to subsection (c)) require a greater vote or voting by class, dissolution is authorized if it is approved:

(1) by the board;

(2) by the members, if any, by two-thirds of the votes cast or a majority of the voting power, whichever is less; and

(3) in writing by any person or persons whose approval is required by a provision of the articles authorized by section 10.30 for an amendment to the articles or bylaws.

(b) If the corporation does not have members, dissolution must be approved by a vote of a majority of the directors in office at the time the transaction is approved. In addition, the corporation shall provide notice of any directors' meeting at which such approval is to be obtained in accordance with section 8.22(c). The notice must also state that the purpose, or one of the purposes, of the meeting is to consider dissolution of the corporation and contain or be accompanied by a copy or summary of the plan of dissolution.

(c) The board may condition its submission of the proposed dissolution, and the members may condition their approval of the dissolution on receipt of a higher percentage of affirmative votes or on any other basis.

(d) If the board seeks to have dissolution approved by the members at a membership meeting, the corporation shall give notice to its members of the proposed membership meeting in accordance with section 7.05. The notice must also state that the purpose, or one of the purposes, of the meeting is to consider dissolving the corporation and contain or be accompanied by a copy or summary of the plan of dissolution.

(e) If the board seeks to have dissolution approved by the members by written consent or written ballot, the material soliciting the approval shall contain or be accompanied by a copy or summary of the plan of dissolution.

(f) The plan of dissolution shall indicate to whom the assets owned or held by the corporation will be distributed after all creditors have been paid.

Section 14.03. Notices to the Attorney General.

(a) A public benefit or religious corporation shall give the attorney general written notice that it intends to dissolve at or before the time it delivers articles of dissolution to the secretary of state. The notice shall include a copy or summary of the plan of dissolution.

(b) No assets shall be transferred or conveyed by a public benefit or religious corporation as part of the dissolution process until twenty days after it has given the written notice required by subsection (a) to the attorney general or until the attorney general has consented in writing to the dissolution, or indicated in writing that he or she will take no action in respect to, the transfer or conveyance, whichever is earlier.

(c) When all or substantially all of the assets of a public benefit corporation have been transferred or conveyed following approval of dissolution, the board shall deliver to the attorney general a list showing those (other than creditors) to whom the assets were transferred or conveyed. The list shall indicate the addresses of each person (other than creditors) who received assets and indicate what assets each received.

Section 14.04. Articles of Dissolution.

(a) At any time after dissolution is authorized, the corporation may dissolve by delivering to the secretary of state articles of dissolution setting forth:

(1) the name of the corporation;

(2) the date dissolution was authorized;

(3) a statement that dissolution was approved by a sufficient vote of the board;

(4) if approval of members was not required, a statement to that effect and a statement that dissolution was approved by a sufficient vote of the board of directors or incorporators;

(5) if approval by members was required:

(i) the designation, number of memberships outstanding, number of votes entitled to be cast by each class entitled to vote separately on dissolution, and number of votes of each class indisputably voting on dissolution; and

(ii) either the total number of votes cast for and against dissolution by each class entitled to vote separately on dissolution or the total number of undisputed votes cast for dissolution by each class and a statement that the number cast for dissolution by each class was sufficient for approval by that class.

(6) if approval of dissolution by some person or persons other than the members, the board or the incorporators is required pursuant to section 14.02(a)(3), a statement that the approval was obtained; and

(7) if the corporation is a public benefit or religious corporation, that the notice to the attorney general required by section 14.03(a) has been given.

(b) A corporation is dissolved upon the effective date of its articles of dissolution.

Section 14.05. Revocation of Dissolution.

(a) A corporation may revoke its dissolution within 120 days of its effective date.

(b) Revocation of dissolution must be authorized in the same manner as the dissolution was authorized unless that authorization permitted revocation by action of the board of directors alone, in which event the board of directors may revoke the dissolution without action by the members or any other person.

(c) After the revocation of dissolution is authorized, the corporation may revoke the dissolution by delivering to the secretary of state for filing articles of revocation of dissolution, together with a copy of its articles of dissolution, that set forth:

(1) the name of the corporation;

(2) the effective date of the dissolution that was revoked;

(3) the date that the revocation of dissolution was authorized;

(4) if the corporation's board of directors (or incorporators) revoked the dissolution, a statement to that effect;

(5) if the corporation's board of directors revoked a dissolution authorized by the members alone or in conjunction with another person or persons, a statement that revocation was permitted by action by the board of directors alone pursuant to that authorization; and

(6) if member or third person action was required to revoke the dissolution, the information required by section 14.04(a)(5) and (6).

(d) Revocation of dissolution is effective upon the effective date of the articles of revocation of dissolution.

(e) When the revocation of dissolution is effective, it relates back to and takes effect as of the effective date of the dissolution and the corporation resumes carrying on its activities as if dissolution had never occurred.

Section 14.06. Effect of Dissolution.

(a) A dissolved corporation continues its corporate existence but may not carry on any activities except those appropriate to wind up and liquidate its affairs, including:

(1) preserving and protecting its assets and minimizing its liabilities;

(2) discharging or making provision for discharging its liabilities and obligations;

(3) disposing of its properties that will not be distributed in kind;

(4) returning, transferring or conveying assets held by the corporation upon a condition requiring return, transfer or conveyance, which condition occurs by reason of the dissolution, in accordance with such condition;

(5) transferring, subject to any contractual or legal requirements, its assets as provided in or authorized by its articles of incorporation or bylaws;

(6) if the corporation is a public benefit or religious corporation, and no provision has been made in its articles or bylaws for distribution of assets on dissolution, transferring, subject to any contractual or legal requirement, its assets: (i) to one or more persons described in section 501(c)(3) of the Internal Revenue Code, or (ii) if the dissolved corporation is not described in section 501(c)(3) of the Internal Revenue Code, to one or more public benefit or religious corporations;

(7) if the corporation is a mutual benefit corporation and no provision has been made in its articles or bylaws for distribution of assets on dissolution, transferring its assets to its members or, if it has no members, to those persons whom the corporation holds itself out as benefitting or serving; and

(8) doing every other act necessary to wind up and liquidate its assets and affairs.

(b) Dissolution of a corporation does not:

(1) transfer title to the corporation's property;

(2) subject its directors or officers to standards of conduct different from those prescribed in chapter 8;

(3) change quorum or voting requirements for its board or members; change provisions for selection, resignation, or removal of its directors or officers or both; or change provisions for amending its bylaws;

(4) prevent commencement of a proceeding by or against the corporation in its corporate name;

(5) abate or suspend a proceeding pending by or against the corporation on the effective date of dissolution; or

(6) terminate the authority of the registered agent.

Section 14.07. Known Claims Against Dissolved Corporation.

(a) A dissolved corporation may dispose of the known claims against it by following the procedure described in this section.

(b) The dissolved corporation shall notify its known claimants in writing of the dissolution at any time after its effective date. The written notice must:

(1) describe information that must be included in a claim;

(2) provide a mailing address where a claim may be sent;

(3) state the deadline, which may not be fewer than 120 days from the effective date of the written notice, by which the dissolved corporation must receive the claim; and

(4) state that the claim will be barred if not received by the deadline.

(c) A claim against the dissolved corporation is barred:

(1) if a claimant who was given written notice under subsection (b) does not deliver the claim to the dissolved corporation by the deadline;

(2) if a claimant whose claim was rejected by the dissolved corporation does not commence a proceeding to enforce the claim within 90 days from the effective date of the rejection notice.

(d) For purposes of this section "claim" does not include a contingent liability or a claim based on an event occurring after the effective date of dissolution.

Section 14.08. Unknown Claims Against Dissolved Corporation.

(a) A dissolved corporation may also publish notice of its dissolution and request that persons with claims against the corporation present them in accordance with the notice.

(b) The notice must:

(1) be published one time in a newspaper of general circulation in the county where the dissolved corporation's principal office (or, if none in this state, its registered office) is or was last located;

(2) describe the information that must be included in a claim and provide a mailing address where the claim may be sent; and

(3) state that a claim against the corporation will be barred unless a proceeding to enforce the claim is commenced within five years after publication of the notice.

(c) If the dissolved corporation publishes a newspaper notice in accordance with subsection (b), the claim of each of the following claimants is barred unless the claimant commences a proceeding to enforce the claim against the dissolved corporation within five years after the publication date of the newspaper notice:

(1) a claimant who did not receive written notice under section 14.07;

(2) a claimant whose claim was timely sent to the dissolved corporation but not acted on; and

(3) a claimant whose claim is contingent or based on an event occurring after the effective date of dissolution.

(d) A claim may be enforced under this section:

(1) against the dissolved corporation, to the extent of its undistributed assets; or

(2) if the assets have been distributed in liquidation, against any person, other than a creditor of the corporation, to whom the corporation distributed its property to the extent of the distributee's pro rata share of the claim or the corporate assets distributed to such person in liquidation, whichever is less, but the distributee's total liability for all claims under this section may not exceed the total amount of assets distributed to the distributee.

Subchapter B: Administrative Dissolution

Section 14.20. Grounds for Administrative Dissolution.

The secretary of state may commence a proceeding under section 14.21 to administratively dissolve a corporation if:

(1) the corporation does not pay within 60 days after they are due any taxes or penalties imposed by this Act or other law;

(2) the corporation does not deliver its annual report to the secretary of state within 60 days after it is due;

(3) the corporation is without a registered agent or registered office in this state for 60 days or more;

(4) the corporation does not notify the secretary of state within 120 days that its registered agent or registered office has been changed, that its registered agent has resigned, or that its registered office has been discontinued; or

(5) the corporation's period of duration, if any, stated in its articles of incorporation expires.

Section 14.21. Procedure for and Effect of Administrative Dissolution.

(a) Upon determining that one or more grounds exist under section 14.20 for dissolving a corporation, the secretary of state shall serve the corporation with written notice of that determination under section 5.04, and in the case of a public benefit corporation shall notify the attorney general in writing.

(b) If the corporation does not correct each ground for dissolution or demonstrate to the reasonable satisfaction of the secretary of state that each ground determined by the secretary of state does not exist within at least 60 days after service of the notice is perfected under section 5.04, the secretary of state may administratively dissolve the corporation by signing a certificate of dissolution that recites the ground or grounds for dissolution and its effective date. The secretary of state shall file the original of the certificate and serve a copy on the corporation under section 5.04, and in the case of a public benefit corporation shall notify the attorney general in writing.

(c) A corporation administratively dissolved continues its corporate existence but may not carry on any activities except those necessary to wind up and liquidate its affairs under section 14.06 and notify its claimants under sections 14.07 and 14.08.

(d) The administrative dissolution of a corporation does not terminate the authority of its registered agent.

Section 14.22. Reinstatement Following Administrative Dissolution.

(a) A corporation administratively dissolved under section 14.21 may apply to the secretary of state for reinstatement within two years after the effective date of dissolution. The application must:

(1) recite the name of the corporation and the effective date of its administrative dissolution;

(2) state that the ground or grounds for dissolution either did not exist or have been eliminated;

(3) state that the corporation's name satisfies the requirements of section 4.01; and

(4) contain a certificate from the [appropriate taxing authority, if any] reciting that all taxes owed by the corporation have been paid.

(b) If the secretary of state determines that the application contains the information required by subsection (a) and that the information is correct, the secretary of state shall cancel the certificate of dissolution and prepare a certificate of reinstatement reciting that determination and the effective date of reinstatement, file the original of the certificate, and serve a copy on the corporation under section 5.04.

(c) When reinstatement is effective, it relates back to and takes effect as of the effective date of the administrative dissolution and the corporation shall resume carrying on its activities as if the administrative dissolution had never occurred.

Section 14.23. Appeal from Denial of Reinstatement.

(a) The secretary of state, upon denying a corporation's application for reinstatement following administrative dissolution, shall serve the corporation under section 5.04 with a written notice that explains the reason or reasons for denial.

(b) The corporation may appeal the denial of reinstatement to the [name or describe] court within 90 days after service of the notice of denial is perfected. The corporation appeals by petitioning the court to set aside the dissolution and attaching to the petition copies of the secretary of state's certificate of dissolution, the corporation's application for reinstatement, and the secretary of state's notice of denial.

(c) The court may summarily order the secretary of state to reinstate the dissolved corporation or may take other action the court considers appropriate.

(d) The court's final decision may be appealed as in other civil proceedings.

Subchapter C: Judicial Dissolution

Section 14.30. Grounds for Judicial Dissolution.

(a) The [name or describe court or courts] may dissolve a corporation:

(1) in a proceeding by the attorney general if it is established that:

(i) the corporation obtained its articles of incorporation through fraud;

(ii) the corporation has continued to exceed or abuse the authority conferred upon it by law;

(iii) the corporation is a public benefit corporation and the corporate assets are being misapplied or wasted; or

(iv) the corporation is a public benefit corporation and is no longer able to carry out its purposes.

(2) except as provided in the articles or bylaws of a religious corporation, in a proceeding by 50 members or members holding 5% of the voting power, whichever is less, or by a director or any person specified in the articles, if it is established that:

(i) the directors are deadlocked in the management of the corporate affairs, and the members, if any, are unable to breach the deadlock;

(ii) the directors or those in control of the corporation have acted, are acting or will act in a manner that is illegal, oppressive or fraudulent;

(iii) the members are deadlocked in voting power and have failed, for a period that includes at least two consecutive annual meeting dates, to elect successors to directors whose terms have, or would otherwise have, expired;

(iv) the corporate assets are being misapplied or wasted; or

(v) the corporation is a public benefit or religious corporation and is no longer able to carry out its purposes.

(3) in a proceeding by a creditor if it is established that:

(i) the creditor's claim has been reduced to judgment, the execution on the judgment returned unsatisfied and the corporation is insolvent; or

(ii) the corporation has admitted in writing that the creditor's claim is due and owing and the corporation is insolvent.

(4) in a proceeding by the corporation to have its voluntary dissolution continued under court supervision.

(b) Prior to dissolving a corporation, the court shall consider whether:

(1) there are reasonable alternatives to dissolution;

(2) dissolution is in the public interest, if the corporation is a public benefit corporation; and

(3) dissolution is the best way of protecting the interests of members, if the corporation is a mutual benefit corporation.

Section 14.31. Procedure for Judicial Dissolution.

(a) Venue for a proceeding by the attorney general to dissolve a corporation lies in [name the county or court]. Venue for a proceeding brought by any other party named in section 14.30 lies in the county where a corporation's principal office (or, if none in this state, its registered office) is or was last located.

(b) It is not necessary to make directors or members parties to a proceeding to dissolve a corporation unless relief is sought against them individually.

(c) A court in a proceeding brought to dissolve a corporation may issue injunctions, appoint a receiver or custodian pendente lite with all powers and duties the court directs, take other action required to preserve the corporate assets wherever located, and carry on the activities of the corporation until a full hearing can be held.

(d) A person other than the attorney general who brings an involuntary dissolution proceeding for a public benefit or religious corporation shall forthwith give written notice of the proceeding to the attorney general who may intervene.

Section 14.32. Receivership or Custodianship.

(a) A court in a judicial proceeding brought to dissolve a public benefit or mutual benefit corporation may appoint one or more receivers to wind up and liquidate, or one or more custodians to manage, the affairs of the corporation. The court shall hold a hearing, after notifying all parties to the proceeding and any interested persons designated by the court, before appointing a receiver or custodian. The court appointing a receiver or custodian has exclusive jurisdiction over the corporation and all of its property wherever located.

(b) The court may appoint an individual, or a domestic or foreign business or nonprofit corporation (authorized to transact business in this state) as a receiver or custodian. The court may require the receiver or custodian to post bond, with or without sureties, in an amount the court directs.

(c) The court shall describe the powers and duties of the receiver or custodian in its appointing order, which may be amended from time to time. Among other powers:

(1) the receiver (i) may dispose of all or any part of the assets of the corporation wherever located, at a public or private sale, if authorized by the court; provided, however, that the receiver's power to dispose of the assets of the corporation is subject to any trust and other restrictions that would be

applicable to the corporation; and (ii) may sue and defend in the receiver's or custodian's name as receiver or custodian of the corporation in all courts of this state;

(2) the custodian may exercise all of the powers of the corporation, through or in place of its board of directors or officers, to the extent necessary to manage the affairs of the corporation in the best interests of its members and creditors.

(d) The court during a receivership may redesignate the receiver a custodian, and during a custodianship may redesignate the custodian a receiver, if doing so is in the best interests of the corporation, its members, and creditors.

(e) The court from time to time during the receivership or custodianship may order compensation paid and expense disbursements or reimbursements made to the receiver or custodian and the receiver or custodian's counsel from the assets of the corporation or proceeds from the sale of the assets.

Section 14.33. Decree of Dissolution.

(a) If after a hearing the court determines that one or more grounds for judicial dissolution described in section 14.30 exist, it may enter a decree dissolving the corporation and specifying the effective date of the dissolution, and the clerk of the court shall deliver a certified copy of the decree to the secretary of state, who shall file it.

(b) After entering the decree of dissolution, the court shall direct the winding up and liquidation of the corporation's affairs in accordance with section 14.06 and the notification of its claimants in accordance with sections 14.07 and 14.08.

Subchapter D: Miscellaneous

Section 14.40. Deposit with State Treasurer.

Assets of a dissolved corporation that should be transferred to a creditor, claimant, or member of the corporation who cannot be found or who is not competent to receive them, shall be reduced to cash subject to known trust restrictions and deposited with the state treasurer for safekeeping; provided, however, that in the state treasurer's discretion property may be received and held in kind. When the creditor, claimant, or member furnishes satisfactory proof of entitlement to the amount deposited or property held in kind, the state treasurer shall deliver to the creditor, member or other person or his or her representative that amount or property.

Chapter 15: Foreign Corporations

Subchapter A: Certificate of Authority

Section 15.01. Authority To Transact Business Required.

(a) A foreign corporation may not transact business in this state until it obtains a certificate of authority from the secretary of state.

(b) The following activities, among others, do not constitute transacting business within the meaning of subsection (a):

(1) maintaining, defending, or settling any proceeding;

(2) holding meetings of the board of directors or members or carrying on other activities concerning internal corporate affairs;

(3) maintaining bank accounts;

(4) maintaining offices or agencies for the transfer, exchange, and registration of memberships or securities or maintaining trustees or depositaries with respect to those securities;

(5) selling through independent contractors;

(6) soliciting or obtaining orders, whether by mail or through employees or agents or otherwise, if the orders require acceptance outside this state before they become contracts;

(7) creating or acquiring indebtedness, mortgages, and security interests in real or personal property;

(8) securing or collecting debts or enforcing mortgages and security interests in property securing the debts;

(9) owning, without more, real or personal property;

(10) conducting an isolated transaction that is completed within 30 days and that is not one in the course of repeated transactions of a like nature;

(11) transacting business in interstate commerce.

(c) The list of activities in subsection (b) is not exhaustive.

Section 15.02. Consequences of Transacting Business Without Authority.

(a) A foreign corporation transacting business in this state without a certificate of authority may not maintain a proceeding in any court in this state until it obtains a certificate of authority.

(b) The successor to a foreign corporation that transacted business in this state without a certificate of authority and the assignee of a cause of action arising out of that business may not maintain a proceeding on that cause of action in any court in this state until the foreign corporation or its successor obtains a certificate of authority.

(c) A court may stay a proceeding commenced by a foreign corporation, its successor, or assignee until it determines whether the foreign corporation or its successor requires a certificate of authority. If it so determines, the court may further stay the proceeding until the foreign corporation or its successor obtains the certificate.

(d) A foreign corporation is liable for a civil penalty of $_____ for each day, but not to exceed a total of $_____ for each year, it transacts business in this state without a certificate of authority. The attorney general may collect all penalties due under this subsection.

(e) Notwithstanding subsections (a) and (b), the failure of a foreign corporation to obtain a certificate of authority does not impair the validity of its corporate acts or prevent it from defending any proceeding in this state.

Section 15.03. Application for Certificate of Authority.

(a) A foreign corporation may apply for a certificate of authority to transact business in this state by delivering an application to the secretary of state. The application must set forth:

(1) the name of the foreign corporation or, if its name is unavailable for use in this state, a corporate name that satisfies the requirements of section 15.06;

(2) the name of the state or country under whose law it is incorporated;

(3) the date of incorporation and period of duration;

(4) the street address of its principal office;

(5) the address of its registered office in this state and the name of its registered agent at that office;

(6) the names and usual business or home addresses of its current directors and officers;

(7) whether the foreign corporation has members; and

(8) whether the corporation, if it had been incorporated in this state, would be a public benefit, mutual benefit or religious corporation.

(b) The foreign corporation shall deliver with the completed application a certificate of existence (or a document of similar import) duly authenticated by the secretary of state or other official having custody of corporate records in the state or country under whose law it is incorporated.

Section 15.04. Amended Certificate of Authority.

(a) A foreign corporation authorized to transact business in this state must obtain an amended certificate of authority from the secretary of state if it changes:

(1) its corporate name;

(2) the period of its duration; or

(3) the state or country of its incorporation.

(b) The requirements of section 15.03 for obtaining an original certificate of authority apply to obtaining an amended certificate under this section.

Section 15.05. Effect of Certificate of Authority.

(a) A certificate of authority authorizes the foreign corporation to which it is issued to transact business in this state subject, however, to the right of the state to revoke the certificate as provided in this Act.

(b) A foreign corporation with a valid certificate of authority has the same rights and enjoys the same privileges as and, except as otherwise provided by this Act, is subject to the same duties, restrictions, penalties, and liabilities now or later imposed on, a domestic corporation of like character.

(c) This Act does not authorize this state to regulate the organization or internal affairs of a foreign corporation authorized to transact business in this state.

Section 15.06. Corporate Name of Foreign Corporation.

(a) If the corporate name of a foreign corporation does not satisfy the requirements of section 4.01, the foreign corporation, to obtain or maintain a certificate of authority to transact business in this state, may use a fictitious name to transact business in this state if its real name is unavailable and it delivers to the secretary of state for filing a copy of the resolution of its board of directors, certified by its secretary, adopting the fictitious name.

(b) Except as authorized by subsections (c) and (d), the corporate name (including a fictitious name) of a foreign corporation must be distinguishable upon the records of the secretary of state from:

(1) the corporate name of a nonprofit or business corporation incorporated or authorized to transact business in this state;

(2) a corporate name reserved or registered under section 4.02 or 4.03 of this Act or section _____ or _____ [(appropriate sections of the state business corporation act)]; and

(3) the fictitious name of another foreign business or nonprofit corporation authorized to transact business in this state.

(c) A foreign corporation may apply to the secretary of state for authorization to use in this state the name of another corporation (incorporated or authorized to transact business in this state) that is not distinguishable upon the records of the secretary of state from the name applied for. The secretary of state shall authorize use of the name applied for if:

(1) the other corporation consents to the use in writing and submits an undertaking in form satisfactory to the secretary of state to change its name to a name that is distinguishable upon the records of the secretary of state from the name of the applying corporation; or

(2) the applicant delivers to the secretary of state a certified copy of a final judgment of a court of competent jurisdiction establishing the applicant's right to use the name applied for in this state.

(d) A foreign corporation may use in this state the name (including the fictitious name) of another domestic or foreign business or nonprofit corporation that is used in this state if the other corporation is incorporated or authorized to transact business in this state and the foreign corporation:

(1) has merged with the other corporation;

(2) has been formed by reorganization of the other corporation; or

(3) has acquired all or substantially all of the assets, including the corporate name, of the other corporation.

(e) If a foreign corporation authorized to transact business in this state changes its corporate name to one that does not satisfy the requirements of section 4.01, it shall not transact business in this state under the changed name until it adopts a name satisfying the requirements of section 4.01 and obtains an amended certificate of authority under section 15.04.

Section 15.07. Registered Office and Registered Agent of Foreign Corporation.

Each foreign corporation authorized to transact business in this state must continuously maintain in this state:

(1) a registered office with the same address as that of its registered agent; and

(2) a registered agent, who may be:

(i) an individual who resides in this state and whose office is identical with the registered office;

(ii) a domestic business or nonprofit corporation whose office is identical with the registered office; or

(iii) a foreign business or nonprofit corporation authorized to transact business in this state whose office is identical with the registered office.

Section 15.08. Change of Registered Office or Registered Agent of Foreign Corporation.

(a) A foreign corporation authorized to transact business in this state may change its registered office or registered agent by delivering to the secretary of state for filing a statement of change that sets forth:

(1) its name;

(2) the street address of its current registered office;

(3) if the current registered office is to be changed, the street address of its new registered office;

(4) the name of its current registered agent;

(5) if the current registered agent is to be changed, the name of its new registered agent and the new agent's written consent (either on the statement or attached to it) to the appointment; and

(6) that after the change or changes are made, the street addresses of its registered office and the office of its registered agent will be identical.

(b) If a registered agent changes the street address of its business office, the agent may change the address of the registered office of any foreign corporation for which the agent is the registered agent by notifying the corporation in writing of the change and signing (either manually or in facsimile) and delivering to the secretary of state for filing a statement of change that complies with the requirements of subsection (a) and recites that the corporation has been notified of the change.

Section 15.09. Resignation of Registered Agent of Foreign Corporation.

(a) The registered agent of a foreign corporation may resign as agent by signing and delivering to the secretary of state for filing the original and two exact
or conformed copies of a statement of resignation. The statement of resignation may include a statement that the registered office is also discontinued.

(b) After filing the statement, the secretary of state shall attach the filing
receipt to one copy and mail the copy and receipt to the registered office
if not discontinued. The secretary of state shall mail the other copy to the
foreign corporation at its principal office address shown in its most recent
annual report.

(c) The agency is terminated, and the registered office discontinued if so
provided, on the 31st day after the date on which the statement was filed.

Section 15.10. Service on Foreign Corporation.

(a) The registered agent of a foreign corporation authorized to transact business in this state is the corporation's agent for service of process, notice, or
demand required or permitted by law to be served on the foreign corporation.

(b) A foreign corporation may be served by registered or certified mail,
return receipt requested, addressed to the secretary of the foreign corporation at its principal office shown in its application for a certificate of authority or in its most recent annual report filed under section 16.22 if the foreign
corporation:

(1) has no registered agent or its registered agent cannot with reasonable
diligence be served;

(2) has withdrawn from transacting business in this state under section
15.20; or

(3) has had its certificate of authority revoked under section 15.31.

(c) Service is perfected under subsection (b) at the earliest of:

(1) the date the foreign corporation receives the mail;

(2) the date shown on the return receipt, if signed on behalf of the foreign
corporation; or

(3) five days after its deposit in the United States Mail, as evidenced by the
postmark if mailed postpaid and correctly addressed.

(d) This section does not prescribe the only means, or necessarily the
required means, of serving a foreign corporation.

Subchapter B: Withdrawal

Section 15.20. Withdrawal of Foreign Corporation.

(a) A foreign corporation authorized to transact business in this state may not withdraw from this state until it obtains a certificate of withdrawal from the secretary of state.

(b) A foreign corporation authorized to transact business in this state may apply for a certificate of withdrawal by delivering an application to the secretary of state for filing. The application must set forth:

(1) the name of the foreign corporation and the name of the state or country under whose law it is incorporated;

(2) that it is not transacting business in this state and that it surrenders its authority to transact business in this state;

(3) that it revokes the authority of its registered agent to accept service on its behalf and appoints the secretary of state as its agent for service of process in any proceeding based on a cause of action arising during the time it was authorized to do business in this state;

(4) a mailing address to which the secretary of state may mail a copy of any process served on him or her under subdivision (3); and

(5) a commitment to notify the secretary of state in the future of any change in the mailing address.

(c) After the withdrawal of the corporation is effective, service of process on the secretary of state under this section is service on the foreign corporation. Upon receipt of process, the secretary of state shall mail a copy of the process to the foreign corporation at the post office address set forth in its application for withdrawal.

Subchapter C: Revocation of Certificate of Authority

Section 15.30. Grounds for Revocation.

(a) The secretary of state may commence a proceeding under section 15.31 to revoke the certificate of authority of a foreign corporation authorized to transact business in this state if:

(1) the foreign corporation does not deliver the annual report to the secretary of state within 60 days after it is due;

(2) the foreign corporation does not pay within 60 days after they are due any franchise taxes or penalties imposed by this Act or other law;

(3) the foreign corporation is without a registered agent or registered office in this state for 60 days or more;

(4) the foreign corporation does not inform the secretary of state under section 15.08 or 15.09 that its registered agent or registered office has changed, that its registered agent has resigned, or that its registered office has been discontinued within 90 days of the change, resignation, or discontinuance;

(5) an incorporator, director, officer, or agent of the foreign corporation signed a document such person knew was false in any material respect with intent that the document be delivered to the secretary of state for filing; or

(6) the secretary of state receives a duly authenticated certificate from the secretary of state or other official having custody of corporate records in the state or country under whose law the foreign corporation is incorporated stating that it has been dissolved or disappeared as the result of a merger.

(b) The attorney general may commence a proceeding under section 15.31 to revoke the certificate of authority of a foreign corporation authorized to transact business in this state if:

(1) the corporation has continued to exceed or abuse the authority conferred upon it by law;

(2) the corporation would have been a public benefit corporation had it been incorporated in this state and that its corporate assets in this state are being misapplied or wasted; or

(3) the corporation would have been a public benefit corporation had it been incorporated in this state and it is no longer able to carry out its purposes.

Index

Numerics

501(c)(3) organization
  adverse determination, 83–85
  political activity limitations, 24
  tax-exempt application, 51–52, 79–83
  tax-exempt organizations list, 69–79
501(d) organization, 77
501(e) organization, 77
501(f) organization, 78
501(k) organization, 78
501(n) organization, 78
521(a) organization, 78
527 organization, 78
9/11 disaster, 35–36

• A •

abbreviation, 62
Abramoff, Jack (lobbyist), 40
accountability
  compensation governance, 98
  for-profit versus nonprofit group, 15
  Sarbanes-Oxley objectives, 184
  Sarbanes-Oxley provisions, 186
  volunteer taxes, 99–100
accountable plan, 99–100
accountant, 144
accounting, 187, 196
accounting firm, independent
  approved services, 147–148
  overview, 142–143
  Sarbanes-Oxley provisions, 197
Ace Hardware (cooperative), 178
ad hoc committee, 136
address, 62
adjournment, 67
adjusted gross income, 42
adverse determination, 57, 58, 83–85
advertising, 252–253
affiliation, 145

agenda, meeting, 67
agricultural marketing cooperative, 170
agricultural organization, 51, 71
airplane, 213
Alabama, 263
Alaska, 263
Alliance for Children & Families, 49
American Cancer Society, 49, 244
American Red Cross (nonprofit
    organization)
  bylaw examples, 64
  recent missteps, 18, 35–36, 132
annuity, 29–31
antique property, 212
apostolic association, 77
*Application for Employer Identification
    Number* (Form SS-4), 55, 80
Application for Recognition of Exemption
    (Form 1023 or 1024), 54, 80
appraisal, 209–210, 212
Arizona, 263
Arkansas, 263
arm's length offer, 207
art, 212
articles of incorporation
  cooperative formation, 174
  Model Nonprofit Corporation Act
      provisions, 289–294, 297
  nonprofit incorporation, 62–63
  tax-exempt application, 80
  tax-exempt revocation, 244
articles of organization, 60
asset
  Form 990 detail, 114, 115
  Model Nonprofit Corporation Act
      provisions, 302–303
  self-dealing, 160
  test, 157
audit
  board function, 120
  definition, 142

audit *(continued)*
  executive salaries, 37
  increase in, 36
  IRS review, 222–226
  recent IRS actions, 34, 36
  Sarbanes-Oxley general provisions,
    133, 184–185
  Sarbanes-Oxley nonprofit provisions,
    190, 191–192
  state-IRS information sharing, 25
audit committee
  CEO/CFO certifications, 148–149
  charter, 144
  complaints, 148
  functions, 139, 142
  independent accounting firm,
    142–143, 147–148
  interaction with management, 144–145
  legal issues, 150
  membership guidelines, 145–146
  overview, 141
  questions to evaluate board
    membership, 237
  rotating audit partners, 149, 185
  sample report, 261–262
  Sarbanes-Oxley general provisions,
    133, 141, 147–150, 185
  Sarbanes-Oxley nonprofit provisions,
    189, 191
  standards, 143
automatic excess benefit transaction
  rule, 96

• B •

backdated status, 57–58
balance of funds, 115
balance sheet, 56
bankruptcy, 38
basis, 43–44
beneficiary, 61, 121
benevolent life insurance association,
  51, 73
Bill and Melinda Gates Foundation, 155
black lung benefit trust, 75
blood donation, 42

board meeting
  director's duties, 122, 124
  guidelines, 66–68
  Model Nonprofit Corporation Act
    provisions, 277–278
  questions to evaluate board
    membership, 241
  Sarbanes-Oxley provisions, 133
board-meeting minutes
  committee meetings, 138
  compensation documentation, 92–93
  director's duty of care, 123
  director's rights, 129
  overview, 67–68
board of directors. *See also* director
  charitable investment regulation, 31–32
  compensation committee tasks, 87–90
  compensation governance, 98
  diversity of members, 64
  election, 119
  evaluation questions, 235–242
  Form 990 detail, 114
  function, 118, 120
  governance, 119–120
  IRS compensation guidelines, 91
  legal obligations, 120–121
  member recruitment, 64–65, 235–242
  mission statement creation, 50
  Model Nonprofit Corporation Act
    provisions, 278–283
  overview, 117–118
  private foundations, 162–163
  Sarbanes-Oxley changes, 131–134, 196
board of trade, 71
BoardSource (Web site), 233
boat, 213
bonus, 187
book donation, 41, 212
bookkeeping
  director's rights, 129
  Form 990 errors, 110, 223
  IRS audit, 223–224
  new legislation, 19
  questions to evaluate board
    membership, 238
  Sarbanes-Oxley provisions, 185

Brand, Myles (NCAA president), 204
budget
  board function, 120
  questions to evaluate board
    membership, 239
  salary issues, 89
Buffet, Warren (charitable donor), 155
bulk purchase, 166
business income, unrelated
  criteria, 201–202, 203
  definition, 13
  exceptions, 202–203
  Form 990, 104, 107–108
  overview, 201
  PPA provisions, 42
  reporting requirements, 204–205
business judgment rule, 122, 128–129, 177
business league, 51, 71
bylaw
  board election, 119
  committee formation, 136
  cooperative formation, 174
  definition, 12
  examples, 257–259
  incorporation process, 63–64
  Model Nonprofit Corporation Act
    provisions, 295–297
  tax-exempt status application, 55

● **C** ●

California, 264
call to order, 67
capital gains tax, 30
capital stock, 74
car, donation of, 213
care, duty of, 122–123
Carnegie Foundation, 158
cash contribution, 214
cemetery company, 52, 73–74
CEO/CFO. *See* chief executive/financial
    officer
certificate of incorporation, 11
chamber of commerce, 51, 71
chapter, 72
Chapter 11 bankruptcy, 38

Charitable Gift Annuities Model Act, 31
charitable investment, 31–32
charitable risk pool, 78
charitable trust, 245
charter, 11–12, 144
chief executive/financial officer (CEO/CFO)
  audit committee, 148–149
  Sarbanes-Oxley provisions,
    186, 187, 190, 192, 197
  selection, 120
  typical day, 127
child care organization, 78
church, 245
civic league, 70
closed membership, 171
clothing donation, 212, 214
collections, 212
Colorado, 264
committee. *See also specific types*
  basic structures, 135–136
  formation, 136–138
  overview, 135
  questions to evaluate board membership,
    237–238
  types, 138–140
common law, 121–125
common treasury, 77
communication
  audit committee regulations, 147
  audit committee standards, 143
  director's rights, 129
  IRS interaction, 217–226, 224
community
  function, 11
  nonprofit's impact, 49
  public charity versus private
    foundation, 156
  relations and outreach committee, 238
  treasury, 77
Community Career Center (Web site), 233
CompassPoint (Web site), 232
compensation
  audit committee membership, 145
  board function, 120
  consultants, 88
  Enron problems, 182

compensation *(continued)*
  excessive salaries, 37–38, 95–97, 98
  Form 990 detail, 115
  governance issues, 97–99
  IRS guidelines, 91–93
  overview, 87
  package creation, 93–97
  PPA provisions, 96
  questions to evaluate board
    membership, 239
  recent scrutiny, 16
  Sarbanes-Oxley provisions,
    132, 133, 187, 196
  self-dealing, 160
  tax exemption revocation, 245–246, 248
compensation committee
  board responsibilities, 133
  duties, 87–90
  IRS guidelines, 92
  overview, 140
compliance check, 97, 220
condominium cooperative, 168
confidentiality, 124, 252
conflict of interest
  audit committee membership, 145
  compensation regulation, 91, 93
  director's duties, 123–124
  Sarbanes-Oxley provisions,
    184–185, 187, 193
  trustee's duties, 128
conformed copy, 55, 81
Connecticut, 264
consulting service, 191
consumer cooperative, 168
cooperative. *See also specific types*
  categories, 167–171
  common issues, 177
  versus corporation, 175–176
  definition, 166
  famous examples, 178
  formation, 173–174
  function, 166–167
  history, 167
  member criteria, 171–172
  overview, 61, 165
  tax benefits, 172–173
  typical operations, 176

cooperative telephone company, 51
corporate governance guidelines, 133
corporation
  versus cooperative, 175–176
  incorporation process, 62–64
  overview, 59
Council of Better Business Bureaus'
    Philanthropic Advisory Service, 32
Council on Foundations, 163
county/municipality nonprofit
    regulations, 32
credit union, 52, 74
crop cooperative, 74
Cumulative List of Organizations (Internal
    Revenue Service), 54

• *D* •

David and Minnie Meyerson
    Foundation, 157
debt, 115
declaratory judgment, 85
deduction, tax
  donations, 12
  notable nonprofit missteps, 38–39
  political activity limitations, 24
  private foundation versus public
    charity, 53
  property donations, 210, 212–213
  qualified appraisals, 210
  versus tax exemption, 52–53
Delaware, 264
determination letter
  request, 221–222
  tax-exempt application, 57, 80, 81, 83
  tax-exempt documentation, 53
direct mail, 23
director. *See also* board of directors
  definition, 117
  function, 118, 121–128
  lawsuits against boards, 121
  Model Nonprofit Corporation Act
    provisions, 283–285
  overview, 121
  questions to evaluate board membership,
    236–237, 240–241
  rights, 128–129

Sarbanes-Oxley provisions, 131–134
state regulation, 25
DIRECTV (television company), 169
disclosure committee, 196
disqualified person, 160
dissention, 129
dissolution provision, 63, 304–315
distributing funds
  compensation governance, 98
  cooperative tax, 172–173
  corporation versus cooperative, 175
  Model Nonprofit Corporation Act
    provisions, 304
  notable nonprofit missteps, 36–37
  private foundation creation, 159
  private foundation versus public
    charity, 153
distribution cooperative, 166
District of Columbia, 264
document shredding
  board duties, 131
  Enron problems, 183
  Sarbanes-Oxley major provisions,
    188, 193
documentation
  director's duty of care, 123
  Enron problems, 183
  Form 990 errors, 110
  IRS audit, 223–224, 225
  IRS salary guidelines, 91, 92–93
  notable nonprofit missteps, 39–40
  overview, 11–12
  PPA provisions, 42–43
  questions to evaluate board
    membership, 238
  Sarbanes-Oxley provisions, 131, 188, 193
  tax-exempt status, 53–54, 55–56, 81
domestic fraternal society, 73
donation. *See also specific types*
  for-profit versus nonprofit group, 15
  notable nonprofit missteps, 35–36
  PPA incentives, 41–42
  PPA provisions, 213–215
  private foundation versus public
    charity, 53
  tax deduction, 12

tax exemption revocation, 246–247
valuation, 205–213
donor
  definition, 11
  lawsuits against boards, 121
  overvalued donations, 211–213
  political activity limitations, 24
donor-advised funds, 96
due diligence, 93
duty of care, 122–123
duty of loyalty, 123–124

• *E* •

earned income, 200
easement, 43, 215
education, nonprofit, 218
educational organization, 70, 78
election law, 23–24
electric cooperative, 168–169, 177
emeritus status, 119
employee
  association, 70
  benefit plan, 61, 76, 94, 128
  employment contract, 95
  firing policy, 125
  identification number, 55, 80
  salary determination, 88
employees, hiring
  audit committees, 139
  board's duties, 125
  compensation package, 93–97
employer withdrawal liability payment
  funds, 76
*Employer's Supplemental Tax Guide,
  Supplement to Circular E* (IRS
  Publication 15-A), 240
employment contract, 95
employment tax, 100
endowment test, 157
Enron (bankrupt company)
  major problems, 182–183
  Sarbanes-Oxley changes, 130, 131
environmental conservation, 42
equity credit, 172

ethics
    Model Nonprofit Corporation Act
        provisions, 279–283
    Sarbanes-Oxley provisions, 193
ex officio member, 119
excess benefit transaction, 96–97
excise tax, 42, 98
executive committee, 138
Executive Order 13224, 247
exempt function, 78
expenditure
    compensation package, 93–94, 96
    Form 990 detail, 112, 115
    notable nonprofit missteps, 39
    private foundation creation, 161
    questions to evaluate board
        membership, 239
    volunteer tax issues, 99
extension, Form 990, 106

• *F* •

facade easement, 43, 215
fair market value, 206, 209
faith-based organization, 70, 77, 105
family foundation, 154
farmer, 42, 78
Federal Emergency Management Agency
    (FEMA), 36–37
federally organized corporation, 70
financial cooperative, 171
financial expert, 146, 191
financial statement
    Enron problems, 183
    notable nonprofit missteps, 35
    tax-exempt status application, 56, 81
firing employees, 125
501(c)(3) organization
    adverse determination, 83–85
    political activity limitations, 24
    tax-exempt application, 51–52, 79–83
    tax-exempt organizations list, 69–79
501(d) organization, 77
501(e) organization, 77
501(f) organization, 78
501(k) organization, 78
501(n) organization, 78

521(a) organization, 78
527 organization, 78
Florida, 265
food donation, 41
Ford Foundation, 155
foreign corporation, 62, 316–323
Form 8718 (*User for Exempt Organization
    Determination Letter Request*), 55
Form 8283, 210, 212
Form 990
    common errors, 109–110
    compensation package, 95
    detail, 112–116
    groups required/not required to file,
        104–105
    IRS audit, 223
    overview, 55, 103–104
    public inspection, 110–112
    recent changes, 17
    salary comparisons, 90
    Sarbanes-Oxley nonprofit provisions, 192
    small nonprofits, 19
    soft contacts, 220
    state statutes, 108–109
    tax exemption revocation, 247
    types, 106–108
Form 990-EZ, 106–107, 115–116
Form 990-PF, 107, 161–162
Form 990-T, 107–108, 204–205
Form SS-4 (*Application for Employer
    Identification Number*), 55, 80
Form 1099, 95
Form 1023 or 1024 (*Application for
    Recognition of Exemption*), 54, 80
for-profit business, 14–15, 92
foundation. *See also specific types*
    board of directors, 162–163
    characteristics, 154
    creation, 159–162
    Form 990 filing, 104
    IRS view, 22
    nepotism, 236
    overview, 12, 153
    versus public charity, 53, 153, 155–156
    rationale, 153–154
    recent IRS audits, 34
    tax deductions, 53

termination, 163
types, 156–159
fractional interest, 214–215
fraternal beneficiary society, 72
fraud
  Sarbanes-Oxley provisions, 186, 188
  state regulation, 26, 29
  USPS regulation, 23
fringe benefits, 94, 248
fundraising activity
  board of directors recruitment, 65
  director's duties, 126
  overview, 12
  public charity versus private
    foundation, 156
  watchdog agencies, 32
funds distribution
  compensation governance, 98
  cooperative tax, 172–173
  corporation versus cooperative, 175
  Model Nonprofit Corporation Act
    provisions, 304
  notable nonprofit missteps, 36–37
  private foundation creation, 159
  private foundation versus public
    charity, 153

• G •

Generally Accepted Accounting Principles
  (GAAP), 144
Generally Accepted Auditing Standards
  (GAAS), 144
Georgia, 265
gift annuity, 30
goal setting
  for-profit versus nonprofit group, 15
  notable nonprofit missteps, 40
  Sarbanes-Oxley implementation, 194
good cause, 106
governance
  board functions, 119–120
  committee, 196
  compensation issues, 97–99
  Sarbanes-Oxley standards,
    20, 133–134, 189
  state regulation, 25, 26

government corporation, 105
government program, 12
grant-making foundation, 153, 158–159
Grassley, Charles (senator)
  IRS scrutiny, 16, 17
  Red Cross controversy, 18, 36
  tax deduction reforms, 38
gross income, 204
group legal service plan, 52, 75
Guidestar (nonprofit organization),
  111–112, 229–230

• H •

Hatch, Michael A. (Massachusetts attorney
  general), 37
Hawaii, 265
health
  cooperative, 169
  insurance, 52, 76, 78
healthcare industry, 37
HealthPartners, Inc. (nonprofit
  company), 37
hiring employees
  audit committees, 139
  board's duties, 125
  compensation package, 93–97
history, 22, 43, 167, 219
honorary member, 119
horticultural organization, 51, 71
hospital, 16, 77
household goods, 212, 214
housing cooperative, 168, 176
Hurricane Katrina, 36–37

• I •

Idaho, 265
illegal activity
  director's duties, 125
  Sarbanes-Oxley provisions,
    130–134, 186, 188
  state regulation, 26, 29
  USPS regulation, 23
Illinois, 265
income tax. *See* tax

income test, 157–158, 201–202
incorporation process, 62–64
indemnified member, 125, 285–289
independent accounting firm
  approved services, 147–148
  overview, 142–143
  Sarbanes-Oxley provisions, 197
independent director, 131–132
Indiana, 266
Individual retirement account (IRA), 41
information return, 103
inspection, public
  Form 990, 104, 110–111
  tax-exempt application, 56–57, 82
intellectual property, 57
intermediate sanction, 98
internal controls
  audit committee functions, 139, 146
  Sarbanes-Oxley provisions,
    188, 192, 197–198
Internal Revenue Service (IRS). *See also*
    specific tax forms
  adverse determination, 83–85
  audit increases, 36
  audit tips, 222–226
  communication tips, 217–226
  Cumulative List of Organizations, 54
  definition, 1
  Employer's Supplemental Tax Guide,
    Supplement to Circular E, 240
  history, 219
  information sharing with states, 25
  overview, 21–23
  recent legislation, 15–20, 34
  revocation of tax-exempt status, 18–19
  salary guidelines, 91–93
  Tax Exempt Status for Your
    Organization, 59
  Tax on Unrelated Business Income of
    Exempt Organizations, 203
  tax-exempt application, 50–59, 79–83
  unrelated business income criteria,
    201–202
  unrelated business income reporting,
    204–205
international law, 31
International Trademark Association, 64

Internet Nonprofit Center, 230–231
Internet Resources for Nonprofits (Web
    site), 233
interview, 250
investment, 31–32
investment committee, 140
Iowa, 266
IRA (individual retirement account), 41
IRS. *See* Internal Revenue Service
issuer, 185

• J •

jewelry, 212
judgment, 122

• K •

Kansas, 266
Kentucky, 266

• L •

labor organization, 51, 71
Land O'Lakes (cooperative), 178
lease, 160
legal issues
  audit committees, 150
  board's obligations, 120–121
  cooperative membership, 171
  cooperative versus corporation, 175
  directors' duties, 121–125, 126
  IRS soft contacts, 221
  negative effects of lawsuits, 34
  questions to evaluate board
    membership, 242
legal service plan, 52, 75
legislative action, 15–20, 33–34. *See also*
    specific laws
Letter of Determination
  request, 221–222
  tax-exempt application, 57, 80, 81, 83
  tax-exempt documentation, 53
liability insurance, 94
Liberty-Ellis Island Foundation, 39–40
life member, 119

limited liability company (LLC), 60
loan, 94, 132, 160
lobbying, 40–41, 114
local associations of employees, 70
location, organization, 49, 90
lodge, 72
Louisiana, 266
loyalty, duty of, 123–124

• *M* •

Maine, 267
management, nonprofit
  audit committee's tasks, 139, 144–145
  director's duties, 125–126
  director's rights, 129
  Enron problems, 183
  for-profit versus nonprofit group, 15
  Sarbanes-Oxley objectives, 184
  Sarbanes-Oxley provisions, 186
margin, 167, 172, 173
market conditions, 207, 208
marketing cooperative, 166, 170
Maryland, 267
Massachusetts, 267
material weakness, 188
media, 126, 249–253
Medicare tax, 240
meeting
  committee members, 137–138
  IRS audit, 225–226
meeting, board
  director's duties, 122, 124
  guidelines, 66–68
  Model Nonprofit Corporation Act
    provisions, 277–278
  questions to evaluate board
    membership, 241
  Sarbanes-Oxley provisions, 133
merger, 297–302
Meyerson Foundation, 157
Michigan, 267
Minnesota, 267
minutes, meeting
  committee meetings, 138
  compensation documentation, 92–93

director's duty of care, 123
director's rights, 129
  overview, 67–68
mission
  definition, 10
  director's duties, 125
  for-profit versus nonprofit group, 15
  overview, 47
  salary comparisons, 90
  tax-exempt status reapplication, 58
mission statement
  board function, 120
  components, 48–49
  definition, 11, 47
  models, 49
  overview, 47–48
  rationale, 48
  writing guidelines, 50
missionary organization, 105
Mississippi, 268
Missouri, 268
model act
  overview, 26–27
  types, 27–32
Model Charitable Solicitations Act, 28–29
Model Nonprofit Corporation Act
  articles of incorporation, 289–294, 297
  board of directors, 277–285
  bylaws, 295–297
  dissolution provisions, 304–315
  distributions, 304
  foreign corporations, 316–323
  indemnification, 285–289
  mergers, 297–302
  organization provisions, 275–277
  overview, 26, 27
  participating states, 27–28
  sale of assets, 302–303
Montana, 268
Musculoskeletal Transplant Foundation, 17
museum, 203
mutual benefit organization, 51
mutual ditch or irrigation company, 51, 73
mutual insurance company, 52, 74
mutual reserve, 52
mutual telephone company, 51

• N •

name, organization, 18, 62
National Association of Attorneys General
    (NAAG), 28
National Association of Insurance
    Commissioners, 31
National Association of Investors
    Corporation, 17
National Association of State Charity
    Officials (NASCO), 28, 232
National Collegiate Athletic Association
    (NCAA), 204
National Cooperative Finance
    Corporation, 171
National Rural Electric Cooperative
    Association, 169
National Rural Telecommunications
    Cooperative (NRTC), 169
National Telephone Cooperative
    Association, 169
NCNA (Web site), 233
Nebraska, 268
nepotism, 236
net assets, 115
Nevada, 268
New Hampshire, 269
New Jersey, 269
New Mexico, 269
New York, 269
New York Stock Exchange (NYSE), 37
news item, 252–253
9/11 disaster, 35–36
nominating committee, 138–139, 196
non-accountable plan, 100
noncompliance, 218
nonexempt activity, 243–244
non-government organization (NGO), 31
Nonprofit @ Adobe (Web site), 233
Nonprofit Academic Centers Council (Web
    site), 233
Nonprofit Guides (Web site), 233
Nonprofit Integrity Act, 34
nonprofit regulation. *See also specific laws*
  county and municipality
      considerations, 32
  IRS considerations, 21–23
  notable nonprofit missteps, 35

political activity limitations, 23–24
Postal Service considerations, 23
state government considerations,
    24–32, 34
nonprofit sector
  characteristics, 10–14
  versus for-profit sector, 14–15
  membership, 1, 9, 10
  types of nonprofits, 59–61
North Carolina, 269
North Dakota, 270
Northumberland Big Sisters Big
    Brothers, 49
notice, meeting, 66–67
NRTC (National Rural Telecommunications
    Cooperative), 169
NYSE (New York Stock Exchange), 37

• O •

Ocean Spray (cooperative), 178
Office of Management and Budget Circular
    No. A-133, 142
officer salary. *See* compensation
Ohio, 270
Oklahoma, 270
OMB Watch (Web site), 233
operating agreement, 60
Operation Rescue West (ORW), 245
operational test, 72
Opportunity Knocks (Web site), 233
Oregon, 270
organizational test, 72
Orton Foundation, 17

• P •

PAC (political action committee), 79
painting, 212
partnership, 60, 245
patron, 166
patronage dividend, 165, 172
payroll tax, 239–240
Pennsylvania, 271
Pension Protection Act (PPA)
  compensation limits, 96, 97
  documentation, 42–43
  donor gifts, 213–215

incentives, 41–42
loopholes, 43–44
overview, 33, 41, 213
provisions, 18–20, 41–44
tax exemptions, 42
pension trust, 75
People for the Ethical Treatment of
      Animals (PETA), 244
performance evaluation, 88, 134
personal property, 214
philanthropy, 22
PipeVine (nonprofit company), 39
planned giving, 31
point person, 224–225
political action committee (PAC), 79
political activity
   exemption revocation, 244–245
   nonprofit limitations, 14, 23–24
political organization, 78–79
PPA. *See* Pension Protection Act (PPA)
PR (public relations) professional, 251
press release, 251
prior gift, 128
privacy, 154
private foundation
   board of directors, 162–163
   characteristics, 154
   creation, 159–162
   Form 990 filing, 104
   IRS view, 22
   nepotism, 236
   overview, 12, 153
   versus public charity, 53, 153, 155–156
   rationale, 153–154
   recent IRS audits, 34
   tax deductions, 53
   termination, 163
   types, 156–159
private letter ruling, 222
private non-operating foundation, 153, 159
private operating foundation, 156–158
programming committee, 237
progressive tax, 205
property donation
   PPA incentives, 213–215
   PPA provisions, 42, 43
   valuation, 205–213

property sale, 160
public
   benefit organization, 51
   confidence in nonprofits, 34
   disclosure of information, 186, 196
public charity
   definition, 52
   versus private foundation,
      53, 153, 155–156
   tax deductions, 53
public inspection
   Form 990, 104, 110–111
   tax-exempt application, 56–57, 82
public relations (PR) professional, 251
Publication 598, IRS (*Tax on Unrelated
      Business Income of Exempt
      Organizations*), 203
Publication 15-A, IRS (*Employer's Supple-
      mental Tax Guide, Supplement to
      Circular E*), 240
purchase price, 207
purchasing cooperative, 170

• Q •

qualified appraisal, 210
questionnaire, 134
quorum, 67

• R •

railroad retirement, 77
raise, 140
rancher, 42
REA (Rural Electrification Association), 169
real estate board, 51
reasonable compensation, 91–92
record-keeping
   director's rights, 129
   Form 990 errors, 110, 223
   IRS audit, 223–224
   new legislation, 19
   questions to evaluate board
      membership, 238
   Sarbanes-Oxley provisions, 185
recreational club, 51, 72
registered agent, 63

registration document, 25
regular meeting, 66
regulation, nonprofit. *See also specific laws*
  county and municipality
    considerations, 32
  IRS considerations, 21–23
  notable nonprofit missteps, 35
  political activity limitations, 23–24
  Postal Service considerations, 23
  state government considerations,
    24–32, 34
religious organization, 70, 77, 105
replacement cost, 209
reporting form, 103
reporting requirements
  recent scrutiny, 16
  Sarbanes-Oxley provisions, 188
  unrelated business income, 204–205
resolution, 136
restricted gift, 128
revenue. *See also specific types*
  Form 990 detail, 112, 115
  salary comparisons, 89
revocation, tax exemption
  notice, 58
  PPA provisions, 18–19, 20
  reasons, 243–248
Rhode Island, 271
Rochdale Society, 167
Rockefeller Foundation, 155
rural electric cooperative, 169
Rural Electrification Association (REA), 169

salary
  audit committee membership, 145
  board function, 120
  committee duties, 87–90, 92, 133, 140
  consultants, 88
  Enron problems, 182
  excessive salaries, 37–38, 95–97, 98
  Form 990 detail, 115
  governance issues, 97–99
  IRS guidelines, 91–93
  overview, 87

package creation, 93–97
PPA provisions, 96
questions to evaluate board
  membership, 239
recent scrutiny, 16
Sarbanes-Oxley provisions,
  132, 133, 187, 196
self-dealing, 160
tax exemption revocation, 245–246, 248
Sarbanes-Oxley Act (SOX)
  audit policies, 147, 148–150
  impact, 193–194
  nonprofit governance, 20
  objectives, 183–184
  overview, 130, 181–182
  provisions, 130–134, 141, 184–194
  standards implementation, 194
  test, 195–198
scholarship trust, 61
school, 105, 203
scope of authority, 126
S-corporation, 43–44
self-dealing
  Form 990 detail, 114
  PPA provisions, 43
  private foundation creation, 159, 160
self-perpetuating organization, 119
selling in bulk, 166
September 11, 2001, attacks, 35–36
settlor, 61
shredding documents
  board duties, 131
  Enron problems, 183
  Sarbanes-Oxley major provisions,
    188, 193
sign-off authority, 147
small nonprofit, 19
social club, 51, 72
Social Security tax, 240
social welfare organization, 70
soft contact, 219–221
solicitation
  Form 990 statutes, 109
  model acts, 28–29
  state regulation, 25
South Carolina, 271

South Dakota, 272
SOX. *See* Sarbanes-Oxley Act
special committee, 136, 137
special meeting, 66
special purpose entity, 183
Spitzer, Eliot (New York attorney general), 36, 37, 132
staff. *See* employee
staggered term, 119
stakeholder
  for-profit versus nonprofit group, 15
  overview, 10–11
  Sarbanes-Oxley provisions, 184
standing committee, 136, 137
state attorney, 25
state government
  cooperative formation, 173
  Form 990 statutes, 108–109
  information sharing with IRS, 25
  nonprofit regulation, 24–32, 34
  private foundation creation, 161–162
  recent legislation, 34
  regulatory authority listing, 263–274
state institution, 105
statement of value, 212
stock
  cooperative formation, 174
  corporation versus cooperative, 175–176
  crop cooperative, 74
  PPA provisions, 43–44
stockholders' equity, 183
subsidiary organization, 105
Suer, Oral (nonprofit CEO), 39
support staff, 88
support test, 158

• *T* •

tax
  assistance, 218
  compensation package, 94, 95
  cooperatives, 172–173
  foundation termination, 163
  history, 219
  public charity versus private foundation, 156

questions to evaluate board membership, 239–240
  refunds, 83
  state regulation, 25
  taxable versus nontaxable income, 199–205
  volunteer issues, 99–100
tax deduction
  donations, 12
  notable nonprofit missteps, 38–39
  political activity limitations, 24
  private foundation versus public charity, 53
  property donations, 210, 212–213
  qualified appraisals, 210
  versus tax exemption, 52–53
Tax Exempt and Government Entities Division (TE/GE)
  compliance checks, 97
  overview, 22, 218
  soft contacts, 220–221
Tax Exempt Status for Your Organization (Internal Revenue Service), 59
tax exemption
  adverse determination, 83–85
  articles of incorporation, 63
  cooperative membership, 172
  eligible nonprofits, 69–79
  overview, 12–13
  payroll taxes, 240
  political activity limitations, 23–24
  PPA provisions, 42
  rationale, 14
  recent scrutiny, 16, 17
  versus tax deduction, 52–53
  tax-exempt status application, 50–59, 79–83
tax exemption revocation
  notice, 58
  PPA provisions, 18–19, 20
  reasons, 243–248
Tax on Unrelated Business Income of Exempt Organizations (IRS Publication 598), 203
Tax Reform Act, 154
Taxes For Dummies (Tyson), 53

teachers' retirement fund association, 73
TE/GE. *See* Tax Exempt and Government
    Entities Division
telephone cooperative, 168–169
Tennessee, 272
termination tax, 163
terrorism, 247
Texas, 272
title holding company, 70, 76
trust, 161. *See also specific types*
trustee
    definition, 61
    duties, 127–128
    state regulation, 25
Tyson, Eric (*Taxes For Dummies*), 53

unearned income, 200
unemployment trust, 74
Uniform Management of Institutional Funds
    Act, 32
Uniform Principal and Income Act, 32
Uniform Prudent Investor Act, 31
Uniform Trust Act, 32
Uniform Unincorporated Nonprofit
    Association Act (UUNAA), 29, 60
unincorporated association, 60–61
United Way (nonprofit organization),
    39, 132
university salary, 37
unrelated business income
    criteria, 201–202, 203
    definition, 13
    exceptions, 202–203
    Form 990, 104, 107–108
    overview, 201
    PPA provisions, 42
    reporting requirements, 204–205
U.S. Postal Service (USPS), 23
USA.gov (Web site), 231
user, 11, 80
User for Exempt Organization Determination
    Letter Request (Form 8718), 55
Utah, 272

utility cooperative, 168–169
UUNAA (Uniform Unincorporated
    Nonprofit Association Act), 29, 60

• *V* •

valuation, property, 205–213
vehicle donations, 39
Vermont, 273
veterans' organization, 75, 76
Virginia, 273
voluntary employees' beneficiary
    association (VEBA), 51, 72–73
volunteer, 15, 99–100

Washington, 273
watchdog agency, 32
Web sites
    BoardSource, 233
    Community Career Center, 233
    CompassPoint, 232
    Internet Resources for Nonprofits, 233
    NCNA, 233
    Nonprofit @ Adobe, 233
    Nonprofit Academic Centers Council, 233
    Nonprofit Guides, 233
    OMB Watch, 233
    Opportunity Knocks, 233
    USA.gov, 231
West Virginia, 273–274
whistle blower, 130, 188, 193
Wisconsin, 274
workers' compensation, 76
workers' cooperative, 170
W-2 form, 95, 100
Wyobraska Wildlife Museum, 206
Wyoming, 274

• *Y* •

Youth Ministries, Inc., 245